7 - 6 -83

IN **Method Madness**

MAURICE YACOWAR

*The Comic Art
of Mel Brooks*

ST. MARTIN'S PRESS
New York

ACKNOWLEDGMENTS

For their help in preparing this book, I heartily thank Bonnie
Bellows, Al Ciceran, Joan Gordon, and Jenny Gurski. Special thanks to
my friend and colleague Joan Nicks, for her help in style and content.

Library of Congress Cataloging in Publication Data

Yacowar, Maurice.
    Method in madness.

    1. Brooks, Mel. I. Title. II. Title: Comic art
Mel Brooks.
PN2287.B695Y3   792.7   81-8753
ISBN 0-312-53142-7   AACR2

Design by Dennis J. Grastorf

Contents

Nietzsche whispers to you: "Without audacity there is no greatness." Freud whispers to you: "Why must there be greatness?" That fight's still going on. And you don't understand either one, because they're both whispering in German.

—MEL BROOKS

Introduction

MEL BROOKS IS A MYSTERY. On the one hand, he is notorious for his wacky public behavior and for his zany films. On the other, some of his public pronouncements show him to be a very serious fellow. While his audiences clutch their sides in helpless laughter, Madman Mel warns us that serious things are going on amid those wild goings-on. This book will attempt to reconcile the public clown and the closet thinker.

First, Mel the wacko. Brooks has a reputation for doing outrageous things. A psychologist friend once called Brooks the sanest person he had ever met; he was tempted to reconsider when Brooks, standing next to him in a men's room, turned and urinated on the psychologist's shoe.[1] Lunacy? Or was Brooks trying to free himself from the man's judgment, albeit supportive? Or was it just a good joke, the kind that a free spirit can (or in this case, *must)* take a shine to?

Then there was the time that Brooks barged into a high-level conference in the RCA Building, jumped up on the table, skimmed his straw hat across the room, and shouted, "Hurray! Hurray! Lindy has landed at Le Bourget!" This was in 1950, long after Lindbergh's flight. While RCA Board Chairman General Sarnoff, NBC President Pat Weaver, and assorted other dignitaries stared on, aghast, Brooks broke into the "Marseillaise." Naturally, Brooks did not crash the executives' conference without a reason: He was curious about their plans for the TV show on which Brooks was a writer.

Then there was the Emmy Awards ceremony, when the award

for best comedy writing was given to *The Phil Silvers Show*. At the time, Brooks was on the writing team for *Your Show of Shows*. In front of the formal assemblage and TV cameras, Brooks leaped up on a table and screamed, "Coleman Jacoby and Arnie Rosen won an Emmy and Mel Brooks didn't! Nietzsche was right! There is no God! There is no God!" As it happens, a tame version of this incident was later used on the *Mary Tyler Moore Show*. Mel Brooks makes his life stranger than fiction.

To his credit, Brooks treats his friends as respectfully as he does the industry moguls. His treatment of Howard Morris is a case in point. Morris was one of Brooks's colleagues on the old Sid Caesar TV shows; he was the diminutive fellow whom Caesar would carry clinging to his leg. One night, when the two colleagues were walking to Greenwich Village, Brooks mugged Morris. He slapped him around and knocked him against a yellow Studebaker. With his finger pointed through his coat pocket like a pistol, Brooks hissed, "Gimme everything you got or I'll kill you!" Morris turned white and handed over his wallet, watch, wedding ring, the works. After Brooks had run off, Morris phoned Caesar. "Oh, he's started *that* again," Sid responded unperturbed. He advised Morris not to visit Brooks's home and to wait till Brooks returned to his senses. For three weeks Morris waited, while Brooks acted as if nothing unusual had happened. He greeted Morris amiably whenever they met and went about their usual business. Suddenly one day, Brooks slapped his forehead and said "Howie! Oh, my God! I robbed you. I'm so sorry." He returned Morris's property.

Three years later, Brooks and Morris were rowing together on the lake in Central Park, enjoying a sunny lunch hour. As they drifted under a secluded bridge, Brooks robbed him again. Again, the finger gun in the pocket, the slap in the face. This time Morris quietly handed over his property, removed his shoes and tied them around his neck, jumped overboard and waded to shore. Brooks plans to rob him again someday, "because robbing Howie is what I do best."[2]

This irrepressible spirit, when expressed in Brooks's films, has won him critical disdain. When *Blazing Saddles* was released, its reception was typified by Pauline Kael's verdict: "intentionally graceless." This, a more sympathetic writer remarked, "is like charging the Atlantic Ocean with intentional wetness." When a *Playboy* interviewer remarked, "You've been accused of vulgarity," Brooks replied, "Bullshit!" What his critics assail as looseness and wildness, Brooks defends as his personal style. "I could do my little Jewish *Brief Encounter* and disguise it—shorten the noses." That is, he could make the more respectable, "serious" film. "But it wouldn't be as much fun as my delivering my dish of insanity. That's what I'm good at." So, "I salute the fact that there's something crazy about me, and that's what people enjoy, and that's what I can give them."[3]

And enjoy they do. While the critics cavil at Brooks's vulgarity and lack of discipline, or worse—ignore him completely in any serious discussion of contemporary comedy—the audiences lap up his work with relish. Despite the critics' harping, Brooks's films have played sprightly tunes on the box-office registers. In *Variety's* 1981 listing of the all-time film rental champions on the North American market, Brooks had four notable successes. *Blazing Saddles* ranked 29th with a gross of $45,200,000, *Young Frankenstein* was 38th with $38,823,000, and *Silent Movie* grossed $21,242,000. *High Anxiety*, his youngest, grossed a respectable $19,163,000. For purposes of comparison: *M*A*S*H* had a gross of $36,720,000, Disney's venerable *Snow White and the Seven Dwarfs*, $26,740,000, and *Clockwork Orange*, $16,000,000. More to the point, Brooks's archrival, Woody Allen, had grossed only $18,093,000 with *Annie Hall* and $16,962,018 with *Manhattan*, his greatest successes. Not only does Brooks have the greatest number of comic hits, his hits have staying power. In 1979 the reissue of *Blazing Saddles* grossed $8,000,000 and *Young Frankenstein* another $4,297,000. In comparison, the reissue of *Animal House* made only $6,530,000. The heart of Brooks's audience is the precollege, college, and young professionals crowd between eighteen and twenty-five years of age. "I also pick up a whole slew of people between forty-five and sixty and . . . a bunch of twelve-year-old kids who really relate to my films because they have seen every old movie that's been made on television and they can understand exactly what I'm satirizing." As he told Digby Diehl, "Kids and intellectuals are still my best audiences. The kids get it intuitively, and the intellectuals can figure out what I'm getting at." So even if the Brooks films were not seriously founded statements, their box-office success alone would justify their serious study. For Mel Brooks is an important phenomenon in contemporary popular culture.[4]

But there is more to the Brooks comedy than meets the box office—or the funnybone. Brooks is a serious fellow. His favorite playwright is Samuel Beckett. He even has highbrow taste in films—Renoir's *Grand Illusion*, Ford's *The Grapes of Wrath*, de Sica's *Bicycle Thieves*. His literary passion is for the Russian philosopher-novelists: "I read *War and Peace* every couple of years. I *have* to because he's tops in taps." Of course, Brooks has his own distinctive way of articulating his respect for the giants of literature: "My God, I'd love to smash into the casket of Dostoyevsky, grab that bony hand and scream at the remains, 'Well done, you goddamn genius.'" Brooks's respect is a clue to his own creative aspirations.[5]

Another clue is Brooks's diligence. To him, the key stage in filmmaking is writing the script. Directing is "a terrible, anxious experience" in which the dream is "diluted very quickly by the slightest ineptness in any of your collaborators." Brooks directs "in self-defense. Basically, I'm a writer. I'm the proprietor of the vision . . . the only way to protect it is to direct it." Also, the comedy is all planted during the writing stage. Because "comedy is serious—deadly serious," Brooks has often warned:

> Never, never try to be funny! The actors must be serious. Only the situation must be absurd. Funny is in the writing, not in the performing. And another thing, the more serious the situation, the funnier the comedy can be. The greatest comedy plays against the greatest tragedy.

In his second *Playboy* interview, Brooks called comedy "a red rubber ball," logically enough:

> If you throw it against a soft, funny wall, it will not come back. But if you throw it against the hard wall of ultimate reality, it will bounce back and be very lively. *Vershteh, goy* bastard? [Translation: Understand, illegitimate gentile?] No offense. Very, very few people understand this.

So it's a "Disaster!" when "directors try to be funny when they do comedy . . . . The writer has to be funny. Not the director, not the actor." The writers on the Sid Caesar TV shows would reject comic sets and tell the designers, "Don't help us! Make the sets real. We'll do the rest." Similarly, "you never do funny music for a comedy. The humor must come from the truth of the situation, the juxtaposition of serious music and bizarre behavior." Brooks's title song for *Blazing Saddles* sounds completely straight, until you listen closely to the lyrics. For *Young Frankenstein* Brooks ordered a simply beautiful Slavic lullaby, in order to establish a "hard" realistic but sentimental base.[6]

Because the comedy is all worked out in the scripting, it is a laborious process:

> Most writers do their story in six months. I can't. I write and rewrite for the kind of comedy I do. I keep pads and pencils all over the house, jotting down new ideas and dialogue that comes to mind any time of the day or night.

The script finished, Brooks adheres to it "word for word. *Blazing Saddles* had no line changes, *Twelve Chairs* had only a couple. You can improvise with rhythms and motions during rehearsals, but you have to keep control."[7]

What? Keep control? Mel Brooks keeps control? Brooks is so successful in his planning that his finished product seems spontaneous, but actually it is scrupulously planned. Close calculation and tight editing lie behind every Brooks film. For example, on *Blazing Saddles* the writing team brainstormed for four months to produce a 412-page script. Then it took another three months to pare it down to 275 pages. Two more years of planning preceded the production. Then came ten months of shooting and ten months of editing.

As Brooks points out, "Being a good comedy editor is as difficult as being a good comedy director." He's scrupulous about the length of time allowed each joke, as well as which to keep and which to cut. During the editing stage, too, he works closely with the music, sound, optical effects, even the color of the titles and the advertising strategy. And the end result? "What you're after is to make a Mount Whitney of a picture. What you settle for is a wonderful snowball." The whole process is "compression, remolding and restructuring—tension, tension, tension."[8]

If Brooks has the reputation for being a fast yet casual worker, he has only his own genius to blame. For one thing, his films pour out with such energy and exuberance that their formal design and order quite escape attention. More important, Brooks is known as a brilliant improviser. From his earliest days as a comic writer and actor, Brooks has displayed an uncanny flair for the brilliant ad-lib.

For example, when his *Playboy* interviewer suddenly asked what advice Brooks would give to someone wanting to quit smoking, Brooks replied, "Suck somebody else's nose." The quip is far-out and absurd, but it has a dollop of practical sense. Sucking someone else's nose is a plausible—nauseating but plausible—alternative to smoking. It would address (and surely cure) one's oral fixation![9]

In another example, he plays a verbal riff around interviewer Philip Fleishman's mention of the Delicious apple:

> Now the Delicious apple I don't like. It's too tall. It's not round enough. It has too much . . . it's fraught with shoulders, so to speak. I prefer McIntosh, which has just a little bit of tartness in the apple. I know more about apples than I do about show business, as many critics are wont to shout.

In one swell swoop, Brooks neatly discriminates among types of apples, humanizes them, imputing mental, physical, and emotional states, and finally rallies back for a dig at the (tart? saucy?) critics. Has anyone described the Delicious apple—or a tall, threatening man, or a critic—better than Brooks's extemporized "fraught with shoulders"? We find the same genius in his rather wishful self-description in a *Playboy* interview:

> I'm crowding six-one. Got a mass of straight blond hair coming to a widow's peak close to the eyes. Sensational steel-blue eyes, bluer than Newman's. Muscular but whippy, like Redford. The only trouble is I have no ass.

Not the magazine to pass by an opener like that, *Playboy* asked "What happened to it?"

It fell off during the war. Now I have a United Fruit box in the back and I shit pears.

From comic vainglory, Brooks effortlessly cruises into an inspired, surreal image. The man with the fruit-box ass—that is an image to conjure with. For that matter, so is his quip about the Japanese erotic aid, "a whole rubber person. . . . Costs as much as a Toyota, but you can't back up in it." Brooks's mind seems perpetually to hover on the brink of the fantastic. So he describes his quiet home life with wife Anne Bancroft. (Anne Bancroft? Mel Brooks's wife? Read on.):

Week nights we stay quietly at home and worry about how we're going to get rid of all our Raisenets. Sometimes a little *jai alai* in the living room with ripe guavas for balls and live pelicans for baskets.

The Raisenets? Brooks received cartons after Hedley Lamarr ordered a box in the cinema in *Blazing Saddles*. The rest of the passage is clear enough.[10]

With this rampaging inventiveness, Brooks simply dominated a 1970 TV show on which David Susskind invited his six panelists to discuss Jewish mothers. With Brooks in full flight, the other speakers could not get an edge in wordwise. Brooks spared no one. David Susskind was born with a cute little nose just like Dick Cavett's, Brooks claimed; Susskind had his lengthened when he decided to go into show biz. In a pseudo-Freudian dream analysis, Brooks explained that the fetal image means getting your feet wet. He snored, sang, danced, did impersonations, and even made up theme songs for the other guests. David Steinberg he summarized as "the Winesberg, Ohio, of Jews."

Steinberg attempted a comic tangent of his own: "Forget about Jewish mothers. Let's talk about sharks." Brooks hijacked the routine, assuming the slow, arch falsetto of a pedant:

A shark could never harm you. The shark is a benign creature of the sea. Of course, if you thrash about in the water or if you wear shiny bracelets, the shark will be attracted to you. On occasion, the shark has followed people out of the water and has gone to their blanket and eaten their beach ball.

By piling up specific details, Brooks makes even the most outrageous premise seem plausible:

> One time, the shark followed my brother Irving home on the Brighton local, and, upon being admitted to the apartment house, the shark entered his apartment—Apartment 4B—and ate his entire family and a brand-new hat. Apart from that, the shark is a pussycat.

This apparent digression turns into an allegory about Jewish mothers. Beginning far away from the topic, Brooks zeroes in on the ambivalent mangle of domestic friendliness and savage destruction that characterizes the post-Portnoy Jewish mother. Later in the show Brooks completed his parallel: "Until they die themselves, [Jewish mothers] *clean* and *kill*." In a seemingly freeform digression, Brooks intuitively developed a metaphor for the subject at hand.

That Brooks is at his best when he is improvising was demonstrated in Michel Minaud's program about Brooks, made for French television in 1978 and shown on Thames TV in the Superstar Profile series in 1980. The program sparkled when Brooks ad-libbed to the audience or broke into snatches of song. But it creaked to a grind when he had to toe some line in order to introduce the film clips.

Brooks developed his genius at improvisation in his series of recordings with Carl Reiner. They won Brooks his reputation as the comedians' comedian, the funniest man in America. But his quick wit may have prejudiced the critics against Brooks's major work, his films, for none have gone beyond superficial engagement.

The present volume is a modest attempt to redress that neglect. Readers who hunger for a critical explication of the Brooks films may well skip past the next five chapters and proceed to the film analyses. There they will find each film analyzed in turn, with a brief plot summary to refresh the memory, a close reading of the film's major themes and strategies, and a scattering of background information about the film. Alternatively, the reader may well prefer to learn more about the artist before proceeding to his art. To this end, the next five chapters will in turn summarize Brooks's own pronouncements about film and the art of comedy, survey his life story, and briefly analyze his early works. Liberal quotations from The Master's works should ensure that the proposed interpretations have some firm base in the material and also that a good time is had by all.

PART I

Background

Chapter 1

The Creed

Because he has such a quick and unpredictable wit, Brooks is a delightful interview. But he would infuriate anyone who craves just a straight and sober answer. Ask him why he makes films and he may reply, "Because they are the only truly complete art form." More likely, he would playfully respond, "My job is you should pay three dollars and not want to spit at the ticket-taker on the way out." Nevertheless, over the years Brooks has tossed out enough serious statements about his art that it is possible to deduce his creed. Surprisingly perhaps, almost every claim he makes is rooted in Freudian psychology.[1]

Foremost is his conviction that comedy can serve a serious purpose. "I maintain there is nothing you cannot deal with in comic terms and make a point. I proved that by spoofing Hitler in

The Producers." Indeed, "often one can say much more important things about human behavior, and especially political behavior, because one has the guise of comedy to hide behind." Brooks often vows never to leave the laugh business (as Woody Allen did in *Interiors*). "I'll never do a serious picture just to make a profound statement. I can make those statements comically. You don't have to stop laughing." Significantly, when Brooks announced his plan to film the noncomic *The Elephant Man*, he restricted his participation to that of producer and assigned the direction to David Lynch.[2]

Brooks's commitment to comedy is partially due to the challenge of the form. It is harder to say something important in a genre that audiences treat lightly, than in one they expect to be "serious." Also, "in comedy you have to do everything the people who make drama do—create plot and character and motive and so forth—and *then*, on top of *that*, be funny." So in Brooks's view, "Why should I waste my good time making a straight dramatic film? The people who can't make you laugh can do that." Instead, Brooks is drawn to the greater challenge, with its correspondingly greater rewards.[3]

As we might deduce from his practical jokes and incorrigible behavior, there is also a compulsive element to Brooks's comedy:

> I don't think in terms of results at all. I think: what next insanity can I shock the world with? What can I say to, for, my fellow citizens of the world? How crazy shall I be? . . . I've got to get this stuff out of my system.

On the other hand, there is calculation behind his craziness:

> In good comedy, there's always a scintilla of reason. In my films I suppose you can say that behind the laughs there's an examination of good and bad, of greed, rottenness, pettiness. It's important for me to have a philosophical base, even though I may disguise it.

The need for a "base" from which to operate has also led Brooks to a fascination with film genres. He parodies genres because "I like a background to work against, a milieu."[4]

The operative word is "against." Brooks works *against* backgrounds, whether it be the rhetoric of a genre he parodies, or a moral or social context. The Brooks comedy is a fight back, a corrective, an awakener. As he told Charles M. Young, "We choose not to be maudlin. As long as I am on the soapbox, farts will be heard." Translation:

> I want to make trouble. I want to say in comic terms, *"J'accuse."* We dealt with bigotry in *Saddles* and with neo-Fascism in *Producers*. Underneath the comedy in *Frankenstein*, the doctor is undertaking the quest to defeat death—to challenge God. Our monster lives, therefore he wants love too. He's really very touching in his lonely misery.[5]

Time and again Brooks returns to the theme of man's need for love. He sees his art rooted in human emotion: "My movies are about people and how they love and hate each other, how they deal with each, but mostly how they *need* each other." This is the quality he reveres in the work of Alfred Hitchcock, which prompted his homage in *High Anxiety*. Hitchcock, says Brooks, "understood more about what the camera could do than anyone. . . . His shots were never just for effect, [but] always to implant some emotion." So too for Brooks, "without love, there's no movie." In the previous quotation, we find this sense of emotional responsibility in Brooks's shift from "What next insanity can I shock the world with?" to "What can I say to, for, my fellow citizens of the world?" Indeed, Brooks goes so far as to say that if he were to teach screenwriting, he "would teach one sentence: What do the leading characters *want?*" For in the character's desire or need lie both his vitality and his significance to the viewer. For Freud, of course, the essence of man lay not in his rational powers (as Descartes argued), but in his compulsive desires.[6]

This quality in Brooks's work has not been widely noted. Indeed the critics have tended to assail Brooks for lack of technical polish and for what they take to be his cruelty and misanthropy. But Brooks is civilized: "Emotion is the essence of a movie—not the shots, not the cinematic aspects of it, but the emotion . . . pictures live because of their humanity."[7]

Brooks admits two debts to the Russian novelists. First, they gave him ambition. They showed him that "it's a bigger ball park than the *Bilko* show. . . . I wanted to be the American Molière, the new Aristophanes." Second, they led him to be committed "to no joy but the joy of observation." The Russians excited him because "they'll look at a tree and cry out, 'Look at that tree!' They're full of original astonishments." In the thrill of original astonishment the great Russian highbrows and the babbling Brooks are one.[8]

The maniacal energy and the scandalous lack of decorum that characterize Brooks's work have a philosophical foundation. In part, it involves his sense that man curtails himself through excessive logic. "We defer too much to our brains, our logic, our powers of rational thought," he told Kenneth Tynan. "That's why we're so vain, so egotistical, always full of complaining." To Brooks, "we are part of an evolving process that has no knowable purpose. What's happened is that we were given too many brains, and our brains have screwed up our biological evolution. If we didn't think so much, we'd know what it was all about." Brooks places his confidence in intuition, instead of in logic. Moreover, he exhorts us to live life as fully as we can in the present, uninhibited by the dark future:

> We're going to die anyway. And because of that, let's have a merry journey, and shout about how light is good and dark is not. What we should do is not *future* ourselves so much. We should *now* ourselves more. *"Now* thyself" is more important than "Know thyself."

This is an existential basis for Brooks's art of improvisation. His brilliant exchanges with Carl Reiner, as we shall see, show the artist [thrilled and blazing] in an art of the *now*, the unscripted thrust and parry without the security of a futured script.[9]

Of course, what works on live exchange and on record may not work on film: "You design specifically for the medium. For records, the best way for me and Carl to do [it] was to just ad-lib it. A movie takes me eighteen months to write, because pieces have to be fashioned together and they have to work smoothly."[10] Still, Brooks labors to make his crafted films *seem* uncrafted, unshaped. He wants them to live as process not as product, as an emblem of life on the fly, in the now and not in some vague tomorrow or frozen past.

Brooks's free-spirited comedy attempts to overwhelm man's

mere logic, to escape the false security of cerebral man, with all the slings and arrows of outrageous repression that the brain is heir to.

Brooks found Freud's work on repressed sexuality inadequate for him as an artist: "That's only one aspect of the world's behavior, and I'm not just into that. There's a lot more happening."[11] But much of Brooks's work, both in theme and in style, seems Freudian in its revolt against repression. Indeed we will find that Brooks's entire canon can be read as an attempt to bring man's subconscious anxieties and impulses to the surface of his conscious awareness.

In this spirit Brooks justifies his antic pose:

> If you're alive, you got to flap your arms and legs, you got to jump around a lot, you got to make a lot of noise, because life is the very opposite of death. And therefore, as I see it, if you're quiet, you're not living. I mean, you're just slowly drifting into death. So you've got to be noisy, or at least your *thoughts* should be noisy and colorful and lively. My liveliness is based on an incredible fear of death. . . . Most people are afraid of death, but I really *hate* it! My humor is a scream and a protest against goodbye.[12]

Translation: "As long as I am on the soapbox, farts will be heard." This affirmative spirit propels Brooks's every sally forth against decorum. In a recent issue of *Feature*, Brooks defined six characteristic "Rules of Dining Etiquette":

1. Always keep your mouth closed while masticating. (Masticating.) Most people get disgusted when other people discharge sardine fragments on them. I say "most people" because there are always a few who like it.
2. Once something is in your mouth, you must swallow it. Yes. Do not remove it to see what it is or what it looks like. Unless, of course, it is a bad clam.
3. When eating with the fingers, do not touch other people to make a point.
4. If you choke on a fish bone, leave the table quickly. However, if you are choking on a chicken bone you may stay.
5. When serving yourself at a buffet, always return the serving spoons to the platter. If, however, you should make a serious

blunder and walk away with the utensils, then bluff it through by saying in a loud voice, "It's just not dinner without a big spoon."
6. Do not shout, "Gangway, all ashore that's going ashore," when the gravy boat comes in.

Here his wild nature smacks through his laborious prescriptions for tameness. Brooks refuses to "sacrifice one laugh." Rather than "leave the Mel Brooks business," he will continue "to make noises that make sense and that make people laugh. Enjoy! Revel! Live! Have yourselves one sweetheart of a good time. That's what my films are saying."[13]

This idea crops up throughout his films. In *The Twelve Chairs* Father Fyodor addresses God: "Are you strict!" In *Blazing Saddles* a gunslinger says of Hedley Lamarr, "Boy, is *he* strict!"—Lamarr has shot a desperado for chewing gum in line. In *High Anxiety* a psychiatrist relishes his S-M sweetheart: "You're so strict!" Brooks's wild recess humor is his antidote to a life quelled by the strictnesses of discipline, dread, and death. As he told Herbert Gold, his message to the world is "Let's swing, sing, shout, make noise! Let's not mimic death before our time comes! Let's be wet and noisy!" Folks call him vulgar.[14]

Brooks also sees comedy as a palliative: "Humor is just another defense against the universe." This is the point of one of his childhood memories. When Mel was a boy, a woman killed herself by jumping off a roof at South Fifth Street and Hooper in Brooklyn. From the crowd, Mel saw the lady's shoes sticking out from under the sheet. They looked like his mother's:

> God, that was the worst moment I ever experienced. I just stood there and the whole bottom fell out of my life. Then my friend Izzie made a tasteless joke: He said it couldn't be my mother, because my mother was so heavy, she would have broken the sidewalk. But you know, it helped a little bit, it really did.[15]

In addition to offering its consoling powers and giving expression to his vision and values, comedy has also been a profession for Brooks. In his remarks about his "job" Brooks shows the same paradoxical balance between chaos and control, between self- and other-centeredness, that characterizes every aspect of his philosophy. On the one hand, he affirms his need for personal style: "There must be a great big explosion—but it must be something that I think is in my personal domain. I've got to be the purveyor of something unique."[16]

On the other hand, Brooks keeps himself out of his work. We see much more of Woody Allen on screen than Mel Brooks. But we have a more personal, intimate communication from Brooks than from Allen. The more cerebral Allen makes films about the issues and metaphysical concerns that preoccupy him; his own personal nature remains unrevealed. In contrast, Brooks's films pour out his emotions, vision and appetites. So we know more of him than we do of the more visible but hidden Allen. Brooks acknowledged as much in the Michel Minaud documentary about his work:

> I don't like to examine me all the time. I like to look out. [Then wheeling upon the camera]: My job as a writer is to observe you, not for you to observe me.

Methinks the kosher ham doth protest too much. In addition, Brooks has a hunger for a wider audience than a personal, esoteric cinema would allow. He claims he would rather have a commercial success than a critical one. Not for the money, though, but "because the commercial success allows you to work again." So Brooks hones his drafts to sharpen "some nuances so that they didn't get out of hand and get too personal or insular or not accessible to Des Moines." As he told Kenneth Tynan,

> I went into show business to make a noise, to *pronounce myself*. I want to go on making the loudest noise to the most people. If I can't do that, I'm not going to make a quiet, exquisite noise for a cabal of cognoscenti.

The *Variety* box-office tallies affirm his success.[17]

Strangely, there is an element of selflessness in Brooks's ideal of the communicating artist. "The only thing I have against [Ingmar] Bergman, one of my gods, is that he's obtrusive. He's always telling you it's a Bergman film, a Bergman shot. Well I saw it; O.K., Ingmar, we heard you. We all know you're there." So too for himself: "I don't know any more than anyone else. What I have is a gift for articulation; beyond that, it's a matter of discipline and technique. Like any other artist, I have the ability to let my essential self float through so that others can enjoy it." Actually, in one of his records Brooks parodies this stance. His mock-humble, inarticulate singer, Fabiola, avers, "We are all singing. I have the mouth."[18]

Brooks does not have a blind idealism about either man or art. As to man:

> We are by nature selfish. It's part of our survival equipment—until certain situations arise and the word "noble" comes in. We are capable of giving ourselves, but it has to be worth it. World War II was worth it. Vietnam was not. Well, World War II was worth it up to the bomb. That was in questionable taste.

Hiroshima was "in questionable taste"? Behind that line sounds the ghost of another indecorous comedian, Lenny Bruce, reminding us that conventions of propriety may be far more damaging to the human condition than indiscretions are. As to art, in Brooks's view "artistry should be a free and unconscious act. The later assessment, that's the world's business. I do what I do because I have to get it out. . . . [But] in thirteen billion years, when they total everything up, they may decide it was tomatoes that were important and all the rest was jerking off." Heedless of fame, fortune, or delusions of immortality, Brooks just goes about his job, his compulsion: "I'm just lucky it wasn't an urge to be a pickpocket."[19]

At other times Brooks takes a loftier view of his enterprise. He claims to put his all into his work so that it will survive: "If you've done a good job, your work will still be sixteen years old and dancing and healthy and pirouetting and arabesquing all over the place. And they'll say, 'That's who he is! He's not this decaying skeleton.'" Again, a Brooks comedy is an explosion of laughter in the face of death, disappointment and decay. In this view, even the vulgar, hearty comedian belongs to a noble tradition. Like a coral island, built by the collection of infinitesimal bits of individual coral that die and pile up together, "writing is simply one thought after another dying upon the one before. Where would I be today if it wasn't for Nikolai Gogol? You wouldn't be laughing at *Young Frankenstein*. Because he showed me how crazy you could get, how brave you could be."[20]

Brooks has an uncommon breadth of spirit. Not many men of achievement could sincerely say with Brooks, "Any man's greatness is a tribute to the nobility of all mankind, so when we celebrate the genius of Tolstoy, we say, 'Look! One of our boys made it! Look what we're capable of!'"[21] More common is rivalry between the greats. And so we have the popular pastime of debating whether Mel Brooks or Woody Allen is the greatest American comedian of our time.

Certainly both men are equals in ambition. Once one admits their differences in tone and style, they are seen to be equally funny. They are also equally intellectual, though, as we have seen, Brooks goes to great pains to veil his philosophical import, while Allen wears his mind on his sleeve. In Brooks's view, Allen "starts out with the idea of making art. He feels that his art is his life. And more power to him. The difference is that if someone wants to call my movies art or crap, I don't mind." Brooks prefers to be considered ". . . beneficent. I produce beneficial things. A psychiatrist once told me he thought my psyche was basically very healthy, because it led to *product*. He said I was like a great creature that gave beef or milk." Brooks avows community with Allen rather than competition: "No wonder Woody Allen and I are great. We are not Brooks and Allen, we are not some *department store*. We are Konigsberg and Kaminsky. Now *those* are names, like Tolstoy and Dostoyevsky." And further: "Woody and I don't get in each other's way—we do different things. His comedy takes a more cerebral tack than mine does. I've always been very broad." Brooks accepts the sobriquet of "vulgar primitive." Among others, Andrew Sarris finds Allen "more cerebral" and Brooks "more intuitive." To Sarris, Allen lacks Brooks's "reckless abandon and careless rapture." In actor Gene Wilder's view, Woody lights separate epiphanies, where Mel wants to "set off atom bombs of laughter."[22]

But Allen and Brooks have a common ground. As New Yorkers, both are attuned to the tensions, concerns, and mythopoeia of the urban American. Both wrote for Sid Caesar and—no connection intended—submitted their fractured psyches to analysis. Both are short, plain people in a tall world that places a premium upon beauty. Both are Jewish, virtually a requirement for the comic drama of modern alienation:

> When the tall, blond Teutons have been nipping at your heels for thousands of years, you find it enervating to keep wailing. So you make jokes. If your enemy is laughing, how can he bludgeon you to death?

So Brooks is not just proud of being Jewish, but "proud and scared."

> O.K., you want me to admit I'm a four-foot, six-inch freckle-faced person of Jewish extraction? I admit it. All but the extraction.

You can take the Melvin out of the *shul* but you can't take the *shul* out of Melvin. All sense of his difficulty in life keeps this focus. Asked if he had trouble getting to direct his first feature, *The Producers*, Brooks quipped that it was "about as hard as it is for a Jew to check into the Cairo Hilton." His common signature, "Your obedient Jew," conjoins humility and self-assertion. As if to confirm the Jewish root of his comedy, he told *Playboy* that he found his humor in a package at South Third and Hooper:

> When I opened it up, out jumped a big Jewish genie. "I'll give you three wishes," he said. "Uh, make it two."

Indeed, for both Brooks and Allen, one might say that comedy works like Mel's description of the legendary egg cream: "Psychologically, it is the opposite of circumcision. It *pleasurably* reaffirms your Jewishness." And thereby hangs a tale. Brooks and Allen both brandish their vulnerability: their physical deficiency, their Jewishness, their sense of alienation in a hostile society and in an unfeeling universe, and their unsilenceable intelligence and spirit.[23]

On the latter point perhaps our heroes diverge. In Allen the intelligence dominates the spirit; in Brooks the spirit overwhelms the smarts. Brooks projects the Dionysian spirit, in contrast to Allen's Apollonian. So Brooks's comedy is orgiastic, open, chaotic, vulgar, instinctual, overflowing; Allen's is restrained, formally ordered and enclosed, discreet, rational, and elegantly defined. In form as in content, Allen's comedy preserves self-consciousness; Brooks's would destroy it. And yet the two share a common strength, as Herbert Gold best summarized: ". . . a bewildered yet focused eye, a language which slips out of the loose grasp of immigrant speech into desperate precision" and the fact that they make their insecurity "comfortable. . . . The audience is implicated, but not bound." Both comics play with nihilism but do not threaten total revolution. As Gold concludes, "There is room for both Woody Allen and Mel Brooks at the top."[24]

If not higher. So enough of (in Dogberry's shrewd phrase) odorous comparisons. On to Mel Brooks himself, the robust rogue and his rich body of comic works.

But one warning: Comics don't ply their craft just for laughs. Jokes mean and mean deep. Indeed the comic may be spinning out a compulsion as profound and somber as any tragedian's. After all, as Shakespeare's great Dane in the mourning proved, you can't make a *Hamlet* without cracking yokes.

Chapter 2

The Life

I**T ALL BEGAN** in the obligatory crowded New York tenement at 515 Powell Street, on June 28, 1926. There Melvin Kaminsky was born to Kitty and Max Kaminsky. "We were so poor my mother couldn't afford to have me; the lady next door gave birth to me."[1] Ahead of Mel were brothers Irving, Lenny, and Bernie. Mother was a Kiev-born, archetypal Yiddish momma. Father was a Danzig emigré who worked as a process server.

When Mel was two and a half years old, his father died of kidney tuberculosis, at the age of thirty-four. This was a profound loss to Mel:

> I can't tell you what sadness, what pain it is to me never to have known my own father. . . . If only I could look at him, touch his face, see if he had eyebrows! Maybe in having the male characters in my movies find each other, I'm expressing the longing I feel to find my father and be close to him.

To support the family Kitty worked ten-hour days in the garment trade in Brooklyn. To make a little extra, she brought home piecework at night. She was a proud woman; the family never went on relief. When first Irving, then Lenny, then Bernie turned twelve, they took part-time jobs in the mill. The Kaminsky family income climbed to $35 per week.

Mel was the family's darling. "I was adored. I was always in the air, hurled up and kissed and thrown in the air again. Until I was six, my feet didn't touch the ground." When his family was all at work, Mel ran the streets. There he turned into a wiseacre, fleet of foot and in phrase.

There is some dispute over what was the first funny thing Mel Brooks ever said. He told one interviewer that it was "Lieutenant Faversham's attentions to my wife were of such a nature I was forced to deal him a lesson in manners." This was addressed to "an elderly Jewish woman carrying an oilcloth shopping bag on the Brighton Beach Express." In a variant history, however, Brooks quotes his first funny line as "da-da-ba-ga-ba-da-da-ba-ba. I was four months old. It got laughs. Do you want me to move a little further than that?" Whichever his first routine, a comic he certainly was. His knack for mimicry brought him stardom, first at the Sussex Camp for Underprivileged Jewish Children, then at P.S. 19. "I always felt it was my job to amuse those around me. Don't ask me why."[2]

But if you do ask him why, he has some suggestions. His looks invited a comic response, so why not feed it? That would change being laughed at to being laughed with. Also, he was a small kid in a world of big roughies. The little Jewish boy found that "words were my equalizer" in the strife of the street. His wit and intelligence gave him an in with the older boys: "Why should they let this puny kid hang out with them? I gave them a reason. I became their jester." He was encouraged by his family's spirit. His mother was a jolly, uplifting, exuberant character; people remember his father as a warm, humorous fellow, too. Finally, Brooks suggests two opposite emotional sources of his comic bent. "Every comic and most of the actors I know had a childhood full of love. . . . They went into show business to recapture the love they had known as children when they were the center of the universe." But an opposite cause could have been Brooks's ". . . pure hate—for the whole world. . . . Getting even in an oblique way through comedy instead of just yelling insults and taunts and getting my head smashed in." A shrewd preference.[3]

In any case, show biz tightened its inexorable grip on the young Melvin. He slipped into the universal initiation rites of the second-generation American—Saturday matinees at the movies. For a dime there would be a serial, a cartoon, a short, a newsreel, two B features, and two, maybe four, trailers to whet the appetite for the next week's gorge. After Mel's *bar mitzvah*, the Kaminskys moved to Brighton Beach, in the shadow of Coney Island. The grip tightened. Free silent films, mostly slapstick comedies, were shown in the lunchrooms on the Coney boardwalk. Free. Up the street lived the Riches. There Mel found a new friend, Bernard, a drummer who had been with Bunny Berrigan and who was just starting to drum for Artie Shaw. Buddy Rich gave Mel drum lessons.

At fourteen Melvin went to work at a resort in the Catskills, the borsch belt, which proved to be the finishing school for two generations of American sage and wit. True, he began as just a busboy, but he branched out into organizing social events. He edged into the limelight with a clowning routine at poolside. Swaddled in a huge overcoat and derby, carrying a decrepit suitcase in each hand, Melvin would climb up to the high board and lugubriously declare: "Business is terrible. I can't go on!" Then he would dive in. A lifeguard would fish him out, of course. After all, where would a Jewish boy from Brooklyn learn how to swim?

In its element of danger, its thrill of risk, that poolside tumble has the seeds of Brooks's later work in comedy. It was also the beginning of his comic exploration of the Jew's pathos. Amid the comforts of the holiday retreat, Brooks sounds the dread of disaster and despair to draw out a laugh. The mature Brooks is also limned when an escapist diversion recalls the human condition. In addition, it was a rigorous act. His suitcases were filled with rocks so that he would sink to the bottom of the pool, before lifeguard Oliver fished him out. As Brooks remembers, the overcoat seemed to absorb twenty pounds of water when he sank. Very early in his career, Brooks found comedy in physical exertion and daring.

Mel remained the clown and free spirit, while his brothers developed into serious students and good, hardworking sons. When he neared high school age, Kitty proposed that Mel study mechanics at Haaron High School of Aviation Trades. But Irving—already a college graduate in chemistry—insisted that The Kid have the same academic advantages that his older brothers enjoyed. So between his Catskill summers, Melvin honed his waggery at Eastern District High.

In the famous summer of '42, Melvin got his first proper (sic) show-biz job. He was drummer and occasional patterer at Ellenville's Butler Lodge. From his perch he could study the lines, inflections, rhythms of the star comedians. And then that familiar story happened again as it so often does, in life as in films. The Star Got Sick. Drummer Melvin was shoved into the breach.

At first Brooks simply repeated the star's routine. It went over well enough, but Brooks wasn't satisfied. So he began to work out his own bits based on the day's events at the resort, as seen through the Brooks glass wildly. In his first venture, he quoted the line that the entire resort had earlier heard a maid calling, when she locked herself in a closet: *"Loz mir arois!"* ("Let me out!"). By quoting it at the start of his act, Mel addressed a common experience, one that he shared with that particular audience and had not dug out of a joke index. Moreover, it cast a spontaneous air over his entire routine; even the familiar parts seemed charged with the thrill of the ad-lib. Incidentally, the line also enabled the nervous amateur indirectly to express his own nervousness about being trapped in the limelight: "Let me out!"

Very early in his career, then, "I realized that all one really had to do was just observe. Observe and slightly exaggerate, and you had comedy. Instead of creating a mythical premise for a stupid joke, I found playing off truth got the best result." The resort life was a rich mine for Brooks's comic fancy. He recalls another early routine, based on the time manager Pincus Cantor unwittingly left on the camp's P.A. system while he railed about some "son of bitch bastard! Filt'y rotten! How dey can leave a sheet so filt'y! That son of bitch! Lat him sleep in it! I vudn't—it's vaaaat? It's on? Oyy! [CLICK]." Here Brooks anticipates his affectionate parody of Yiddish rhythms, colloquialism, and the sense of being an embarrassed stranger in an even stranger land, all of which culminated in his classic Two-Thousand-Year-Old Man series.[4]

These early routines also prepared Brooks for his rigorous activity later. The Catskills load was seven two-hour shows a week: "One show a week on television, one picture a year in the movies. Are you kidding? I've spent the last twenty years catching up on my sleep." And he learned to take chances. He developed his skills at improvisation. Sometimes he may have winged it too far for his audience to follow. More often, he held his audience the way he was used to commanding attention, from the Kaminsky kitchen gabfests to the street-corner raillery. But he took his chances. In his ad-libs as in that kamikaze pool dive, Brooks relished the risk: "Look, I had to take chances or it wasn't fun being funny."

The die was cast. The comic drummer was snared. When Melvin Kaminsky graduated from high school, he was already a hilarious wit and a polished mimic. In a more respectable vein, he held a seat on the Class Day Committee, spent a term as Dean's Assistant, and had been a member of the fencing team! But the native cheek (Yiddish: *chutzpah)* shone through. Beside his yearbook picture was his declared ambition, "To be President of the United States." Well, we may have done worse.

Brooks also had his show-biz persona. Ostensibly to fit the marquee (but really, to oblige the industry's demand for nonethnic names), he trimmed down to Mel and adapted Brooks from his mother's family name, Brookman. As biographer William Holtzman shrewdly puts it, the new name "rolled nicely off the tongue and just cleared the teeth with a click. It was its own punctuation, not unlike a rim shot."[5] Brooks also had his own theme song. It anticipated his later modesty:

> *Here I am, I'm Melvin Brooks,*
> *I've come to stop the show.*

Then there's a pinch of candor:

> *Just a ham who's minus looks,*
> *But in your heart I'll grow.*
> *I'll tell you gags. I'll sing you songs.*
> *Just happy little songs that roll along.*

Then the payoff, an open clutch for affection:

> *Out of my mind, won't you be kind?*
> *And please love Melvin Brooks.*

Thus armed, Brooks finished high school and went to war. At seventeen, he reported to Virginia Military Institute, where he acquired his country club polish: "I rode a horse and cut down sticks with a saber. I couldn't believe it, a little Brooklyn Jewish kid on top of a big red horse."[6] Big red horses and sabers, you see, are Suburban WASP. Just after Brooks enlisted (no connection implied), the Allies launched their D-day assault. By the time Brooks completed his basic training at Fort Sill, Oklahoma, Paris was liberated. When Brooks landed at Le Havre in February 1945 for duty as an artillery forward observer, the German resistance was crumbling.

So though Brooks went to war, he did not get deeply entrenched in battle against the Nazis. He may still carry some subconscious frustration as a result of this. That might explain his continual reference to the Germans in his comedy routines. In virtually every film he takes a dig at the Germans, even if it is only implicit, as in the Germanic tones of Cloris Leachman's Frau Blücher in *Young Frankenstein* and Nurse Diesel in *High Anxiety*. Brooks, of course, denies any such obsession:

Me? Not like the Germans? Why should I not like Germans? Just because they're arrogant and have fat necks and do anything they're told so long as it's cruel, and killed millions of Jews in concentration camps and made soap out of their bodies and lamp shades out of their skins? Is that any reason to hate their fucking guts?

In light of this cool denial, I withdraw my suggestion. Anyway, Brooks played a rather spirited German scientist in his cameo appearance in *The Muppet Movie* (1979). Alternatively, Brooks's jokes say more about the Jews' sense of vulnerability than about the Germans. In the Minaud documentary, Brooks suddenly falls into a wary crouch: "A Jew never stands up straight. A Nazi stands up straight. A Jew is always bent—just in case there's trouble: 'Where? Where?'"

After the war Brooks stayed overseas as a corporal in the Occupation Forces, Noncom in Charge of Special Services. Translation: he ran officers' clubs and camp variety shows. One of his specialties was a bawdy three-man parody of the Andrews Sisters. This Patti, LaVerne, and Maxine had hairy legs and cheeks and wore army garb. Rather than risk being shot by his own celebrating countrymen, Brooks spent V-E Day on a twenty-four-hour binge in a secret wine cellar. His postwar service showed the same strategy and fortune.

When Mel returned home, he did occasional work at the Abilene Blouse and Dress Company and enrolled for a brief stint at Brooklyn College. Then show biz beckoned again. He hired on as stagehand with the Red Bank Players, a summer-stock company on the North Jersey shore. He roomed with actor John Roney and John's cousin, Will Jordan, who later became an important comedian, best known for his original Ed Sullivan impersonation and as a source for many other comedians' routines. At Red Bank, Jordan and Brooks would often extemporize impersonations to entertain the house when there was a delay in the curtain. Mel also became a director when the original appointment left suddenly. The season over, Brooks went back to the Catskills, where he worked his way up to Grossinger's, the acme of the borsch-and-bagel belt.

It was then that Brooks crossed paths with Sid Caesar, the major influence on his career. Mel knew Sid as a tenor saxophonist at Yonkers High School. Caesar went on to play with the Charlie Spivak, Claude Thornhill, and Shep Fields bands. By hanging around his father's diner, Caesar mastered an atlas of dialects. Like Brooks, musician Caesar also edged into the comedy of ad-lib and mimicry. When he enlisted in the Coast Guard in late 1942, Caesar found his career accelerated. He was cast in the recruiting review *Tars and Spars,* starring Victor Moore and directed by the veteran showman Max Liebman. After its national success on tour *Tars and Spars* was filmed. Caesar was the sole holdover from the original cast. When Caesar went on to play the Copacabana, Brooks was reintroduced to him. They sensed a kindred spirit.

Liebman helped get Caesar started in the new medium of television. In turn, Caesar kept trying to get Brooks hired on as one of his writers, but this was some time in coming. Starting in January 1949 Caesar starred in a nineteen-week series, *The Admiral Broadway Review.* Mel hung around the writing crew, usually lurking in the hall, where Sid could find him when he needed an extra gag or ten. Caesar paid him $50 a week from his own pocket. When the show was resurrected in February 1950 as *Your Show of Shows,* Mel remained an unofficial member of the writing retinue. But his persistence—and omnipresence—paid off. On the seventh show he was credited for "additional dialogue." By the second season, Brooks was a fully credited writer of *Shows*, along with Liebman, Caesar, Lucille Kallen, and Mel Tolkin.

Your Show of Shows was more than just a TV series. It was a phenomenon. From February 25, 1950, to June 5, 1954, every Saturday night at nine o'clock, all America tuned into NBC for ninety minutes of high-powered music, dance, and comedy. The show made household names of stars Caesar and Imogene Coca. The series bulged with talent. Marge and Gower Champion were the dancers on Caesar's Admiral show; they were replaced by Mata and Hari. James Starbuck did the choreography. The stock company of singers included Bill Hayes, Jack Russell, and the Billy Williams Quartet. Weekly guests included the stellar likes of Gertrude Lawrence, Fred Allen, Rex Harrison, and José Ferrer. And the writers! Caesar's stable of comedy writers came to include Howard Morris, Carl Reiner, Doc Stein, Larry Gelbart, Tony Webster, brothers Neil and Danny Simon, and Brooks, who recalls: "Mike Stewart typed for us. Imagine! Our *typist* later wrote *Bye Bye Birdie* and *Hello, Dolly!* Later on, Mike was replaced at the typewriter by somebody named Woody Allen." This roster reads like a Who's Who of American comedy.

From their madhouse brainstorming emerged scripts that brought a new sophistication, intelligence, originality, and pace to TV comedy. Of course, they worked under terrific pressure, with a ninety-minute spectacular to write and produce each week. As Tolkin recalls, "We were too young to know it's impossible." The "we" there could refer to the brash, new, ravenous medium as much as to the present crew. Also, the show went on live every week. As Andrew Sarris observes, "Their opening nights were thus not only their closing nights but also their eternal incarnations." Little wonder that the show proved a crucible for the forging of so many brilliant comic talents. When ten highlights from the kinescopes were released as the feature film *Ten from Your Show of Shows*, many called it the best comedy of 1973.[7]

As well as advancing his career, the TV show advanced Brooks's education. When the company went to Europe, he took the opportunity to visit John Huston's shooting of *Moulin Rouge*. From Mel Tolkin, a closet highbrow, Mel picked up his passion for classic literature, especially for the nineteenth-century Russians. Tolkin also helped Brooks come to terms with his new success, his self-doubts, and the usual baggage of all-American guilts, by introducing him to psychoanalysis.

Brooks spent six years in analysis ("but I always took my shoes off"), two to four sessions weekly. "It was a choice of that, or suicide," he recalls. "I had low blood sugar, a chemical imbalance, plus the normal nervous breakdown everyone goes through from adolescence to adulthood. It comes from the suspicion that only an incredible amount of failure is there to greet us."[8] His anxiety was brought on by what he calls his "fear of heights," his unsettlement by his rapid climb to the top of the comedy business. His salary soared from Caesar's $50 a week to $250, to $1,000 when he was only twenty-four years old, then to $2,500, then to $5,000. These anxieties brought on (of all things!) an underactive thyroid.

Now Brooks is glad that he had that early breakdown:

> If you can fail between the ages of twenty and thirty, it's fabulous. Too much early success and the rest of your life becomes a measure of repeating it. If they had praised *The Potato Eater*, Van Gogh never would have painted *The Starry Night*.

He is also grateful for the deep and lasting benefits of his experience with psychoanalysis.

> In addition to relieving that early duress, analysis helped me later in my life with my writing, because I'm less inhibited and more in touch with unconscious realities. . . . If it did nothing but crush my societally taught sense of shame . . . that was enough; that was plenty to free me.

But as we shall see, his high regard for psychoanalysis does not inhibit his satirizing it at every opportunity.[9]

In 1952 Brooks collaborated with Ronny Graham on sketches for the traditional Broadway review *New Faces of 1952*. The bright young cast featured Graham, Eartha Kitt, Paul Lynde, and Carol Lawrence. Brooks wrote the show-stopper, a parody that mixed Odets's *Golden Boy* with Elia Kazan's epochal production of Arthur Miller's *Death of a Salesman*. Paul Lynde played the Willy

Loman figure, a washed-up burglar whose ambitions are shattered when his son comes home with a straight-A report card and resolves to take up the violin instead of a life of crime. The boy's mother reaffirms her faith in him: "I know, deep down inside, down where it really counts, you're rotten." But the boy persists in his wrongheaded, stubborn virtue. The father has a heart attack. Prophetic of his later film career, Brooks parodies a well-known work; his tone aligns it closer to seamy life than to the sentimental illusions of the original.

Also in 1952, Brooks married dancer Florence Baum. In three years they had daughter Stephanie and son Nicky (named after Gogol), then son Eddie. The couple separated in 1959: "We had married too young. I expected I would marry my mother and she expected she would marry her father."

In the meantime, Brooks's professional life also floundered. The happy professional family on *Your Show of Shows* broke up over Caesar's desire to leave the successful series. Brooks declined an invitation to write for his new show, *Caesar's Hour*, in order to apply himself to writing for the (as the trade puts it) legitimate stage. But he relented in order to try to save the flagging Imogene Coca show. That partnership—and the show—failed. In 1955 Brooks rejoined Caesar for the second season of *Caesar's Hour*. Although it was cancelled because of poor ratings, it posthumously dominated the 1957 Emmy Awards. Caesar and his merry band still had their quality, but they had lost their huge audience. Brooks stayed aboard for an ABC attempt to reunite Sid and Imogene in a thirty-minute Sunday evening series, *Sid Caesar Invites You*. But after a great start, it too lost out in the ratings race against *The General Electric Theater* and *The Dinah Shore Show*—no soft touches. Brooks's salary plunged from $5,000 a week to unemployment compensation. For four years he averaged $85 per week. According to even his own recollection, he turned into a compulsive yapper and a pain in the ass.

In 1957 Brooks was hired to help rewrite *Back Alley Opera*, a musical based on Don Marquis's book about a cockroach and an alley cat, *archy and mehitabel*. Carol Channing and Eddie Bracken had starred in the original musical by Joe Darion and George Kleinsinger, which was also released as a record. Then John Morris was hired to augment the musical routines and Brooks to plump up the book into a full-length Broadway feature. When *Shinbone Alley* opened, it starred Bracken and Eartha Kitt, with Chita Rivera and Tom Poston as understudies. The production suffered several problems, including the last-minute departure of the director, Norman Lloyd. It closed after forty-nine performances.

Brooks remains proud of his work on *Shinbone Alley*. He recalls it as a "rather Brechtian" work that dealt with social inequality and hypocrisies. For example, his archy is constantly threatened with being squashed by his romantic rival, Big Bill, a bully tomcat. Archy is a severe moralist who suffers cruel treatment. Mehitabel throws him out of her new house where cockroaches are forbidden. Archy is seduced and rolled by some siren ladybugs. Thus archy is haunted by the idea of suicide. The play overall takes an acerbic view of respectability and prefers the lively vagaries of street life. At the end archy is reformed to tolerance and humanism by his acceptance of the fallen mehitabel.

The critics appreciated only bits, not the whole. The *Time* reviewer praised mehitabel's scene as a drama-school tyro jazzing up Shakespeare, but complained about the "plotless proceedings" and lack of "episodic lift." Clearly the reviewer did not know "Brechtian." *Mirror* critic Robert Coleman applauded the authors' "amazing job" of adapting the esoteric original into an "intelligent, sophisticated and sexy" show. *Theatre Arts* dismissed it as "a very noble try" with occasional "genuine inspiration," such as the *Romeo and Juliet* parody, obviously a Brooks touch. Brooks Atkinson acknowledged the play's ambition, its "sly and original" point of view, mingling "sardonic fantasy" and "ironic improbability," but found a failure in the play's "aimless last act." In a lengthier article later, Atkinson cited several moments of illumination in the character of mehitabel but defined a basic abandonment of the original spirit of the work. Brooks subordinates Marquis's "humorous comment on human nature" to the rather hackneyed notion that archy is in love with mehitabel, "the line of least resistance on the musical stage." Equally mixed reviews greeted John David Wilson's animated feature film of the play, *Shinbone Alley*, when it was released in 1971.[10]

With this failure, Brooks slipped further into his professional doldrums. Jerry Lewis hired him to write a script for *The Ladies'*

Man, then rejected it completely. At this point Brooks's marriage was over and his writing career at a standstill. Then his resurrection began—with a party act.

Two Sid Caesar alumni, Brooks and Reiner, used to entertain friends by improvising comic interviews, in the manner of the popular "Nonentities in the News" routine on *Your Show of Shows*. Carl would be the questioning reporter, while Mel Brooks would ad-lib replies in whatever persona he happened to be assigned (usually Jewish and curmudgeonly). In one of these routines Brooks was introduced as a two-thousand-year-old man. This particular routine proved the sensation at an October 1959 party that Random House threw at Mamma Leone's restaurant to celebrate the publication of Moss Hart's autobiography, *Act One*. Given their enthusiastic reception by Hart, Steve Allen, Kenneth Tynan, and George Burns (who warned, "Listen, you better put that on a record, because if you don't, I'll steal it"), Reiner and Brooks took their party act more seriously. So in 1960, before an improvised audience, World Pacific Records recorded Carl and Mel mixing some old routines with new ad-libs for two hours of comedy. This was trimmed down to a forty-minute LP and released as *2,000 Years with Carl Reiner and Mel Brooks*. Some twelve and a half minutes feature the old man himself. Various satiric interviews round out the album, which was laundered of raunchiness for general consumption. Several radio stations featured the recording, and it sold astonishingly well. Because World Pacific couldn't keep up with the demand, they sold the title to Capitol Records. At one-year intervals came *2001 Years with Carl Reiner and Mel Brooks* and *Carl Reiner and Mel Brooks at the Cannes Film Festival*. The old man was revised in 1973 in *2,000 and Thirteen*. In 1973 a boxed set of the first three was released as *The Incomplete Works of Carl Reiner and Mel Brooks*. The records became a cult classic, as was evidenced by Gilda Radner's closing homage in *Gilda Live* (1980). George Burns was finally an accomplice in the promised theft; his titular role in the *Oh, God!* film series is based on the two-thousand-year-old man.

The success of the records gave Reiner and Brooks new life. They made all kinds of TV appearances on talk shows and with Ed Sullivan. Brooks quickly established himself as a brilliant ad-libber. When he appeared on Johnny Carson's very first *Tonight*

Show on October 1, 1962, he dominated costars Rudy Vallee, Tony Bennett, and Joan Crawford.

Brooks's quick and unpredictable wit and his two-thousand-year-old man character also led to a classic series of radio commercials that he made with Dick Cavett for Ballantine beer. True to form, Brooks's beer commercials were inspired originals. As the Ballantine company's two-thousand-year-old brewmaster, Brooks would continue his old man's satiric trot through time. Unique in the advertising industry, Mel had full creative authority over the ads and he improvised them. He and Cavett would take a premise, then wing it, taping everything, and then carve out the ads. Brooks saw Cavett as "a bright, young, incredibly Gentile person . . . a marvelous foil for me. He's innocent and guileless and he just aches to be cut to pieces. He reacts beautifully during the interviews, especially when I call him 'company rat,' 'pusher,' 'marshmallow,' 'fluffy,' 'sellout.'" These were not your usual ads. Not when they could burst into a Brooksian genius. To wit: "My tongue just threw a party for my mouth."[11]

Hard upon this success, Brooks was invited by Charles Strouse, the Tony-winning composer of *Bye Bye Birdie*, to write a musical-comedy stage adaptation of Robert Lewis Taylor's novel, *Professor Fodorski*. *All-American* opened at the Winter Garden Theatre on March 19, 1962, directed by Josh Logan and starring Ray Bolger, Eileen Herlie, Anita Gillette, Ron Hussman, and Fritz Weaver. It closed after eighty-six performances. The common complaint of the critics—one shared by director Logan—was the weakness of the second act. Indeed the director and others rewrote the second act themselves when Brooks failed to come up with an adequate rewrite. As Mel explained the failure, "We had an unfortunate stroke of luck. It opened in New York when there was no newspaper strike."[12]

Of all the reviewers, John Simon was probably the most irresponsible. "If *All-American* is not the all-time low in musical comedy, it is not for lack of trying," he preened, in a review that is totally spent on the author's self-display. The *Time* reviewer more responsibly noted the play's first-act parody of "the old-fashioned football college comedy" and its second-act satire of Madison Avenue. John Chapman acknowledged the "solid humor and satirical wit" in the book, but John McClain found it "labored and spotty," and Howard Taubman, "ponderously written."[13]

But this setback paled beside the new light in Brooks's life. While working with Strouse on *All-American,* Brooks tagged along one day to visit Strouse's friend, Anne Bancroft, at a rehearsal for *The Perry Como Show.* According to legend (which in Brooks's case means it is absurd enough to seem true), Brooks stood at the back of the hall listening to her sing "Married I Can Always Get." At the end, he applauded loudly and cried "Bravo!" and "Terrific!" He strode onstage, grabbed her hand, and announced, "Hi. I'm Mel Brooks. I would kill for you."

Maybe she figured he didn't say that to all the girls. In any case, the vulgar, homely, brash, irrepressible Jewish clown besieged the elegant queen of Broadway (fresh from her triumph in *The Miracle Worker*). He found a sympathetic soul. After all, she was herself the daughter of Italian immigrants. Her real name was Italiano. She too had a warm, homey, sensitive nature and a bubbling sense of humor. They had a long, romantic courtship.

Business was also booming for Brooks. He appeared on Andy Williams and Jerry Lewis specials and he launched a hit TV series, *Get Smart.* Its reruns are still with us. He was rushed in to doctor an ailing comedy series, *Nowhere to Go but Up,* but it went down. He failed to get funding for a screenplay, discreetly titled *Marriage Is a Dirty Rotten Fraud,* but in 1967 won a writing Emmy for a Sid Caesar special. He wrote, directed and starred in a trailer for a United Artists film, *My Son the Hero,* that *Variety* declared to be more entertaining than the film itself.

On August 5, 1964, Mel and Anne were married at City Hall. There were no religious problems: "She don't have to convert. She's a star!" In June 1972 son Maximilian Michael Brooks was born. The subject of his blissful marriage frequently arises in Brooks's interviews (*e.g.,* "I know you're wondering how the hell I got her"). Brooks also has three children from his first marriage. He remains a devout family man. Hence his rhapsody about man's need for children:

> Think what a barren existence it would be without the constant asking for money and the sarcasm and the laughing at you and telling you, "Pop, there's all kinds of stuff hanging out of your nose."

In his own sentimental way, he told *Playboy* that he'd like to have eight children: "That's enough to carry me to my grave comfortably when I die of the heart attack they've brought on."

All sense of Bancroft and Brooks as an odd couple disappears when one sees Anne Bancroft's debut as a feature film director with *Fatso* (1980). Dom DeLuise stars as a self-indulgent glutton who suddenly is struck down by the fear of cholesterol. His shrill sister (Bancroft) and kid brother (Ron Carey) drive him to diet. His campaign is eased when he falls in love with Candice Azzara; as his passion soars, his waistline shrinks. For the course of fat love never did run smooth.

The film shows Bancroft's family background to be quite the same as Brooks's. The strength of *Fatso* lies in its image of American immigrant families in all their lively excitement. The shrieking, the embraces, the flagellation, the tight religion, the effulgent emotions overflowing mannerly bonds, and the sense of a hot and ardent minority community set against the abstemious WASP America—this is a philosophical territory common to Bancroft the Italian and Brooks the Jew. In *Fatso* Bancroft contrasts the immigrant family's emotional and culinary excesses with the abstemiousness of the American society. The hero is simply too hearty and effusive to fit into the slender frames of modern American style. For, in his experience, love was expressed through food.

The film has some deft gags that show Bancroft capable of holding her own in comic matrimony. When his fat cousin dies, the hero wails, "He was like a mother to me. He always had something on him to eat." So too the physical comedy of tubbies trotting, waddling, jiggling, and succumbing to a faceful. But primarily, in *Fatso* Bancroft played out the spirit and energy of her Italian background. That odd couple now seems as harmonious a union as cream cheese and lox, or pepperoni and provolone.

In 1970 Brooks appeared on Anne Bancroft's CBS special, *Annie, The Women in the Life of a Man*, which won two Emmys; he played Anne's psychiatrist. He participated in Marlo Thomas's recording and TV show, *Free to Be—You and Me;* Mel provided the gravelly voice for a Carl Reiner–Peter Stone skit about a newborn boy and girl exploring each other. In December 1977 Brooks joined 145 celebrities, including Anne Bancroft, Dustin Hoffman, Tony Randall, and Stacy Keach, for a five-day reading of *War and Peace* on noncommercial WBAI radio in New York. Then there is his own movie career. After winning Oscars for *The Critic* and *The Producers,* Brooks became a box-office success. By the end of 1976 he was the fifth biggest box-office attraction in America, topped only by Redford, Nicholson, Hoffman, and Eastwood. He would phone Burt Reynolds and say, "Hello, Six. This is Five speaking." That year he was named Director of the Year by the National Association of Theater Owners. In 1977 Brooks slipped to seventh, to Reynold's fourth, but in the uneven match-up between glamor and comedy, Brooks was doing alright.

In other words, it's time to leave off the Mel Brooks biography and turn to the analysis of his works.

PART II

The Early Works

Too often, studies of popular artists respect only their mature artistry; the early work gets the bird. But an artist's early efforts may well illuminate the later. When the artist is Mel Brooks, the early works have their own delight and spirit. Unfortunately, when the medium is television, early works are unavailable. The old shows are lost. Nonetheless, before we consider the mature films, we will examine the themes and styles of Brooks's early work for television, recordings, theater, and film.

Chapter 3

The Television

B ROOKS'S FIRST CREDIT on *Your Show of Shows* was for an interview with Stanislavski disciple Ivano Ivanovich (Sid Caesar), who illustrated Method acting by impersonating a pinball machine and playing both leads in *Romeo and Juliet*.[1] The skit depended on Caesar's extraordinary facial and vocal dexterity. But it is also quintessential Brooks. For one thing, the writer turned his growing enthusiasm for "high culture" into popular entertainment. Of course, the jokes did not depend upon prior acquaintance with either Stanislavski or the Bard, but rewarded whatever knowledge the viewer had. Whether the viewer knew his Shakespeare or not, the work complimented his intelligence by assuming that he did. Finally, Brooks's skit combined the basic forms that dominated the show's comedy: the interview and parody. These proved the basis for Brooks's mature art.

Film parodies were the single most popular form of skit on *Your Show of Shows*. There were over one hundred in all. This may have been due to the talents and interests of Caesar himself. One of his first routines, pre-TV, was a one-man spoof of Hollywood pilot movies, with Caesar as Smilin' Jack, the pals, the enemy, and even the planes. But the predominance of the parody skit may also have been a response to the nature of the medium. Television was at that time a wholly new experience for its audience; mostly, it seemed a stay-at-home version of the movies. But its small, grainy, black-and-white image and tinny sound diminished its equivalence to films. By showing parodies of films, TV acknowledged this shrunken scale. While these parodies affirmed the medium as an alternative to film going, they exploited its reductive effect. As the parody of films deflated the characters and plot of a large-screen drama, it validated the shrunken scale of the TV image. The smallness was no longer a limitation of the medium, but an amusing aspect of the total conception.

For example, Fred Zinnemann's 1952 Western, *High Noon*, with its rather grandiose ethics and self-importance, was given a thoughtful rebuttal when the Caesar crew parodied it as "Dark Noon." The parody acknowledged the central thrust of *High Noon*, in which a heroic sheriff feels betrayed by his weak and cowardly community. But the parody put the point in comic terms:

> HOWIE MORRIS: Before he became the sheriff, this town was a wild, lawless town full of drinking, gambling, and shooting. Since he's been the sheriff, it's different! [Shouts of 'Yeah!'] He closed down the saloon, he cut out the gambling, he stopped the drinking!
> TOWNSMEN: [As one] Kill the sheriff!

In making the same point as the original film, the parody seems closer to the real springs of human motivation than to the idealistic rhetoric of the original Western. The comedy derives from the gap between the conventional form of this scene and its "honest" deflation here. Similarly, when Sheriff Slim (Caesar) waxes heroic he bogs down in his wax:

When a man flies outa the cage and coyotes [are] howlin' in the tumbleweed, when a horse can't rightly cross the bridge, when a cow is, that is, a man oughta if the moon is high in the cactus and . . . when a coyote is chompin' in the corral . . . when a jackrabbit can't . . . unless there's a . . . [to wife Coca] You better go. You'll miss the train, Mary Ellen.

This blather blends the Gary Cooper convention of reticence and inarticulateness with the clichés of the genre. So too the hero's unheroic admission later. "How can you stay here and wait for a man to come and kill you?" Mary Ellen asks her man. His reply? "'Cause I'm stupid, Mary Ellen." He is resigned not just to his role as hero but to his stupidity in resigning himself to that role. This skit is a solid contribution to the modern literature of the antihero.

As well as the American popular successes, the show parodied European art films. Even Brooks's favorite, de Sica's *The Bicycle Thief*, was parodied as "La Bicycletta," with peasants Caesar and Coca stealing friend Reiner's shiny new bike. Other parodies such as "Hate," "Le Grand Amour," "Au Revoir, Ma Cherie," and "I Love You Strongly" parodied French films. In these shows American innocence was implicitly played against the worldliness and frankness of the French cinema. "Frere Jacques" took off from the romantic subplot of Renoir's *Le Grand Illusion*. Of course, most of the home audience had probably never seen the original film. But the comedy was broad enough not to be obscure. As Brooks recalls, the parody worked on two levels: "for the 7,000 who had seen [the original film], and for those who understood fear, hunger, lust, anger—everything human that was in those films." Moreover, these parodies probably did more to sell the foreign art film to American audiences than any sober ad campaign could have done. For they introduced in a light and palatable way the fact of a foreign cinema, its characteristic themes and styles, and—most important—the sense there could be an alternative to the familiar American models.

Always the parodies expressed affection and respect. It became an honor to be parodied on *Your Show of Shows*. Once producer Sam Spiegel threatened to sue over an impending parody of his

On the Waterfront. But he liked it so much that he later asked Caesar to rerun the parody when the film was being re-released, and he offered to send him the script of his upcoming feature *Bridge on the River Kwai* to facilitate its parodying, too. As Brooks observes, "You cannot have fun with anything that you don't love or admire or respect."[2]

The quality of the film parodies on *Your Show of Shows* has still not been surpassed. As Andrew Sarris explains, the Caesar company's parody was "unique in going beyond the surface of performance to the substance of characterizations." In "A Trolleycar Named Desire," for instance, "Caesar did not so much evoke Marlon Brando as expose Stanley Kowalski." Because it was all done live, "no recapitulation of *Your Show of Shows* can fully reproduce the exquisitely wrought emotional tension of the original experience," with the constant "suspenseful possibility of human error" and the performer's intensity. This tension remains at the heart of Brooks's improvisational genius.[3]

Brooks's other formal inheritance from the Caesar shows was the celebrity interview. As The Professor, Caesar played a rumpled German pedant whom a persistent young reporter (first Tom Avera, later Carl Reiner) would exercise and expose by questioning. Given Brooks's assurance that he has nothing against Germans, no further comment is necessary.

Brooks claims that he actually had a fist fight with Caesar before the star finally consented to do one Brooks interview, Dr. Siegfried von Sedative's advice to insomniacs. It's so good, it should be recorded in full. The opening shows Brooks's precision in language:

> Well, first of all, flop into bed. Don't sneak into bed, flop. And then you relax all the parts of the body. Say good night, toes, shhh. Quiet, go to sleep. And soon the toes drop off.

That's the wild basic premise, based on common advice about putting oneself to sleep. The idea of talking yourself to sleep by concentration is extended into a ludicrous dialogue with oneself:

> And then you say, ankles, shh, go to sleep, ankles, the toes are sleeping. And the ankles fall asleep. And then you say to the knees, all right, put on the sleeping caps, go to sleep. And they fall asleep.

The quick listener will appreciate that the knees wear caps—a Brooks routine rewards all levels of audience.

> And soon the whole leg is asleep. And you say to the stomach, all right, stop the mixing, it's time to go to sleep, put away the tools. Toora . . . loora . . . loora.

From simple concentration to dialogue, to lullaby—the basic premise grows increasingly absurd. There is also a characteristic touch in the ensuing infantilism:

> And then the arms go to sleep. And the chest, all right, stop breathing, beddy bye, and the throat, stop swallowing, don't talk no more, good night. Then the brain, go to sleep, good night.

But all is not quiet on the internal front. The logical conclusion of the basic premise is that if a person can talk to himself, why, then he will probably start arguing with himself. Conflict seems to be the inevitable result of communication, for man's mind will not be stilled:

> Will you go to sleep, will you go to sleep? Come on now. Now stop that and go to sleep. What's the matter with you? My brain is out of its mind . . . Shh. You'll wake up everybody. Look, the toes are awake. Look, toes, go to sleep. Fall asleep, toes. Shhh. . . . Now will you stop that? . . . Now wait. . . . What are you, a wise guy? All right, everybody up. I'll show you. Someday you're gonna wanna sleep. I'll walk the body all night.

Typical of the interviews—and of Brooks's later work on his own— a confident authority is exposed as suffering the common failures, insecurities, and anxieties of the average human wreck.

Even skits that we don't know to have been written by Brooks often have his tone, as sure as a fingerprint. A case in point is an interview with mountain-climbing expert Professor Sigmund von Fraidy-Katz, author of *Mountain Climbing: What Do You Need It For?* Brooks's stamp is on the book's title, with its colloquial undertow. It's also in the first image: The professor enters with a rope around his waist, looks at its frazzled end and sadly remarks, "What a sweet guy!" Like "pussycat," "sweet guy" is a Brooks phrase. And it's like Brooks to give the character such a playfully morbid introduction.

More important, the entire skit plays a fugitive allegory on the idea of psychoanalysis, from the professor's name to his profession of scaling heights from which his comrades plunge to doom. The professor's advice on what to do in an emergency is simple: "Scream and keep screaming all the way down" so "they'll know where to find you." Alternatively, "as soon as the rope breaks, you spread your arms and begin to fly." To the interviewer's skeptical, "But humans can't fly," the professor responds: "How do you know? You might be the first one. Anyway, you can always go back to screaming. That's always working for you." The entire discussion of the sport of scaling heights can be taken as a fun-house image of the psychoanalytic exploration of our depths. Because Sigmund von Fraidy-Katz is too afraid to be Freud, he speaks only of the safer heights.

Another typical Brooks touch is to set out a closely detailed, persuasive fantasy and then suddenly to withdraw from it. The viewer is left stranded, embarrassed for having committed himself to the vision he was fed. This occurs in the interview with Professor Filthy von Lucre (Caesar), author of *Money Talks, So Listen!* This authority claims that cavemen used rocks for currency: "It was the ice age. Plenty of ice cubes, but no rocks." Plausible enough, so he details the ice-age economy along the familiar lines of our own: a "nice, two-room cave" costs six boulders, eight rocks and twenty-four pebbles, in an age when you could get a nice dinosaur steak for eight rocks and six pebbles. The exactness lends weight; one believes that the man has actually studied ice-age menus and real-estate ads.

His parallel continues. Counterfeiters would debase the currency by painting mixtures of cement and clay to appear to be rocks. They were called "rocketeers," of course. One man contrived to become a millionaire by making faces at people till they threw rocks at him (Don Rickles?). But times change. Ice ages thaw. When fish became the official currency, you could smell a rich man a mile away. Yiddish humor obtrudes into the caveman fantasy. Ultimately fish was abandoned as currency because people refused to work in the bank. Now, after we have been completely drawn into the logic of the absurd parallel, the character reverts to real logic: "You think the government is going to take rocks and fish? They want the cash, boy!" The whole skit is a trick. The character's persuasive fantasy draws us into a ridiculous position, and then he traps us.

One may also detect Brooks's hand in the character of Professor Kurt von Stuffer, author of *Food Can Be Habit-Forming*. He has a Brooksian theory that we are what we eat:

> PROFESSOR: When a person eats fluffy eats, little cakes, pastry and fancy little things, then that person is also fluffy. . . . I had a patient once who was so fluffy, so light, that I prescribed a diet of meats and strong foods, and in a couple of months the patient was six feet tall with muscles and a big, flowing mustache.
> INTERVIEWER: That's wonderful.
> PROFESSOR: No, that's terrible. She was a woman and her husband didn't like it.

His most interesting case was "a terrible sight"—"thin, emaciated, small—weighed twelve pounds. So I examined him and found out why. He was just a baby. He was born yesterday." Brooks likely figured in the creation of Professor Hugo von Complex, author of *Animals, Their Habits, Habitat, and Haberdashery*; Professor Ludwig von Fossill, author of *Archaeology for Everyone or, Don't Lift Heavy Rocks*; Professor Lapse von Memory, author of *I Remember Mama—But I Forget Papa*; but probably not Professor Hugo von Gezuntheit, whose book, *The Human Body and How to Avoid It*, seems anathema. But in "I'm in Love," a parody of *The Blue Angel*, Caesar's Professor Ludwig von Brenner (Translation: Ludwig of the burner) is a clearly Brooksian psychoanalyst:

> My theory about the brain is that the brain is bigger than the mind. The brain is everything. The whole shooting match. But the mind is nothing. You want to cross your legs you need the brain. The mind can't make up its mind. And the heart is just a pump and the liver is just for laughs. The brain is everything.

This professor is ruined by his love for a waitress, Ivy (Imogene Coca), a brassy "*gelt* digger."

Of course, not even Mel Brooks won a cigar every time he swung at the bell. Sometimes his waggery was a tad far out, as in the case of this animal psychologist's line:

> You see that snake in dere? Ja? Vell, he don't vant to be in dere. I passed by the snake cage and that snake whispered to me "You gotta get me outa here. This place is full of snakes!" And I looked at him and said, "Vhat you vant out for? You're a snake, too!"

For some reason, that story never gets a laugh. But I find it strangely touching, with the unsettling wit of an Escher drawing.[4]

There was often a Jewish inflection to Brooks's contributions, even when he was not revealing that he has nothing personal against the Germans. For example, there is a Jewish cultural inflection in the opening of "Strange," a parody of the classic Western *Shane*. In the Brandon de Wilde role, Imogene Coca asks the wandering cowboy, "You seem mighty thirsty. Have a long ride?" "No—I had a herring for breakfast." Again, prosaic reality undermines the rhetoric of the genre.

In addition to the parody and interview formats on *Your Show of Shows*, Brooks cultivated his characteristic tone. He turned a simple, candid, deflating perspective upon large, pretentious characters and situations. In this light it is useful to quote Andrew Sarris's distinction between Sid Caesar, and Mike Nichols and Elaine May; it's a difference of class consciousness as well as of period. Caesar appealed to "a fundamentally popular common sense" with his "every bellow of outrage." But with Nichols and May, "an elitist *frisson* of intellectual and cultural superiority was cultivated at the expense of our most sacred cows." Sarris considers this split the beginning of "the civil war between the Jewish intellectuals and the Jewish philistines, and also the beginning of an era of cultural affluence and alienation and of increasing fragmentation of audience sensibilities."[5] Those are sweeping battle lines, but Sarris's point is verified by the polar camps of "intellectual" Woody Allen and "philistine" Mel Brooks. Brooks carried away from the Caesar show the compulsion to connect with a mass audience and a modesty about his own advantages in knowledge; Allen addressed the more specialized audience.

Brooks proved this knack in the series he developed with Buck Henry in 1964, *Get Smart*. Producer David Susskind hired the two writers to develop a parody of the James Bond fad that exploded with the film *Doctor No* (1963). ABC declined the series because it was "too wild"; program chief Edgar Schrick wanted something more "warm and human." So Brooks added a dog (asthmatic). The series was snapped up by NBC, on the prescience of producer Grant Tinker (later sire of the Mary Tyler Moore stable of snappy comedies). When *Get Smart* debuted on September 18, 1965, it was an instant success. Having developed the project and coauthored the hilarious pilot, Brooks left the series, because he feared otherwise he'd "run dry very soon." The series ran until September 11, 1970, by which time the spy drama had dwindled into domestica. But the show proved Brooks right in his confidence that there was an audience waiting for his peculiar gifts:

> Somewhere between those who sop up the gelatinous, brain-scrambling nonsense of *Petticoat Junction* and the intellectuals who catch *Basic Hungarian* at six A.M. is a vast segment of the population that wants intelligent entertainment. Without morals. . . . I mean they want TV without little sermons. For years *The Danny Thomas Show* was doing the Ten Commandments. Every episode had a little message to deliver: Don't lie, don't kill your neighbor, don't covet your neighbor's wife, don't uncovet your neighbor's wife. . . .

Brooks's TV series delivered humor with intelligence and without condescension.[6]

Get Smart focuses on an incompetent WASP secret agent, Maxwell Smart (Don Adams) and his lovely, capable aide, Agent 99 (Barbara Feldon). This leading man is a hopeless blunderer, who drives to distraction the Chief (Ed Platt). Smart's every success is due to luck, his enemies' frustration, and the skills of 99. Smart works for the secret American agency CONTROL, against the international enemy, KAOS. (The CONTROL agent lacks control and causes chaos with his every move against KAOS, get it?)

In the pilot episode, the bumbling hero is up against the notorious Mr. Big, who, typically, is played by a dwarf, Michael Dunn. The authors' literacy shone through the conventional

script: Mr. Big had kidnapped a Professor Dante and his dooms-
day melting machine, "The Inthermo." The show had a crackling
pace of one-liners, a sophisticated level of address, and yet a
simplicity that won even preteenagers.

As Brooks explained, "I wanted to do a crazy, unreal comic-strip
kind of thing about something besides a family. No one had ever
done a show about an idiot before. I decided to be the first." He
contrasted his series to the conventional comedy shows, such as
the Ozzie and Harriet Nelson programs, with "lovable boobs" as
heroes. Max Smart is "dangerously earnest" and commits "monu-
mental goofs." Despite creating a comic-strip tone, Smart's
failures made his series more lifelike than the pastoral idylls of the
various Nelson and Anderson family sagas:

> In their supposedly true-to-life little episodes, they avoid anything
> approaching reality. For years I've always wanted to see an honest
> family TV series—maybe something called *Half of Father Knows
> Best*. The other half of him was paralyzed by a stroke in 1942 when
> he suspected we might lose the war.

Get Smart was as close as Brooks could get to placing that
antiheroic conception on a network comedy show.[7]

The series had several recurrent comic devices. The most
obvious was the hero's inability to live up to his role as secret
agent. The comedy derived either from the spectacle of his failures
or from the discrepancy between his pretensions and his incompetence. The latter is the point of his "Would you believe—"
catchline. Typically, the routine would begin with Smart pretending to a huge power (*e.g.*, "Would you believe I can break eight
boards with one karate chop?"). When his grandiose claim was
doubted, Smart would return with reduced pretensions ("No?
Would you believe three boards?"). Finally, he would be reduced
to a claim of absurd triviality ("Would you believe a loaf of
bread?"). This routine exposes Smart's extreme naïveté, his
grandiose rhetoric, and his helplessness. Because he begins with
such an inappropriate heroic pretense, he is unable to affirm
anything. He can only look for what level of deception his
antagonist is willing to grant him ("Would you believe . . ."). This
transparent trickery recalls the fantastical traps that we found set
in Brooks's interviews for *Your Show of Shows*.

In minor comic patterns, Smart continually proved unable to handle even the simplest of instructions or information. In the second episode, in which his antagonist was a one-armed Chinese villain, The Claw, Smart couldn't pronounce the villain's name to his satisfaction. Smart also revealed his usual dependence upon conventions of his genre:

CLAW: Do you know what they call me?
SMART: Lefty?

In the same spirit, Smart was continually encountering—but being defeated by—the kind of ladies that laid siege to James Bond. Indeed Smart's very dependence upon 99 was an implicit counterpoise to Bond's way of loving and leaving. Smart also had an armory of tricky gadgets, in emulation of Bond. But Smart's were ludicrous and he never could use them properly. He was continually embarrassed by his phone ringing in his shoe at inopportune moments. In addition to these parodies of Bond, the general plot line of *Get Smart* allowed for individual episodes to develop specific parodies. A typical week of the program's reruns today may turn up parodies of *Bonnie and Clyde, The Maltese Falcon,* and the like. Beyond its origin in Bond, the series dramatized the average nincompoop's inability to live up to the rhetoric of the entire American heroic mythology. The greater his aspiration, the more spectacular the defeat, the more pathetic our hero's resigned attempt to make amends: "Sorry about that, Chief."

This sense of futile heroism, a simple human exposed by his attempt to live an impossible mythology, was the central theme of the series. Its point was that man must accept himself and be responsible for himself, free from the fantasies of genre entertainments. This may be what Brooks had in mind when he described the series as "a show in which you can comment, too. I don't mean we're in the broken-wing business. We're not social workers, but we can do some comment such as you can't inject in, say, *My Three Sons*."[8] The "comment" in the *Get Smart* series is the fallacy of trying to live by the conventions of our film heroes and their genres. That very idea propels Brooks's feature films.

In 1975 Brooks attempted to apply this principle to a comic Robin Hood series that writers John Boni and Norman Stiles had proposed to producer Norman Steinberg. With Brooks's clout from the success of *Blazing Saddles*, ABC eagerly launched the series, *When Things Were Rotten*. The show dissolved into shallowness and repetitiveness, though Brooks could not be blamed, because he had a very brief and limited association with the series. The half-hour series ran from September 10 to December 24, 1975.

The pilot show declared its essential device, anachronism, with a barrage of signs: "Nottingham Next Three Exits," "Welcome— No Poaching, Scrambling, Frying or Hard-Boiling." In the treasury there were two signs: "Positively No Personal Cheques Cashed" and "Foreign Exchange: One of Ours for Two of Theirs." These gags assume the universality of man's ways by projecting specifics from our own day upon the legendary past. By firing contemporary dialogue, situations and knowing into a remote, indeed mythic, period, the series emphasized the mythic nature of the original. Each anachronism reminded us that myths such as the Robin Hood one are not an image of their own nature, time, and place, but a projection of the perceiver. The meaning of a myth lies in what it tells us about the mythologizer.

So *When Things Were Rotten* was not really about Robin Hood, but about the process by which a society develops such myths. Brooks gave a comic explanation of the title: As there were no laundromats in Robin's day, when they rode the bus they smelled rancid, but "rotten fits better into the title."[9] Rather, the title works by ironic reversal. The real Robin Hood myth expresses our society's nostalgia for a golden age in the past, when against an evil social force an idealistic hero could arise and lead a noble life. Brooks's title is an implicit rebuttal to the golden-age nostalgia of the Robin Hood myth. His point is that despite the glories of our myths, in the olden days things were as rotten as they are today. There is no salvation to be had in a retreat to myths.

That is the point in the flood of anachronisms: medieval Sherwood Forest is presented as a projection of today and here, without the remote ideality that it conventionally has. Thus, in the bow-and-arrow contest, Lord McDonald of the Golden Archers wears a T-shirt emblazoned "Over 1,000,000 Dispatched." A sign at a county fair reads "Horse Parking—We Validate." A genial, goateed, white-haired gentleman hawks "Kensington Fried Pheasant—It's Knuckle-Lickin' Good." At the climactic joust, one of Robin's fans advises him to "Buckle up for safety." Of course, every medieval knight had his buckler.

In a related motif, a medieval situation or phrase is inflected toward modernity. A sedate court entertainment erupts into a torrid performance of "Babaloo." Often an archaic metaphor is treated literally, as if forced into a modern sense. When the evil Sheriff of Nottingham (Henry Polic II) commands the peasants to hold their tongues, they grab them. When a tax collector orders that a reluctant peasant be "Put . . . in his place," four henchmen sledgehammer him into the ground: "He's in his place, Sir!"

Overall, the show played against the conventions of the legend. Often a familiar situation would be ballooned into absurdity. For example, Gaspard the Spy was disguised as a tree, one day apple, one day mixed fruit. When the sheriff orders him paid, his aide asks, "From the spy fund or the forestry fund?" Similarly, when Bertram is led blindfolded to Robin's camp, his horse is also blindfolded. When Robin (Dick Gautier) robs the rich, he doesn't give all to the poor; he keeps some to run his administration. The tone through all this is modern and debunking.

The entire cast of characters was undermined by this antiheroic spirit. Apart from his bureaucratic compromises, Robin was a clean-cut, fatuous simpleton in this series. Alan-a-Dale (Bernie Kopell), the traditional balladeer-reporter, was here presented as a Las Vegas comedian type who made frequent cliché-riddled addresses directly to his audience. Friar Tuck (Dick Van Patten) was "a man of cloth and violence," with mainly alimentary interests. When he dueled with a sword in one hand and a piece of chicken in the other, he stabbed his opponent with the chicken, then bit his own sword. Prince John (Ron Rifkin) was played as a mincing gay. The evil sheriff loved the groaning sounds from his dungeons: "It's the only place I can really unwind." At his behest, chained prisoners sang "Forget your troubles, come on, get happy." Maid Marian (Misty Rowe) was a spy in Prince John's household, but secretly yearned to marry Robin and become a simple housewife in the new model subdivision Rancho Sherwood Estates.

From another legend altogether, Richard Dimitri played identical twins separated at birth (as in *The Corsican Brothers*)—

Bertram the Bad, a parody of Laurence Olivier's characterization of Richard III, and the virtuous Merry Man Renaldo. This addition to the Robin Hood story is particularly significant. In transplanting characters from other myths, the series again undercut the historical pretense of the Robin Hood saga. Moreover, the double-natured character of the actor's opposite roles points to the central motif of the series—the double life of a legend, as it exists in both reality and myth, eternally revivable and expressive, yet rooted in its viewer's time.

The individual episodes allowed for the same kind of individual parodies as *Get Smart*. In one episode, the sheriff hires a mad inventor, along the lines of Dr. Strangelove, to murder Robin with his Ultimate Weapon; we see an ominous twelve-foot trigger. In another, Robin saves Marian from conscription into a harem. When the heroes are away on holiday, the sheriff discredits them by recruiting a band of evil look-alikes. In another episode heroes and villains are quarantined together with the bubonic plague. In these silly gimmicks, the series was set tongue-in-cheek to carry on forever, playing formulaic variations in the manner of success-ful films and TV shows—and the evergreen myths of our culture.

Chapter 4

The Recordings

THE FOUR RECORDS that Mel Brooks made with Carl Reiner show a wit of unbelievable dexterity. Simply, there is nothing else quite like Mel Brooks's fancy in flight. He extemporizes better than most comics can laboriously write.

In large measure the power of these routines lies in their extemporaneity. As Brooks admits, "It's the pressure that somehow helps catalyze comedy—the insanity. . . . There's something in the voice, the excitement, the fighting for your life when Carl traps you. He chases me like I'm a mouse." Although the genius was Brooks's, much credit is due his interviewer-straightman, Reiner, whose clear, normative tones provided an important foil to the gravelly-voiced Brooks. More important, Reiner had his own lively, ranging mind that would spur Brooks on, challenging him, impelling him. He "always tried for something that would force him to go into panic," Reiner recalls, "because a brilliant mind in panic is a wonderful thing to see."[1]

But Brooks would rise to every challenge. When Reiner suddenly introduced him as a Jewish pirate, Brooks proceeded to whine about the rising cost of sailcloth and galley crews. Introduced as Carl Sandburg, he extemporized reams of plausible but fake Sandburg poetry. As a rather small-world wrestling champion from Israel, he explained his success against larger opponents: "I give them a soul kiss and they're so shocked they collapse." This much may be logical, a revision of the David–Goliath affair. But Brooks followed up with one of his specialties, a wild image that goes beyond all logic: He can distinguish between kissing wrestlers and his wife because his wife "is the only one I know who kisses from the inside out." What does that mean? Who knows? But it somehow sounds precise, so Brooks got himself off Reiner's hook again.

Once the duo worked out a family comprised of a Jewish mother, a black father, and a homosexual son. Brooks played all three roles without confusing their separate identities. Then came Reiner's curve: "Why is your son white-haired when you are not?" Brooks answered, in the mother's voice:

> I told him always to stay inside the building because it's full of Jews. One day he went out and saw a whole bunch of Gentiles on the next block and his hair turned white overnight. It was his own fault. He should have stayed indoors.

Brooks's reply is consistent with the comic character and with his own entrenched world view. His body of set attitudes, upon which he could play infinite variations, fuels his off-the-cuff brilliance.

At other times he could free-fall in absurdity without relation to familiar material. Introduced as novelist Irving Schwartz, he was suddenly asked why his novel was published in a triangular shape. Brooks replied, unperturbed: "I'm glad you noticed that. It's a one-breasted seersucker jacket. The name is on the label—Irving Feinberg." When Reiner confronted him with the discrepancy in names, Brooks checked his driver's license: "My name is William Faversham." Why did he write a book under the name of Schwartz? "I think somebody stole my wallet." Here both men kept topping each other's nonsequiturs. When all was said and done, the interview seemed a plausible extension of the separate lunacies in real-life celebrity conversation.

Kenneth Tynan, who reports these unrecorded exchanges, quotes Mel Tolkin's memory of one party at which Brooks was off on a brilliant monologue—and couldn't find an adequate punch line. In the middle of a sentence he stopped and left the room. The guests waited. When Tolkin eventually left to look for him, he found that Brooks had gone home in self-disgust. He had left a note on a table: "A Jew cries for help!" Clearly, to Brooks there was more at stake in these routines than just laughs. His self, genius, identity, and soul were constantly on the line.

In the sample of these flights that survive on record, there is a good deal of simple satire. As Philip Heineker, author of *Taxes, Taxes, Taxes: What Do They Want from Us?* Brooks spins straightforward variation on the *Your Show of Shows* interviews. Heineker declares the whole population of Romania as his dependents, because nobody else does. Besides, he sends them things: socks, books, old *Time* magazines. Heineker's authority is the Hipaccountant's Oath; that the government of, by and for the people is taking too much money from the people. Dieting expert Dr. Felix Wheird warns that wearing undershirts is the biggest cause of overweight: they make you feel like drinking beer and singing Polish songs. Fish are good, this nutritionist advises, because they never started a war. He closes with a trenchant moral: only poor people dig their graves with their teeth. Though these silly interviews highlight trivial subjects and foolish authorities, serious concerns cast their shadow nonetheless.

On Brooks's first album, an entire sequence satirizes the heroes of modish pop culture. Fabiola typifies the blown-out, laid-back, inarticulate, bored dolt that becomes a generation's bard: "I am them. They are me. We are all singing. I have the mouth." As he explains his success, "I don't know my life, my purpose, that's why I'm loved." His music cannot be classified as jazz or swing: "It's dirty, man." The entire characterization is encapsulated in the contrast between interviewer Reiner's tone of animated energy ("You're dynamic. You're exciting. You're vibrant.") and Fabiola's deadly soporific, "I've heard that." The skit bemoans the death of liveliness in the lively arts.

Then Brooks and Reiner shift into an interview with "an astronaught." The spelling emphasizes that the model image of the astronaut is really a cypher, a void. This subject has a perky, eager voice and a candor that distinguish him from the cool blankness of the real astronauts. As he informs us, the government publicizes a few professional models as astronauts, so that the real and ugly ones like himself will not make the U.S. lose face before Russia. "None of them are them. . . . They can't take pictures of us. We're monkeys, man." This candid astronaut reveals the unglamorous truth behind the experiments of space travel. He accepts officers' insults with a "Thank you, Sir!" Otherwise they would tear his nose off. A four-star general once tore out our hero's tooth ("Whap!") as punishment for giggling on the parade ground.

So much for giggling. To our naive hero, space travel means going "into the blue, up beyond the buildings." As he is a latrine cleaner, his science is limited. He can't recall whether it's the moon or the earth that does not revolve around the sun! He concludes: "Sixteen out of nineteen people revolve around the sun." There is safety in numbers. He even blabs the secret launching time, because "I'm gonna die anyway; I don't care . . . I haven't got a chance." And he tells us that after three or four minutes in the flight simulation machine, you "puke your guts out." He sticks on that phrase, because it is a hard, visceral truth—ballast against the puffery of glamor, illusion, and dehumanized science: "Excuse me. I've got to get in the machine and puke my guts out." But he keeps his pride. When the interviewer suggests that the astronaut may be "ill equipped" for his job, our hero bristles: "Whaddya mean? I got gloves and everything . . . a heavy fur hat, everything." This skit restores the flawed, bathetic humanity to a sterilized image. Of course, one finds this antiheroic candor in Brooks's own war memoirs too:

> I spent a lot of time in the artillery. Too noisy. Could *not* take the noise. All through the war, two cigarette butts stuck in my ears. . . . And then *they* started shooting. "Incoming mail!" Bullshit. Only Burt Lancaster says that. We said, "Oh, God! Oh, Christ!" Who knows, he might help. He was Jewish, too. "MOTHER!"[2]

Often the early recordings seem bowdlerized versions of the party act. Kenneth Tynan recalls a 1959 skit about a psychoanalyst from "The Vienna School of Good Luck," who was analyzed by Freud himself ("Lovely little fellow . . . wearing a nice, off-the-shoulder dress."). This analyst is shocked when the interviewer tells him about the Oedipus complex ("when a man has a passionate desire to make love to his own mother"): "That's the dirtiest thing I ever heard. Where do you get that filth?" He recovers when he learns that Sophocles was Greek, not Jewish: "With a Greek, who knows? But with a Jew, you don't do a thing like that even to your own wife, let alone your mother." On record, Brooks plays another Puritanical analyst, Dr. Hall-Danish. When his patient runs out screaming, the doctor orders: "Nurse, I don't want that nut in here again. . . . She spoke filt'y. . . . In *my* house, in *my* rooms." The "filth" was her admission that she dreamed she kissed her father. When interviewer Reiner admits that he kisses his own daughter, Dr. Hall-Danish gives him a curt dismissal: "It's been nice talking to you, good-bye." Earlier, Dr. Hall-Danish reported two successful treatments. He cured one boy, Arnold, who loved his dog: "I said, 'Hey, you can't do dat. What are you, crazy?'" He also cured a lady of her obsession, tearing paper: "I told her, 'Don't tear paper. What? A nice girl like you? Don't tear paper.'" He had to live with her for a while to slap her hands whenever she started to tear paper. Brooks's psychoanalysts have two basic characteristics: they practice Jewish homilies instead of abstruse theories, and they are all physicians in need of healing.

So too his panel of analysts from the New Technique Psychiatric Society, each with his own neurosis. Dr. Akiba ben Hollywood from Israel is confident: "I never practice, I'm good at it." He gave hope to an entire army division simply by saying, "Good-bye and good luck" to them. He prescribes codeine for between-meals pep and to overcome feelings of inferiority. Dr. Buck Mitchison from Texas wields Texan magniloquence, guns, and exuberance. He loves handshaking because "the human hand is one of the great instruments for shaking." Rather than studying, he ordained himself an analyst, swearing with one hand on a Texas stone. But he is insanely worried about his eyes. "Stay away from my eyes," he continually shrieks at everyone. Dr. Sabu Panchali from India dreads shrinking: "I question nothing. I'm very short." He wakes up from a sudden nap with a startled "Don't hit me; I have one tooth." His countrymen's main fear is of growing even shorter. He urges us to contemplate the inner man, not the "ball-bearing" industrial man. His theory is that his nation's dire poverty is due to its people being poor. A concluding anthem dedicates the profession to overcoming nervousness and sadness, but these specimens provide little hope.

In the 1973 album, *2,000 and Thirteen*, the changing times allowed for spicier routines. But in the earlier ones, decorum was served, in generous helpings, with just a little spice. On *Carl Reiner and Mel Brooks at the Cannes Film Festival*, Federico Fettucini is a Greek director (real name: Mercurio Mercurochrome) whose new film, *Rape*, typifies the industry's prurience: "We're trying to say that there's much immorality in our country." So all his films have orgies and rapes. Even when a virtuous hero, an avocado grower, brings a whole town to contrition, on their way to the church they are all raped by the whole Turkish army. Now Fettucini promises a quiet, pastoral film, where a quiet little shepherd boy rapes a little girl quietly while his sheep wander quietly off. In contrast, Tippy Skittles is the Angry Young Man, angry because his films don't make money. His *Sunday Night and Saturday Morning* will be a week more advanced than Tony Richardson's *Saturday Night and Sunday Morning*.

After these gibes at the pretensions of the film industry, the next subject jars with a harsh reminder of one of Brooks's continuing concerns, the Nazi (not that he has anything personal against the Germans, of course). Adolph Hartler from the Narzi Film Company embodies the new Germany's attempt to dissociate itself entirely from its past. The Nazis were "our worst enemies," he now claims. "In my own home we hid a Jewish family. We hid them for a while and then we turned them over to the Gestapo." His SS tattoo really stands for "Simon Says" ("I take the game very seriously"). The film *Judgment at Nuremberg* was "unfair"; it was all a misunderstanding. After all, "you send a few people to camp, don't you? In the summer?" He does admit that Hitler made "some terrible errors," notably "losing the war." Suddenly a light satire on film biz explodes into an abrasive caricature of Nazi apologists.

On another record, Brooks plays a Peruvian coffee plantation owner named Lopez de Vega Diaz "whatever," who keeps lapsing into German accent and confession. "I was only a sergeant in the Peruvian Indians." "We took Poland in nineteen days." "Crushed France in twenty-seven days . . . I mean, the beans can be crushed and ground in twenty-seven days." When Reiner identifies him as a Nazi, the fellow genially admits, "Well, you found me out." His cheek is as horrifying as his nature. In these routines, as in *The Producers*, the comic keeps alive the drama of the Holocaust.

The early skit, "In a Coffee House," is a survey of frustrated desires in the modish society. One person is "mainly depressed" because "I'm not pretty." The interviewer offers consolation: "You're as attractive as nine out of fifteen people I know. . . .

You're a good-looking man, sir." But "I'm not a man, I'm a woman!" Then comes a Levi-wearing cross between Marlon Brando and Joanne Woodward, with his own confusions: "I'm a lesbian," he says for "thespian," and "The greatest actor in America is Tallulah Bankhead." Well, in terms of a deep, manly voice. . . . His parting line is "I hope I am an actor." Next comes Corin Corfu, a painter who, notwithstanding his Greek name and accent, says "I hope I am Greek. I would like to be Greek very much." This identity crisis spreads to his art, which is confused first with the air conditioner and then with his supper. ("If you really like it, I can lacquer it up and give it to you for forty dollars.") This skit concludes with the uninvited singer, Charlie Great, whose entire repertoire consists of one-note variations on "Twenty-two men fell down and hurt their knee." He extemporizes other songs: "Twenty-two German soldiers fell down and hurt their knee," "Twenty-two Calypso men fell down and hurt their knee," and for a topical—and prophetic—climax: "Big Dick Nixon hurt his knee." There is a similar bathos in poet Laurel Bellew's "Inauguration Poem for John Kennedy":

> *President, President,*
>   *Lea—der!*
> *Rickety zack, rickety zack,*
> *Bring that glory back!*

Of course, Brooks has a rather homey conception of the poet laureate: "I would kill for a ripe cantaloupe."

For Brooks, comedy and man's sense of his insecure existence are not separate concerns. Indeed much of his comedy confronts the various forms of human dread. In raising man's nightmares, Brooks's comedy helps us to face, not to forget, our sources of anxiety and terror. It is healthier and more responsible to joke about the Holocaust than it would be to forget it.

Brooks stares down dread. His interview with the puking, terrified astronaut is a case in point. So is the first skit (uncredited) that Brooks wrote for *Your Show of Shows*. This was an interview with a jungle boy (Sid Caesar) found roaming the New York City streets in a lion skin:

INTERVIEWER: What are you afraid of more than anything?
JUNGLE BOY: Buick.
INTERVIEWER: You're afraid of a Buick?
JUNGLE BOY: Yes. Buick can win in death struggle. Must sneak up
    on parked Buick, punch grille hard. Buick die.

Of course, the modern viewer knows that the Buick will survive
any punch to its grille. The jungle boy's dread should be even
greater than he realizes.

Dread is the organizing and compelling theme of Brooks's
masterpiece, his series of interviews as the 2,000-year-old man. In
his first appearance he guards against a punishing fate: "October
the sixteenth I'll be two thousand years young. How we say:
young! Not to curse ourselves, you know?" Indeed his very first
recorded words are "Oooooohhh boy!" as if to express relief at
having survived a millenium. The two-thousand-years-and-six-
months man is still anxious about his appearance and health: "I
don't look more than sixteen or seventeen hundred, right?" He
prays "fiercely" for twenty-two minutes daily "that a ceiling
shouldn't fall on me and my heart shouldn't attack me." Later the
2,002-year-old recommends garlic for longevity. By his "scientific
explanation" of mortality, the Angel of Death can be driven away
by a garlic-breathed "Wwhhhooo is it?" So although Brooks's two-
thousand-year-old man is a marvelous survivor, he remains a
creature of dread. That's the human condition, Brooks style. For
"as long as the world is turning and spinning," man will be dizzy,
nauseous, confused, and doomed to errors and—worse—his sense
of vulnerability.

According to the two-thousand-year-old man, man has always
been dominated by dread. Before man had a God to fear (two
years before, for that matter), they quaked before their leader,
Phil. They prayed: "Ohhh, Phillip. Please don't take our eyes out
and don't pinch us and don't hurt us. *Ooo-main!*" What begins as
Caliban's fear of pinching demons ends in the Yiddish "amen."
Then a bolt of lightning proved "there's something bigger than
Phil!" According to our authority, the Lord was first named
Gevalt, which is the Yiddish word for "my goodness!" Over the
years it changed to the more familiar *Yahveh*, then *Yahvay*, then
Your-way, *His-way* and finally *Lord*. This etymology presents God

as a dread force felt first, then named, then submitted to *(Your-way, His-way)* and only recently domesticated as the comfy *Lord*.

The two-thousand-year-old man explains that all man's advances and achievements were due to fear. "Everything we do is based on fear." The nicety of the handshake was originally a check to see whether the friend was carrying a hidden stone or stick. From that ploy grew dancing; its "complete immobilization" meant that your partner can't kick you. Even love, "mainly love," originated in fear: "What do you need a woman for? To see if there's an animal behind you." Nationalism also sprang from fear. People huddled in caves and chanted their anthems. (To wit: "Let 'em all go to Hell except Cave 76.") Singing originated in man's "help songs," lilting cries for aid (*e.g.*, "A lion is eating my foot off; would somebody call a cop."). So too did language: "Two hundred years before Hebrew was the Rock language, or rock talk. . . . [For example:] 'Hey, don't throw that rock at me! What you doing with that rock? Put down that rock!'" Apparently the discourse was limited but expressive. Fear was also the chief means of transportation; man would see some threat and run away. In Brooks's history of man, there is no transport of delight, just the driving force of fear.

But Brooks's hero is living proof that man can survive, however terrified and anxious he may be. Constantly aware of his own vulnerability and degeneration, he survives as a hearty, warm, wise, unconventional spirit. Like the doctor in Brooks's *Young Frankenstein*, the two-thousand-year-old man "is undertaking the quest to defeat death—to challenge God."[3] In this character, Brooks confronts man's mortality but affirms his faith in the quirky human spirit.

The single most striking characteristic of the old sage is that he's Jewish. His Jewishness serves several functions. For one thing, it concentrates all his varieties of vulnerability. The Jewish comic figure—in Brooks as in Kafka and Woody Allen—is helpless before hostile man as well as before nature and God. So the old hero observes how hospitals were the same in the caveman days as they are today. The same medical principles were practiced: "the principle of people walking past you when you're screaming and not caring . . . the same wonderful indifference to the sick and the dying." He's so accustomed to an antagonistic society that he has always considered Paul Revere "an anti-Semite bastard" for yelling "The Yiddish are coming! The Yiddish are coming!" Corrected, the old man has a touching remorse: "Oy, my God! I'm going to have to send his wife a note."

The Jewishness in these improvisations was extremely personal for Brooks: "I really wailed. I could hear my antecedents. I could hear five thousand years of Jews pouring through me." In addition, Brooks sees this comic Jew as a way to preserve a dying voice, a fading culture:

> Within a couple of decades, there won't be any more accents like that. They're being ironed out by history, because there are no more Jewish immigrants. It's the sound I was brought up on, and it's dying.

While history presses the uniform, Brooks's two-thousand-year-old man sustains the kinks of an individualistic human nature. "It's not a Jewish accent," he notes, but "an American-Jewish accent." And the documentary realism of the old man is Brooks's defense against any charges of that old bugbear "questionable taste." "He may be pompous at times; he may be a nut, but he's always honest and compelling. And the accent is always accurate." This is what unites the Brooks of the two-thousand-year-old man's Yiddish hominess and the Brooks who loves the Italian neorealist cinema.[4]

Much of the old man's humor derives from traditions of Jewish stereotypy. For example, he is the universal Jewish parent, loving and abandoned melodramatically: "I have over forty-two thousand children and not one comes to visit me. How dey forget a father?" But he's proud: twenty-one thousand doctors, seven hundred accountants, and two entertainers, including the excessive Boom Boom Crosby. In this comedy of stereotype and scale, a domestic sentiment survives massive amplification. He also envies Moses' parents; *he* gave *them* those famous tablets to put over the mantelpiece in a forty-dollar frame, to awe the TV repairman (Commandment 11-b, perhaps: Thou shalt not flaunt thy kid's diploma). Now you don't have to be Jewish to have this mad, hungry affection for your children, or to need their successes to justify your own life. But it helps. Similarly, when the old man's father visited, he would stand outside the cave in the rain and look in: "I'm awright. We just want to look at you. . . . No, we can stand. Awright. . . . Naw, we ate on the way, on the dinosaur." Now the old man repeats that behavior, because "we mock the thing we are to be." As Brooks explained on the famous David Susskind show, "Jewish parents don't want to be a bother. So they overcompensate by being insane." But a key lesson is the warning that the two-thousand-year-old man embodies: We mock what we will become, if we're lucky.

As he is an eternal outsider, Brooks's old man stands apart from social trends and reflects upon them. His idea of a natural organic menu is just what God made: clouds and stars. A simple, homey sense pervades his teachings. He ascribes longevity to never ever touching fried food and never running for a bus ("There'll always be another."). He has also lived at a slow pace of development, which had its own rewards: "I breast-fed for two hundred years. . . . I used to con a lot of ladies into doing it. They took pity on me." Often this man of universal experience falls back on the simplest of homilies. Thus he survives by "will to live," but even here there's nothing high-faluting: it's advice from his doctor, Will Talive. So too is his advice for mankind's survival: "If every human being in the world played a violin, we'd be bigger and better than Mantovani."

This comic bathos animates the old man's naive but often wise versions of the origins of our knowledge. In the old days, "we was so dumb we didn't know who was the ladies." The female was finally discovered by one Bernie, who said, "Hey, dere are ladies here. . . . One morning he got up smiling" and reported how "in the night I felt thrilled and delighted." Our hero still blushes at Bernie's tale. On a less important plane, the old man recalls the early professions: "Hitting a tree with a piece of stick was awreddy a good job. If you could get it." So was looking at the sky or watching each other.

At times we may doubt the old man's veracity, such as when he recalls his ancient Hebrew: "Oh hi dere! How are you? Awright." But he usually seems trustworthy. He refrains from giving examples of early herbal medicine because "I don't wanna throw the whole ethical drug field into chaos. . . . Certain bark from certain trees would make you jump in the air and sing 'Sweet Sue.'" Similarly, early physicians would check their patients by sticking a finger in the patient's nose: "If he doesn't say 'Aw, take your finger out of my nose,' he's dead." With equal logic, he traces tennis back to ancient Egypt, when live skunks were batted back and forth between the pyramids. Later, cats were used. Their racket, when you pull out the catgut, explains why the implement became known as a "racquet."

The old man also delivers Brooks's most concise statement on comedy. He recalls the great comedian of the caveman days, Murray the Nut. When a tiger sauntered in, Murray pulled its tail and yelled "Yaha, yaha, yaha." To the hilarity of all the onlookers, the tiger ate Murray up. He obviously liked salted nuts. As the old wag explains, "To me tragedy is if I cut my finger. . . . Comedy is if you walk into an open sewer and die. What do I care?"

Whatever one's doubts about the old man's veracity, then, one can trust his sense of proportion. In his history of human fashion, the hat predated the fig leaf. After all, if God wanted man to protect his private parts more than his brain, He would have put the skull down there. Anyway, having a stranger caress your genitals is nothing. After a while, the effect is over. But you don't want anyone to caress or scramble your brains!

As well as man's mythic history, the old man draws upon actual historical characters and events. He used to produce Stars of David, by having six men run together with separate points, fusing them in the heat of their collision. "We'd make only two a day, because of the accidents." He rejected Simon's proposal of the cross, even though that would have saved four men's work: "I thought it was too simple. I didn't know then that it would be so eloquent." Had he only gone for that "winner, a big seller," our hero would be rich today: "I'd have over a hundred dollars." He remembers Christ: "a nice boy, lovely, thin, wore sandals. . . . Came in the store. Never bought anything." There's a satiric thrust to his memory of the disciples, Ben, Murray, Al, Richie, Saul, Abe—"No, that's the William Morris Agency. Same stuff." He has little new light to shed on Christ: "He was a carpenter. . . . If I knew it was gonna be Him I'da made Him a partner in the store. Who knew it was gonna be a hit?" In addition to fusing religion and show biz, the two-thousand-year-old man shows in this routine that he is not to be overwhelmed by anyone.

He brings everything down to his own range of experience and understanding. So he survives.

Both his debunking spirit and his affirmation of an essential, indomitable humanity characterize his memories of other great figures. Robin Hood "stole from everybody and kept everything," but his press agent, Marty, built him a fine image. King Arthur was more than a king; he was a landlord, with four apartment buildings! His famous round table was really just oval, but extra leaves were added when the knights came for dinner. Shakespeare was "a pussycat. . . . Oooh, was he good and smart [but] not a good writer at all. . . . Every letter was cockeyed and crazy. He had the worst penmanship I ever saw in my life." Our hero invested in Shakespeare's thirty-eighth play, *Queen Alexandra and Murray*, but "it closed in Egypt." With a Jewish hero and dialogue—

QUEEN: What ho, Murray. . . .
MURRAY: Vat are you hollering? You'll wake up da whole castle.

—little wonder! Rembrandt painted with a roller ('sawright: "just the backgrounds"). Benedict Arnold stood up our hero when they were supposed to have a double date. Our man was a "counterspy" at Valley Forge; he sat at a restaurant counter, then told General Washington what he saw. Custer, Washington, Eisenhower, Cornwallis, Patton, all were "fags"—Federal Army Generals. Churchill prolonged the war for years by his pronunciation; people ran away looking for "Narzis" and forgot all about the Nazis. Lord Byron lured away one of the hero's wives with his poetry: "Hark, I hear . . ." Indeed, "he harked her right out of my life. He's probably still harking her."

Of course, American presidents are all highly sexed. And it's a good thing: "If they don't do it to their wives they'll do it to the nation." In the old man's memory, chivalric knighthood was in weed rather than in flower. Sure, knights jousted for their ladies' handkerchiefs, doing battle with spear and "horseys. . . . A handkerchief was one of the big fights . . . because there was no Kleenex. . . . And once a knight got that handkerchief, he blew his nose pretty good." Sigmund Freud was "unnoticed for his greatest thing, basketball." Freud "was short but he could dribble good." Aptly, Freud concentrated on setting up other people's shots rather than shooting for himself. The old man also knew Napoleon at Elba ("Every day, a shrimp used to go down to the water and cry."). He didn't recognize Napoleon in his swimsuit, because "he had no place to put his hand." He considers Napoleon a dummy for taking his advice and attempting to regain France.

The old man was also an accomplished matchmaker. Among his successes was the coupling of Madame Curie and Benjamin Franklin: "What you think, he flew a kite all night? . . . She liked him too. She gave him radium." When our hero recalls *Antony and Cleopatra,* he means seeing the real "original cast," the historical Antony and Cleopatra charging people a few drachmas to watch them kiss. Cleopatra died at eighty-six from a stroke. There was only one good war, our man opines, only one just war, the War of the Roses. When they woke up one morning, someone had stolen all the roses. They had to fight back. Otherwise, wars are better described by a Brooksian battlesong:

> *Let's go out and lose an eye.*
> *Let's lose a foot.*
> *Let's go to war and lose our brains.*

"That should be the song. They make nice songs." In all these gags, the old man debunks the mythic. He is unimpressed by the great. After all, he is human, just as they were, so why should he be awed? This is the Brooks who thinks of Giuseppe Verdi as just another Joe Green.

In one of these routines there is an especially touching moment. Sure he knew Joan of Arc. Indeed, "I went with her, dummy, I went with her." She was "a cutie," his "Joanelleh" (Yiddish for "little Joan"). Of course, her career came between them. "She used to say 'I've got to save France.' I'd say 'I got to wash up.'" Suddenly interviewer Reiner throws him one of those curves: "How did you feel about her being burnt at the stake?" "Terrible." To that event in his sweetheart's life, we expect a volume of response. But the single word suffices. There's no pause, no grope, no thought, just the direct and simple word: "Terrible." Here lies the secret of the two-thousand-year-old man's commerce with the great and famous. He's not ennobled by their contact. Because he's already the essential human being, he needs no further ennobling. On the contrary, the famous are humanized and ennobled by their contact with him.

From this perspective, the old man takes an ambivalent view of human progress. As he concludes his first recording—

> Hello dere. This is two thousand years talking to you from the depths of back there when we was and where I'm still and they're not,

—the survivor struggles to identify where in time and space he may be—

> and I just want to say, keep the smile on your face and stay out of a Ferrari or any small Italian car. Stay out of them.

—we recall that other naive outsider, the jungle boy, with his fear of the deadly beast Buick—

> And I want to tell you, it's been a wonderful two thousand years and you've been a wonderful civilization and it's been a thrill living for two thousand years and eat a nectarine, it's the best fruit ever made.

He speaks for tradition and the joy of life. But he has a mixed view of man's progress. On the one hand, man's slick machinery is a danger. Even in Ferraris, man's transport is still a matter of fear. On the other hand, man has made some marvelous inventions, improving even upon God's nature, as the nectarine exemplifies: "A helluva fruit . . . I love it . . . I'd rather eat a rotten nectarine than a fine plum, what do you think of that?"

Well. *I* think that Mel Brooks probably loves nectarines. And that he has certainly noticed the Jewish American's penchant for fruit. Even a house without a mezuzah would have its bowl of fruit on the kitchen table. But also, he knows the nectarine to be a man-made fruit, a product of cross-fertilization. So its praise is a paean to man's improvement upon nature.

In a minor key, from the vast range of human achievement, he declares man's biggest advance to be the invention of Saran Wrap. Not only can you wrap sandwiches or olives in it, you can see right through it, "you can touch it and put it on your face and fool around with it . . . whatever you want, it clings to you." So it serves a variety of emotions and appetites. But what about man's discovery of space? "That was good," he concedes, but Saran Wrap serves more immediate human needs. Similarly, he contends that man's greatest medical discovery is liquid Prell. A heart-lung machine falls out of the medicine cabinet, it breaks, but the plastic jug of Prell survives. More important, it is healing fractured families. As our hero has gleaned from TV, no doubt, mothers and daughters who have never had common interests can now start talking to each other about their liquid Prell. To be fair, one should note that in his 1966 *Playboy* interview, Brooks showed he had outgrown his sense of what is man's most important legacy. As he had "become a lot more mature since then" and "also grown with the times," he now nominated—Glad Bags. Brooks then expressed his ambivalent view of man's advances: "The way I see it, progress is progress. The old has to make way for the new." Hence the federal government's Department of People Renewal should be established. Agents would walk the streets, picking out the old people who look "particularly tired and useless." On them would be hung signs reading "Condemned—This person is being demol ished to make way for a modern, new baby." To keep it humane, the old person would be allowed time to settle his affairs before he is torn down: "Of course, he'll have to do it with an X painted across his face." This rather violent joke is based upon the Jew's experience. It reminds us that Brooks's two-thousand-year-old man is his attempt to sustain a human tradition against the murderous forces of time and an inhuman, homogenizing "progress."[5]

This is also the ethical basis for the old man's vulgarity; it registers an independent, kinky spirit of difference. So there is something brave when, asked what he still regards as an important mystery to be solved, the old man wonders why "after I eat asparagus and I make Number One, there is such an odor! Such a nutty flavor! Why is that?" From this candor, he proceeds to rue society's assault upon man's individual, natural odors. Our loss of human rights is less significant than our loss of personal smells in a society of death by deodorizing: "under the arms, in the nose, in the crotch. You don't know who you are. Everyone smells like a strawberry. You walk by a fruit stand, you get hot. What the hell is that? That's no way to live." So this oddball exalts the rough and smelly individuality that a vegetable society is threatening to supplant and suppress. Hence his romantic, gorgeous poetry, his exercise in "the shorthand of beauty": "Beans, beans, the musical fruits; The more you eat, the more you toots."

Brooks's hearty, vulgar, open heroes contrast to his Warren Bland, the ad man in the skit, "The L.M.N.O.P. Ad Agency." For Bland, Brooks drops his Yiddish and dons the Ivy League drawl of a George C. Scott. He enthuses about his company's heavily minted cigarette, Fags, and their new radar deodorant, that "starts beeping when it reaches the smelly part." He studied at the West Point Advertising School of White Bread. This is homogenized, sterilized America, in every way antithetical to the garlic-pumpernickel accent of Brooks's vulgar, Jewish, or vulgar-Jewish heroes. In Bland's home town, Connecticut, Connecticut, the citizens send their children to Hartford to be raised by Italian and Jewish families, who like children. Bland has neither passion nor ethics. His agency handled both the Nixon and the Kennedy election campaigns: "We kept it very close. Nobody complained. Nobody was hurt." The implication is that where there is no passion there can be no ethics. Now the company's biggest campaign is promoting cholesterol: "We're trying to move cholesterol into the American heart. . . . Advertising is bigger than life."

In contrast, the two-thousand-year-old man craves moral consistency. He requires it even of incidental language. In several routines, Brooks plays on man's search for logic in everyday life. In one he claims that all our words derive their meaning from their sound. "Shower" combines the water's "ssshh" with our "Ow!" when the water hits. "Egg" is the sound the chicken makes when he lays one. When Reiner tried to trip him up by asking the onomatopoeic origin of "nose," Brooks held fast: "What are you gonna blow, your eyes? It makes sense to me." In another routine, he states his theory that fruit can cure all diseases. Eat bananas or a mushy pear for hardening arteries. Blueberries will stain TB bacteria so you can find and kill them. And for diarrhea? Cling peaches!

Similarly, Dr. Felix Wheird, author of *Hey, Fatso!* recommends that we eat our vegetables according to the sound of their names. "You brock up a little [broccoli], then you eat it." As for succotash, "First you suck it, then you tash it. You don't just tash it." The self-styled Third Best Poet in the United States, Laurel Bellew, complains about inapt words. "Bed" sounds "hard . . . tiny, too small to lie down on." "Staircase" inhibits walking up one. "Strawberry" is "eighty times too big"—it should be called a "pleep." In these characters, the quest for logic in language seems silly. But the old man's ethical core makes his routine an affirmation of lost logic, simplicity, and integrity.

However, in the final analysis the two-thousand-year-old man is still just an old fogey. With the fastidiousness of the aged, he rejects Michelangelo because "you can't hang a naked in your living room." Now "we're modern and dirty. Then we were clean and cute." When he remembers Onan as a "great inventor" who discovered himself—"I think he was falling and he grabbed onto himself and that's how he fell in love with himself"—he's offended by Reiner's use of the word "masturbation." The most our hero will say is that contrary to the Bible's injunction that we be fruitful and multiply, Onan "was fruitless and subtracting." Our hero also says "gentles" for "genitals," both out of propriety and because the things must be handled gently. But he stays a step ahead of us. We may think he is erring when he says he didn't get his "public" hair for two hundred years, but no, he means "public," all right—the hair the public sees; his "pubic" hair came early. In the end, this old man is beyond judgment and attack because he is a simple, warm and candid human being. He's a *mensch.* That's the really endangered species, in Brooks's view of the world.

In another sketch, Brooks develops a parallel opposite to his venerable aged. He plays a two-hour-old baby who was born with the powers of intelligence and speech. He comes on with an irrepressible openness, much like the peppy old man's:

> Hi. Are you my dad? I haven't met my dad yet . . . I haven't met Mom but I know Mom. . . . I haven't seen her outside yet. . . . I don't care what she looks like. I'm not going to date her. I'm her child. . . . I know she's good. Because you can tell a person by what they are inside and I've been there. I've been inside and looked around. I know she's great.

This character has a healthy and open spirit. He expresses the natural warmth that should prevail in a human relationship.

This child evades the problems that adults hire analysts to solve.

He skirts the Oedipal tension neatly ("I'm not going to date her. I'm her child."). His father's muffled "When awreddy? When awreddy?" he innocently takes to refer to his delivery, not any possibility of sexual tension. He has no regrets about losing the tail he enjoyed as a fetus, because he accepts its replacement, his nose: "You can't blow your tail, you know what I mean?" He misses his umbilical cord, but he'll get a keychain when he grows up. There is even a jovial acceptance of fun over earnestness; he knows Cary Grant (from the movies Mom took him to) but is sure the unfamiliar Pandit Nehru probably is "a hell of an actor" too. He can even understand why his mother was queasy: "I think the moment they realize that there's a living creature in them, they puke. . . . Wouldn't you be nauseous if somebody was running around inside you? It's a frightening thing." He even survives a sexual identity crisis. First, he thinks he's a girl ("Hey, I'm a girl. . . . it's adorable"), but he readily accepts the news that he's a boy: "Well, that's alright. I'll play ball and get drunk and things. I'll be fine." He's further consoled when he learns that Burt Lancaster is also male. This is a healthy, reasonable kid.

Then this healthy spirit breaks down. The kid with all the answers and the healthy openness discovers his vulnerability. Once he starts to talk about his father, his language lapses into baby talk: "I feel that Dad is the kind of guy that—gaga san. . . ." He dissolves into normal helplessness when he begins to look forward to playing with his dad.

The Brooks records are distinguished by their witty comedy and by a considerable dramatic polish. His characters are so fully characterized by their voices that any visual representation—such as the animated TV version of the two-thousand-year-old man—is grating. Brooks gives tired, bloodless voices to his cerebral WASPS, and energy, sparkle, and unpredictable logic and spirit to his simple, vulgar heroes. Especially in the old man and the infant, the energy and the intuition are moral qualities, because they escape our normal torpor and passivity. Finally, the most astonishing element in these routines is the fact that they were largely extemporized. Their most moving and illuminating effect is our sense that Brooks's jokes wing out of the deepest corner of his heart and mind; that they express the ideas he holds most ardently and the losses and desires he feels most profoundly. Brooks's quick, tripping comedy plumbs a considerable soul.

Chapter 5

Mel Brooks, All-American

B ROOKS'S TWO-THOUSAND-YEAR-OLD MAN is a classic in a fading tradition of American humor, dialect comedy. One type contrasts the educated norms of urban grammar with the colorful eccentricities—and often superior wisdom—of rural patterns. Thus Artemus Ward's shrewd observation, "She broke in two tears," for instance. These regional or personal deviations provide color, liveliness, wit, and sagacity. In another type, the comedy uses immigrant language patterns as a sign of the diversity of culture that is feeding into the American melting pot.

The Marx Brothers can serve as a model in this respect. Chico's ersatz Italian accent casts him as the newly arrived and hustling immigrant, playing with and struggling through the language to get one up, if not ahead. Groucho is the immigrant who has mastered the language. He talks circles around the Establishment, who, born into the language and its power, have grown fossilized in it. At the opposite extreme, Harpo has such primitive energy that he does not need language. As Groucho is the most civilized—the most proficient with language—Harpo is the most savage—he expresses his emotions, fears and desires physically instead of verbally. The same pattern works in their respective kinds of music. Chico's piano-playing has an individualistic fingering style that is as eccentric as his language. The silent Harpo plays the most celestial of instruments, the harp, while Groucho subverts the lyrical conventions of singing as he does the civilities of conversation.

As we have seen, Brooks uses Yiddish as a means of reviving a lost past. His Yiddish-flavored recordings keep alive a dying human accent. In addition, they keep alive a memory from his own childhood. Raised among Yiddish-speaking relatives and neighbors, he now uses Yiddish with a double-edged effect. Insofar as it recalls the world he knew as a child, it revives childish emotions. On the other hand, Brooks's Yiddish makes him feel that he has finally grown up:

> When I was a little boy, I thought when I grew up I would talk Yiddish, too. I thought little kids talked English, but when they became adults, they would talk Yiddish like the adults did. There would be no reason to talk English anymore, because we would have made it.[1]

Paradoxically, Brooks finds his adulthood, his maturity, in a stance of childhood.

Moreover, Brooks's use of Yiddish posits a second paradox, this one social. It establishes him as a member of the Jewish culture; it's a badge of membership. So there is a kind of in-ness in his Yiddish address; the in-jokes give a sense of shared community. At the same time, however, the Yiddish reaffirms his distinctness from the Gentile society. Brooks's Yiddish is a declaration of independence from the dominant tone and style of his country (much as his effusive energy and vulgarity are, for that matter, and his tendency to play *against* conventions of film genre). Consequently, Brooks's comedy can be taken both as an extremely personal form of expression and as a social document. It reaffirms the nation's basis in individualistic styles and values, against the pressure of uniformity. These points can be found in two of Brooks's earlier works that have not received the attention they deserve, his play *All-American* and the cartoon film *The Critic*.

All-American is a college comedy with a variety of satiric thrusts. The bulk of its action is set at Southern Baptist Institute of Technology. Engineering professor Fodorski becomes a hero when he starts translating his engineering lectures into football terms. This makes the students begin to enjoy their work. Indeed one of the songs informed the Broadway audience that "It's Fun to Think."[2] The professor enjoys even greater success when he begins to coach the football team using his academic savvy. His learning reverses the losing team's fortunes. Southern Baptist

Tech proceeds to trounce Texas Mohammedan, the Alabama Agnostics, and the Louisiana Zen Buddhists. In the process, he wins the attention and heart of dean Elizabeth Hawkes-Bullock. But *en route* to True Love he must evade the blandishments of commercial celebrity. Another romance blossoms in the subplot between the school's two "brains," Susan Piedmont and Edwin Bricker. Susan praises Edwin as "a truly non-chauvinist man," but he wins wider appreciation as a cunning place-kicker.

There are some minor Brooks touches in the school scenes. An anticipation of Buddy Bizarre in *Blazing Saddles*, Fodorski's predecessor is Coach Hulkington Stockworth, a loud-mouthed runt with a megaphone who exhorts the football team in surprisingly sexual tones: "Kill! Kill! Don't make love to that man, Cooper, knock him down. . . . Okay, ladies, back to the bench! Come on, girls, shake a leg. Your den mother is calling."

More significant is the play's focus on the heterogeneous makeup of America. For one thing, Brooks plays against the title image of the college All-American. Southern Baptist Tech, the Texas Mohammedans, the Alabama Agnostics, the Louisiana Zen Buddhists: these are a far cry from the usual teams in a college comedy. Rather, they redefine "All-American" in terms of religious and cultural diversity.

Brooks introduces this theme in his opening scene, where Fodorski is among a horde of immigrants who arrive at Kennedy Airport. This college comedy follows the immigrant's success in America. In the opening scene, even the customs officer seems to have an immigrant's accent. At least, he is not formally correct in his English, though he may be at home with the language:

> Dis here's a democracy so we're gonna divide you into your own ethical groups. Now all you Krauts over dere . . . all you frogs dere . . . Limeys there and the rest of you gooks right here.

The customs officer's language betrays his reflex of prejudice. But his colloquialism reminds us that the language, like the country, is a matter of individualistic, not uniform, expression. Moreover, his confusion between "ethnic" and "ethical" is a classic malapropism. That is, what seems to be a mistake in word choice actually conveys a surprising wisdom; the word that seems inappropriate proves apt. As we know from Brooks's two-thousand-year-old man, the immigrant outsider often possesses an ethical superiority over the WASP natives, the Warren Blands. So "ethnic groups" may well be the "ethical groups." In *All-American*, Professor Fodorski illuminates the moral as well as the intellectual lives of his students.

In that opening scene, the immigrants are unfazed by the antipathetic customs man ("He's nice . . . so efficient . . . etc."). Indeed, they burst into song about the anticipated splendors of America in "The Old Immigration and Naturalization Rag."

> *Put us in*
> *Your big American Melting Pot and*
> *Melt us!*
> *Melt us!*
> *Oh, say, can't you see*
> *We're ready to be . . .*
> *Joe DiMaggios . . . Sal Mineos . . .*
> FODORSKI: *A regular Joe College . . . that's me!*
> ALL: *Don't mean maybe,*
> *Hot dog, baby,*
> *We're regular Joes*
> *In spite of our clo's.*

The style of America is a meld of ideals, celebrities—and clichés.

The play's central metaphor is the bridge. In a key speech, Professor Fodorski stops talking about the "bridge out of text-books" and rhapsodizes:

A bridge is something more. A bridge is communication. . . . A bridge is beautiful. It is symmetry and grace. It is a functional poem of steel and stone. It is man at his best. Reaching across the alien gap . . . creating unity where once there was separateness.

Fodorski's success involves his bridging the high culture of the classroom with the low culture of the football field. He also manages to bridge the ignorant adolescent with knowledge and the immigrant's Old World ethics with the pragmatic American business world.

The hustling career woman, H. H. "Hildy" Henderson attempts

to turn Fodorski into a franchise. She plans to cash in on his fame as a football coach by selling a new game, Fodorskiopoly:

> It's a game all about immigration. So many points for leaving Europe. So many points for getting to America. A hundred points and you're a citizen. If you lose you go back to a concentration camp.

Fodorskiland health clubs will be advertised as places "where losers can become All-Americans." Professor Fodorski Austro-Hungarian Fried Chicken will be sold as "napkin-schmearing good." As Ms. Henderson warmly reflects, "He's sweet and warm and sensitive and touching and we're gonna promote the hell out of him." Eventually, Fodorski's example brings about Henderson's reform. However, there remains a hint of Brooks's cynicism in the extremity of her expression: The "gentleman of the old school . . . makes me ashamed of my surface rottenness that hides my inner core of rottenness. But I'm going to be different." Her reform seems a matter of genre convention more than a realistic expectation of a human being.

In any case, the play ends happily. When Fodorski wins his highest goal, American citizenship, he cancels his despairing plan to return to Europe: "Do you know how they treat American tourists in Europe? It's disgraceful." The persecuted European finally becomes an American when he takes the American's persecuted view of Europe.

Despite its reputation for breaking down in the second act, then, *All-American* does have a thematic unity. The play is at its strongest when it centers upon Brooks's immigrant spirit; this concern continues—albeit muted—in the satire of the second half. The play might have worked better had it worked up to a frontal attack instead of seeming to taper off into satire. As Brooks recalls the play: "It was about a European immigrant with a dream in his heart. A dream—it should have been an attack."[3] In any case, some significant ideas and several vintage Brooks routines animate this neglected play.

These virtues thrive in *The Critic*. Brooks got the idea on a spring evening in 1962, when he overheard an elderly man muttering about the Norman McLaren short they were watching.

"He was very unhappy, because he was waiting for a story line and he wasn't getting one." Brooks commissioned cartoonist Ernest Pintoff to make up three minutes of McLarenesque animation—various dances among rectangles and triangles, some wavy lines, some play with prickly dots—to which Brooks ad-libbed a running commentary. Pintoff showed a knack for satirical forays against art in his earlier cartoons, *The Violinist* and *The Interview*. Brooks asked him not to give any warning about the images: "Just give me the mike and let them assault me." In this way Brooks hoped to recapture the rich tension of his interview with Carl Reiner.[4]

Brooks responded in 4 voices; the critic, a meek man, an indignant woman, and a gruff brute asking for silence. Actually, the brute shushes a shusher. But the hero yaps on: "I'm seventy-one. I got a right to be loud, lady. I'm gonna die soon." Brooks's "critic" is his familiar old Jewish incorrigible, articulating his own naive, confused, headstrong and individualistic response to the strange, newfangled phenomenon before him.

The satire in this routine cuts in two contrary directions. For one thing, the work itself is directly satirized for its abstract and abstruse nature. It is very tempting to laugh at the obscure film with the spirited old gent. However limited, the man's understanding condemns the film as inaccessible. This reading works to justify the commercial path that Brooks later chose for his film career, in contrast to what one might loosely declare the Nichols-May-Allen road. In this light, the elderly Jew is a film version of Brooks's two-thousand-year-old man upholding the sense of the essential human being against modish abstractions. The Jewish immigrant upholds the narrative tradition against the bland obscurity of WASP modern art.

On the other hand, the old man does speak drivel. More to the point, his layman's befuddlement parallels the response of critics to works that do not satisfy their expectations. So Brooks's title for the film is both ironic and precise: The layman is not really a critic, but his comments typify those of professional critics.

The entire film is based upon a variety of contrasts. Within the audience there is an implicit contrast between the cultured first two complainers and the uncultured brute and critic. Within the hero's title there is another contrast, for he is not a "critic," a professional filmgoer, but an average citizen who has drifted into an unfamiliar style of film. Pintoff's visuals also deal with the motif of contrasts. One section plays different shapes against each other, another foreground against background, and a third, two similar shapes. Moreover, the modernistic image plays against the score, classical harpsichord music, as well as against the outspoken resistance of the old man. With all these tensions and oppositions, the film dramatizes the gap between currents in a culture (such as those which Fodorski sought to "bridge" in *All-American*).

In addition, the film satirizes the professional critic's failure to accept a work on its own terms rather than imposing his own values and expectations. In this respect, *The Critic* is a solid statement about the nature of the artistic encounter. First, the hero tries to find a label for the film, a pigeon hole in which to imprison the exotic bird: "Vot da hell is dis? Must be a cartoon." Even his praise is begrudging: "Dis is cute. Dis is cute. Vot da hell is it?" To define the meaning of the work, he falls back upon the vagaries of his own limited experience. He reads one image as "birt" because he remembers, "back in Rossia, in biology class," a lesson about birth and death. Then there is the consumer complaint: "Two dollars I paid for a French movie, for a foreign movie, and I got to see dis?" He then proceeds to deduce sexual import from the film: "Two t'ings dat like each odder. Could dis be da sex life of two t'ings?" Here Brooks twits the puritanism of the filmgoer who is attracted to the lubricious promise of a French film but inveighs against the sexual reference that he eagerly perceives: "See? Even if dey don't wanna, dey get dirty." So, too, in his concluding judgment: "Lips . . . doit and filt'. . . . I don't know much about psychoanalysis, but I'd say dis was a doity picture." Even when he picks up a relevant term, he turns it into a weapon of abuse: "It must be some symbolism . . . I t'ink it's symbolic of junk!" He essentially imposes himself and his own values upon the work, instead of allowing it its own life and character:

Dat fella dat made dis . . . Vat does he vaste his time wit dis? A fella like dat, he probably could drive a trock, do somet'ing constructive. Make a shoe.

This is judging a work of art by irrelevant criteria. Indeed the entire commentary is a confused and willful attack upon a work that might reward if it were openly received.

The film's savaging by the impatient reviewer recalls the fate of Brooks's two plays at the hands and fangs of the Broadway reviewers, and anticipates the begrudging receptions that his feature films were to receive. As Brooks would later complain, "Some critics are emotionally desiccated. . . . It's easy to say shit is shit, and it should be said. But the real function of a critic is to see what is truly good and go bananas when he sees it." No such enthusiasm or attempt to understand is forthcoming from Brooks's typical critic. As Brooks has complained, critics tend to temper their pleasure with niggling complaints:

> I would prefer open outrage or clear applause. They don't like the movie [in this case *The Twelve Chairs*] because they have to grapple with it. The picture becomes not a friend but an enemy.

This is also the situation in *The Critic*. In his later interviews, Brooks took to referring to the corps of reviewers as "crickets," a malapropism that rather suits critics who speak in unison, from the dark, and through their hind legs.[5]

The Critic was well received by these crickets, however, because they could take it as a paean to their own qualifications and a satire against those less sensitive and informed than they. It was shown at the Cannes Film Festival. John Gruen declared it revolutionary for a cartoon, "sophisticated, funny, and informed with a civilized malice."[6] It won Brooks the Oscar for the Best Animated Short in 1964 and marked his promising debut in films. His next film—and his next Oscar—came three years later: *The Producers*.

PART III

The Feature Films

Chapter 6

The Producers (1967)

M AX BIALYSTOCK (Zero Mostel) is a Broadway producer down at the heels, his luck, and the mouth. He makes love to elderly widows in return for financial support for his theatrical failures. But a nervous young accountant, Leo Bloom (Gene Wilder), gives him an outrageous idea: By raising more money than he needs for a show, he could make more from a flop than from a success. Leo's "little academic economic theory" is converted into a scheme of "creative accounting." Max steamrolls Leo into partnership. Max sells his old ladies 25,000 percent of the profits of his play, confident that it will close immediately. He picks the worst play he can find, *Springtime for Hitler*, a nostalgic romance by a maniacally unassimilated Nazi, Franz Liebkind (Kenneth Mars). He hires Roger DeBris (Christopher Hewett), who is "the only director whose plays close on the first day of rehearsals." For the lead role Max hires Lorenzo St. DuBois (Dick Shawn), alias L.S.D., who has difficulty remembering his own name, and who has questionable theatrical experience:

What have you done?
About six months. But I'm out on probation.

To ensure successful failure, Max offers a blatant bribe to the *Times* critic (John Zoller).

But alas, the best-laid plans *gang aft agley*—especially on the Great White Way. At first stunned, the audience hails the play as a classic comedy of bad taste. Irate at the betrayal of his vision, Franz tries to kill his producers, but is persuaded to blow up the theater instead. When even this backfires, all three men are sent to the state penitentiary, despite Leo's and the ladies' pleas on Max's behalf. We last see them rehearsing—and overselling—a new prison musical, *Prisoners of Love*.

Despite the familiarity of the plot—it dates back at least as far as George S. Kaufman's *The Butter and Egg Man* of 1926—Brooks considers *The Producers* "probably my most private film." Wild Bialystock and timorous Bloom are aspects of Brooks's own nature, with Max "the perfect id" and Bloom the "pure, spiritual ego." Bialystock is clearly an id figure, a wild energy bent only upon its own gratification, without morality or judgment. At his wildest, Bialystock plots to murder the cast but is tempered by Bloom:

LEO: Actors are not animals. They're human beings.
MAX: Oh yeah? Have you ever eaten with one?

As the healthy psyche achieves a balance between id and ego, Max and Leo have salutary effects upon each other. In psychological terms, Max teaches Leo about life and pleasure. In return Leo imposes some moral checks on the rampaging Bialystock and cultivates his fraternal sentiments. As Brooks puts it in social terms, "Bialystock taught Bloom the ways of greed, and the monstrous ways of capitalism, and Bloom taught Bialystock the ways of love." In Kenneth Tynan's reading, the film is a comedy of humors in the manner of Ben Jonson: "Cupidity (Mostel) seduces Conformity (Wilder); in each, a single trait is exaggerated to the point of plethoric obsession, and beyond."[1]

Alternatively, one can take the film as a dramatization of pressures in art. In this view, it is a frontal assault upon an audience that has grown blasé and callous about the way art reflects life. An audience must be suspect if it accepts as entertainment "a gay romp with Adolf and Eva at Berchtesgaden."

Brooks assails the assimilation of the horror of the Holocaust. His two Jewish heroes briefly don Nazi armbands to please their playwright partner. Director DeBris is moronically thrilled at the script, out of ignorance: "I never realized that the Third Reich meant Germany. The whole play is just *drenched* with historical goodies like that. . . . That whole third act has got to go. They're losing the war! It's too depressing!" One implication of the stage full of auditioning Hitlers, Hitlers of all size and activity—dancing, singing, cowboys, bodybuilders, jugglers—is the easy assimilation of this historic figure. In this respect Brooks's comedy anticipates the plethora of Hitlers in the epic Syberberg film *Our Hitler*. The monster becomes a repeatable image. Hence the ambiguity—man or play?—in the moronic telegram that our heroes receive: "Congratulations. *Hitler* will run forever." This sense of a society that has lost its hold on history is also expressed in L.S.D.'s audition song, "Love Power." It expresses a faddish morality that is shallow and inconsistent because it lacks any historic, ethical, or realistic base. In Bialystock's wail—"I was so careful. I picked the wrong play, the wrong director, the wrong cast. . . . Where did I go right?"—the film indicts a world of unreliable judgment, a society inured to tastelessness and oblivious to historical responsibility.

The audience is stunned at the first part of the play, because it is unaccustomed to hearing enemy propaganda. The opening scene is a musical spectacular that some Nazi Busby Berkeley might have devised. Against a procession of statuesque chorus girls, we hear the snappy lyrics:

> *We're marching to a faster pace.*
> *Look out: here comes the Master race. . . .*

Winter for Poland and France,
Springtime for Hitler and Germany,
Germans: go into your dance.

I was born in Dusseldorf.
That is why they call me Rolf.

Don't be shtoopid, be a schmarty,
Come and join the Nazi party.

This straightforward Nazi propaganda horrifies the audience ("Well, talk about bad taste!") because it's a different kind of politics than theirs. In several shots Brooks shows the entire audience aghast, mouths frozen open. When one man applauds, the others beat him up—an act of dubious democracy.

But the audience is held and pleased when L.S.D. appears as Hitler. It's not surprising that L.S.D.'s performance turns around the play's reception: When he first wandered into the audition, he was looking for the try-out for a play about backfiring, *Boomerang Baby*. In his first appearance, this stage Hitler grows impatient with his Eva's game of *Er liebt mir, er liebt mir nicht"* ("He loves me, he loves me not"): "I *lieb* you, baby. Now *lieb* me alone." He turns back to his blues:

Gonna crush Poland. And I'm gonna take over France.
Then I'm gonna take over Poland, And then I'm gonna crush
 France.
Then I'm gonna cross that English Channel—Wow!
And then I'm gonna kick those cats in the pants.

In later scenes he is surprised: "Hey, man, you're German!" He modernizes his lines: "Danke schöen, baby." And a later riff:

One and one is two.
Two and two is four.
I feel so bad
'Cause I'm losin' the war.

The audience finally approves the play, because playing the Hitler character as a blown-out buffoon coheres with their politics. Once their own prejudice is appeased, they are satisfied.

Bialystock's expensive lesson is that there is no moral absolute that he can confidently offend, either on Broadway or in Western Civilization (As We Know It). There is no sure distinction between Right and Wrong in his society's ethics, even for the hardy criminal spirit who wishes to pursue the Wrong. So what he thought would upset his audience pleased them immensely. When the jury declares our heroes "incredibly guilty"—a judgment better applied to the play's hero than to its pathetic progenitors—such is the moral void in which they are sentenced that they are able to repeat their scheme in prison. With yet another "captive audience," similarly weak in will and decrepit in taste, our producers may well find themselves stuck with another success on their hands, another failed failure.

In his first feature Brooks seems to be edging toward the type of comedy that will bring him his greatest success, genre parody. Specifically, *The Producers* contains an insightful analysis of the American musical. Two particular subtypes are evoked. One is the backstage drama, such as Lloyd Bacon's classic *42nd Street* (1933) and Charles Walters's *Summer Stock* (1950). Brooks's plot is a funhouse-mirror distortion of this type, where the characters start with "Hey, why don't we put on a show?" then spend the film doing it. The second type is the musical romance, such as the Astaire-Rogers films of the thirties and Stanley Donen's *Funny Face* (1957). The romantic element aligns the musical with the comic archetype, which celebrates spring, fertility, and the harmonious renewal of the community spirit. The very title, "Springtime for Hitler," alerts us to the context of resurrection.

But Brooks plays against the assumptions of both these types. For one thing, the musical typically ends with its characters' success because the American musical celebrates the triumph of individual ambition, skill, energy, spirit, and luck *cum* destiny. The astonishing success of *Springtime for Hitler* not only imputes tastelessness and amorality to the camp audiences of the late sixties, but accedes to the formal demands of the American musical. The show must be a success. In other words, Max lives in a genre, as well as in a society, that demands success (and "all I can offer is failure"). When our heroes stage *Prisoners of Love,* they are still entrapped in the musical's dreams of success and magic. According to their new song, "Hearts in love will always be free," but the freed lovers are still prisoners of love. The same paradox applies in their social situation. Although they are in prison, they are "free" to repeat what got them there. Hollywood's musical fantasy and the American insistence upon success are ambivalent forces; although they may liberate the timid, they restrict and compel the dreamers.

Brooks also plays against the romantic tradition of the musical. Not for Brooks the love stories usually played by the likes of Dick Powell and Alice Faye. Bialystock's seduction of the wrinkled, parched old ladies is a grotesque parody of the conventional romantic plot. Max's romances with the older ladies are all played as slapstick. They knock him down and spill drinks over him. One urges him to speed on a motorcycle; the next one spends an eternity undoing her myriad locks against a possible burglar. Another is so deaf that Brooks must shout his "I love you," to the amused delight of an entire park. When he hires a Swedish sexpot, Ulla (Lee Meredith), as receptionist/toy, he blatantly amplifies the convention of the casting couch. "Smart as a whip," Max observes, as the dense dish bats her lashes and clips his cigar.

In addition to these grotesque images of heterosexuality, Brooks fills *The Producers* with kinky instances of homosexuality. All the relationships are remote from the boy-meets-girl pattern of the Hollywood musical. The extreme case is director Roger DeBris (whose surname means "garbage" in English but can be read as "the circumcision" in Yiddish), living with his bitchy valet, Carmen Giya (Andreas Voutsinas). Equally strange is L.S.D., who tosses flowers and sings of "Love Power" without knowing what he's talking about; he calls his all-girl band "fellas."

The only character associated with love is Franz Liebkind. His name means "love child," as if a reminder of the illegitimacy of his love for Adolf Hitler (who could "dance the pants off of Churchill"—a gruesome image). Because Liebkind's love is forbidden, he is a schizoid lunatic. He alternates verses of "Deutschland Uber Alles" with "I'm a Yankee Doodle Dandy." His conversation is punctuated with defensive reflexes: "I was only following orders. . . . My papers are in order." Even his bursts of confidence end in timid check: "My play? You mean, Springtime for You-

Know-Who?" Later, before the opening curtain he confidently tells his producers, "Tonight Broadway, tomorrow—" and with his hands sculpts "the world" in complicitous silence.

As Bialystock brings Bloom a new openness, both producers bring Liebkind a chance to express his forbidden love. For all that he is humiliated, at least he has dared to speak his love. Moreover, at film-end he has profitted from having expressed his forbidden passion. With Bialystock and Bloom, the Nazi finds a new enterprise, fraternity and home. Their common enterprise in prison shows that Bialystock has not lapsed into the insularity that he threatened earlier: "Next time I produce a play—no author!"

The most important love story in *The Producers* also plays against the musical norm, because it is both homophile and nonsexual. This is the love that blossoms between the energetic and effusive Bialystock and the suppressed Bloom. Their relationship is distinguished from homosexuality by two scenes: their meeting with DeBris and Carmen, and Ulla's giggling at the fallacious idea that Max is taking Leo to a motel. These scenes dissociate the two producers from possible inferences of homosexuality.

In addition, their entire relationship is a parody of the traditional Hollywood romance. Bloom discovers Max with "another" woman. Max inveigles Bloom into his scheme by a series of romantic, even sexual images. He sweeps his "Darling Bloom, Glorious Bloom" off in a romantic tango ("Oh Rio, by the sea-o"). To the innocent Leo's plea, "I'm an honest man," Max counters romantically, "No, it's fate, Kismet." In the climax, Leo lies on the floor between Max's spread legs, terrified that Max will leap on him, as Nero killed his wife. The seduction threatens to become rape.

Max then courts Leo with a day-long date. They enjoy a variety of truant pleasures but of which even a too-earnest, too-sheltered, too-good little boy may have been deprived in his adolescence. They enjoy a hot-dog lunch *("al fresco")*, a walk in the park, a balloon, merry-go-round rides, a boat trip, and his first blue movie. The latter, *War and Piece*, leaves Leo sucking his thumb, in shock, because it violates his cultural expectations derived from the title. Max summarizes success and affluence as "wine, women and song—and women!" Leo's entire relationship with Max is a process of expanding worldliness and diminishing innocence. At first shocked to see DeBris wearing a dress, Leo begins to open up. After computing their debt, he acknowledges his union with Max by sharing his sacrosanct security blanket. He smokes before the preview and drinks during the show. Later the two men have a lover's spat (Leo harps on Max's fatness), but they make up.

Leo begins the film as a neurotic, hyper-timid dolt, fixated on his own state of being: "I'm hysterical . . . I'm wet . . . I'm in pain." Max teaches him how to live. Through Max, Leo discovers a new state of consciousness:

> LEO: I feel so strange.
> MAX: Maybe you're happy.
> LEO: That's it. I'm happy!

The Innocent has received his first taste of Experience. The cost will prove great, but its benefit is adult, human community. So Leo quite rightly tells the court that Max deserves all the credit for "making me what I am today." This criminal adult is a better, fuller human being than the sheltered but neurotic child was.

In addition to a romantic exchange, Max and Leo's relationship can be taken to represent the relationship between the musical and its audience. Bialystock personifies the musical genre. For in Max as in the musical genre, exuberance, energy, and openness are moral virtues. They are in contrast to the dullness and covertness of the villains. Beyond that, they express the zest for life and the vital senses that are the ethical priority of the musical. Max even sings and dances when he walks across his office alone— at the nadir of fortune in which the film first finds him. He also lives by the principle of style: "That's it, baby, when you got it, flaunt it!" Even in poverty Max clings to remnants of his lost style: the ascot, smoking jacket, leather couch. His sense of loss takes the form of style: "Look at me now: I'm wearing a cardboard belt," he snaps. Max Bialystock is the musical.

As well as these charms, Max embodies the dangers of the musical. This point is made when Leo, having enjoyed Max's day of pleasures, exudes: "I want—I want—I want everything I've ever seen in the movies!" Behind him the Revson fountains at

Lincoln Center erupt in harmony with his new happiness. Leo has succumbed to the lure of life, success, happiness, and affluence that Max and the movies have shown. Max, like the musical fantasies, feeds Leo's dreams.

In the trial later, Leo defends Max (and implicitly, the fantasy mill of the musical) because he repaid his gulls with pleasure. Even as he exploited them, he allowed the ladies (as Max earlier put it) "to grab a last thrill on the way to the cemetery." He made them "feel young and attractive and wanted again." For his part, Max was the first person who ever called Bloom Leo: "Even in kindergarten, they always called me Bloom." Max granted Bloom his personality, free from anti-Semitic innuendo. For Franz Liebkind, too, Broadway promised the "joy of joy, dream of dreams," which Max delivered as fulfillment and community.

Consistent with this reflection upon genre, everyone in the film is involved in some kind of role-playing. For Ulla, "going to work" is redefined as doing a sexy, solo twist. Other characters have other roles, other twists. Often the character is dominated by his role, such as the "conci-urge" (Madlyn Cates). So too is the character who responds to Bialystock's complaint:

> How can you take the last penny out of a poor man's pocket?
> I have to. I'm a landlord.

Bialystock is continually playing roles, partly because he is the embodiment of the genre. So he meditates aloud: "Shut up! I'm having a rhetorical conversation." He is the only character to acknowledge our presence, which he does in asides (for which he prepared by confiding in first a statue, then a flower pot). Of course, he plays a variety of lover roles to win his ladies' "checkies." But their relationship is a matter of roles for them too. One doddering dolly (Estelle Winwood) has reduced their every meeting to an artificial performance by her catchline, "Hold me, touch me." She runs the wrung-out Max through a variety of little dramas: Finders Keepers, Pussycat and Old Tom, Peeping Tom, the Innocent Little Milkmaid and the Dirty Stableboy, the Contessa and the Chauffeur. True to the larger pattern of genre criticism, she both condemns and embraces Max's role: "Rudolfo! You dirty pig! Pull over." With these ladies' money, Max starts to live out his own fantasies. He hires a chauffeur whom *he* calls Rudolfo. In another parallel to his ladies' lot, he clings to Ulla's erotic pleasures despite his sense of mortality ("You'll bury me!").

More negatively, a character can be reduced to his role. In "The Abduction and Cruel Rape of Lucrezia," the lady will be Lucrezia; "I'll be Rape," Max sighs. He is resigned to be reduced to his act. Though their fantasy is liberating for them both, it also debases them by detracting from their individual identity. In a variation upon this joke, when Leo and Max toast "Failure," a stranger down the bar thinks they are drinking to him: "Oh, thank you. That's very kind of you." True to form, before long Max has the lonely failure join them in merriment.

Leo is a role-player out of nervousness and inexperience. When he first comes upon Max in *flagrante delicto*, Bloom reacts stiffly: "Excuse me." Max replies "You mean 'oops,' don't you? Just say 'oops' and get out." Max senses that Leo can't react freely but speaks as if quoting a learned role. He's proved right later, when Leo tries to get his attention by saying, "Cough, cough." Leo grows from making these "cartoon noises" to being able to make open responses. In a visual equivalent, Max commands Leo: "You have just ten seconds to change that look on your face from one of disgusting pity to one of enormous respect."

But even in this liberation Leo remains trapped in a role. After all, even those who love freely are prisoners of love. Leo Bloom's name is a straight theft from James Joyce's hero in *Ulysses*. As Brooks told Tynan, "I don't know what it means to James Joyce, but to me Leo Bloom always meant a vulnerable Jew with curly hair."[2] The allusion makes Bloom represent the more traditional literary context, as Bialystock represents a film genre. Moreover, it suggests that in *The Producers*, Leo Bloom's life in New York has the same multitude of levels—personal, fictional, social, psychological, mythical—that Joyce's Bloom had in *Ulysses*. Finally, as Leo (named from high culture) meets Max (a man of low culture) both achieve a fulfillment but both remain creatures of role and fate. Leo flees the accountant's role into another role, that of entrepreneur or producer. They fail at trying to stage a failure, because the musical genre, their artistic as well as their social context, requires a success.

For his part, although Bialystock lives an irresponsible, self-seeking life, even he is tied to larger powers. His initials bear the stamp of his maker. Moreover, his name, Bialystock, has a double signification. It can be taken as a summary of his present con; "buy all his stock." This is the sense in which he sells himself to his ladies. Indeed, Max plays a similar game with the name of Leo's profession:

> So you're an accountant, eh? So account for yourself. Do you believe in God? Do you believe in gold?

Then he plumps Bloom's vanity: The word "count" comes from his "noble profession." And when he has won Bloom over, Max enjoys a sly elision: "I knew I could con you." The "count on" has turned into a "con." At a deeper level, Bialystock is the name of one of the major ghetto uprisings of Polish Jews against the Nazis. So Max Bialystock's cavorting with the Nazi Liebkind (to the point of wearing Nazi armbands) is a denial of his past. Or a transcendence? That depends on whether one believes in God or gold—or in Brooks's own implicit alternative, the brotherhood of man.

The Joyce reference also recalls Brooks's confidence that a popular entertainment can make as valid an artistic statement as more respectable forms of art. Brooks obviously had serious purposes in view for this film. He stresses its attack on bigotry:

> More than anything, the great holocaust by the Nazis is probably the great outrage of the Twentieth Century. There is nothing to compare with it. And . . . so what can I do about it? If I get on the soapbox and wax eloquently, it'll be blown away in the wind, but if I do *Springtime for Hitler* it'll never be forgotten. I think you can bring down totalitarian governments faster by using ridicule than you can with invective.[3]

Brooks's "Springtime for Hitler" number is the highlight of the film, an unforgettable scene, and one of his greatest achievements. It demonstrates how well popular art can deal with the concerns of high culture. In that number, an escapist spectacle assumes political force. In addition, Brooks imputes dangerous political potential to an ostensibly innocent genre. His pro-Nazi statement is very naturally conveyed by the musical rhetoric. In another conflation of show biz and politics, the helmeted Liebkind turns upon the elegant first-nighter who tried to hush his mutterings: "*You* shut up! You're the audience, I'm the playwright. I outrank you."

Brooks's Broadway show is a specific parody of the film musicals staged by Busby Berkeley, whose career enjoyed a nostalgic revival of interest in the sixties. The uniformly marching chorus girls, wearing headpieces and bras of giant beer mugs and pretzels, all spangled and feathered and deprived of human character, recall any number of Berkeley spectaculars, especially "The Lady in the Tutti-Frutti Hat" from *The Gang's All Here*. Military processions in dance are familiar from the "Remember My Forgotten Man" number in *Gold Diggers of 1933* and "All's Fair in Love and War" in *Gold Diggers of 1937* (both Berkeley hits). The last stageshot, with the cast amassed under painted guns, recalls "Swingin' the Jinx Away" from Roy del Ruth's hyperspectacular *Born to Dance* (1936), with an additional echo of *Battleship Potemkin*, a nonmusical piece of film propaganda. So too does Brooks's inclusion of gunshots, bombs and goose-stepping in his musical, and the down-shot on the dancers forming a swastika image. Like the Berkeley originals, this shot violates the pretense of a stage presentation.

More important, the individual identity is subordinated to the abstraction in the total effect. To put the case at its extreme, Busby Berkeley's popular extravaganzas suggest a fascist rhetoric of deindividuation. So Brooks's outrageous idea of a musical about Hitler reveals the latent fascism in the American tradition of mass spectacle. Max's plot fails because political concerns prove quite at home in the supposedly innocent musical, provided that what is ridiculed is a familiar target. Brooks's parody is a shrewd critique of its genre.

In Brooks's view, there is no distinction between art of concern and art of diversion. In his comedy of a failed failure, man's various levels of concern converge: Politics, history, psychological development, social adjustment, dreams, disasters, all form the single life which propels the individual soul and which art reflects in its time. Hence a Broadway comedy about Hitler can unite in warm fraternity a Jewish con man, a Jewish wimp, and a Nazi nut. When Kenneth Tynan objects that L.S.D's Hitler "not only mixes up too many incompatible jokes but destroys the bedrock plausibility of the plot," he unwittingly points to the heart of the film's intention.[4] In its literary allusions and its genre parody, *The Producers* surveys the radical and pervasive ways that art affects its audience. Like Max, the popular genres of entertainment are most dangerous when they pretend to innocence. Like Leo, the maturity of the musical, indeed any popular genre, derives from its conscious development beyond the vacancies of innocence.

BACKGROUND

Brooks took his title *Springtime for Hitler* from the Edward Everett Horton summer-stock perennial *Springtime for Henry*. Originally Brooks planned to write the work as a novel about the nice, misunderstood Viennese boy who used to be a nifty dancer but grew up to be Adolf Hitler. One obvious source was a Will Jordan routine about show-biz moguls casting a replacement for Hitler; Lenny Bruce's version can be found in "Hitler and the MCA" on *The Sick Humor of Lenny Bruce*. Gradually Brooks changed his mind about the novel format: "It talked so much I thought it might be a play. Then it talked so much in so many different scenes I knew it was a film."[5]

Brooks started with a 150-page outline, which grew to 400 pages, which he pared down to a 122-page shooting script. For his writing and directing he received a total payment of $35,000. But he was grateful for this first directing assignment. Initial financing of $600,000 was arranged by Sidney Glazier, Oscar-winning producer of *The Eleanor Roosevelt Story*, who recalls choking with laughter at Brooks's oral summary of the proposed film. Joseph E. Levine provided the other $500,000 and consented to let Brooks direct and have the right of the final cut. But he persuaded Brooks to change the title, because he was certain *Springtime for Hitler* would prove anathema at the American box office. Brooks rejected a compromise title, *Springtime for Mussolini*. (In Sweden it's a huge hit under the original title.)

According to Brooks's editor, Ralph Rosenblum, the production was a nightmare. Brooks was at war with Mostel, whose ego did not fit Brooks's ideal of ensemble. Worse, as a neophyte director Brooks had no idea how to organize a production and was subject to worsening explosions of frustration and temper. After harsh and violent disagreements, though, Rosenblum's last sight of Brooks was the director's warm thanks for the film's professional finish. Reports from the sets of Brooks's later features suggest that he has become an enjoyable director to work for. He has overcome his confusions about the incredibly complex business of filming and his insecurities about the job. Indeed, despite Brooks's reported difficulties with the production and his cast, Mars and Wilder have become regular members of his stock company.[6]

In his present view, Brooks would recut *The Producers* to avoid the anti-climax. The film should end about four minutes after the "Springtime for Hitler" number, with the later material coming in before, to be explained by the climactic show.

Brooks had the major parts cast in his mind when he wrote the script. Mostel was an old friend whose all-out acting style and combination of gross physicality and delicate gestures were perfect for the ambivalent character. Mostel's performance was quite in key with his character's theatricality and also with his own principle of acting: "The best guide to acting is Bernard Shaw's phrase 'the life force.' When all the elements of art enter into it— the distortion, the reality, the naïveté—you have the life force."[7]

Brooks promised Wilder the Bloom role when they first met, three years before the call came. Anne Bancroft helped find the actors for the L.S.D. and Carmen Giya roles. Strangely enough, Dustin Hoffman wanted the Franz Liebkind role but had to go to work on *The Graduate*, the film that launched both his career and his persona, just before Brooks began production. (One can speculate the course of Hoffman's career had he played the comic Nazi instead of his Ben Braddock!) Brooks considered playing Liebkind himself, but then cast Kenneth Mars.

The critics drew their battle lines against Brooks with this first feature. Andrew Sarris criticized its anticlimax, its "thoroughly vile and inept" direction, its mugging by the lead actors, and its violation of "the realistic conscience of the medium." At least the two last objections must be accommodated to the film's function of genre parody, which licensed the extravagance. Far more wrong-headedly, Renata Adler charged Brooks with misanthropy: "The audience laughs with apparent misery at all the lewd, hideous tumble of old ladies at the start. . . . One can feel the relief when the much more comic, much less cruel, Hitler scenes occur later on." To Pauline Kael, the film only seemed "unconventional" because it was "so amateurishly crude, and because it revels in the kind of show-business Jewish humor that used to be too specialized for movies." She called Mostel "a one-man obstacle course." Because "Brooks has almost no idea where to put the camera," he keeps "almost everything (including Mostel) on top of us." Dan Bates began his review rather promisingly ("Granted, it is tasteless, eccentric, perverse, audacious, outrageous and offensive. All to the good."), but declared it "possibly the worst film of the year," because of its lack of art and humor and Mostel's obnoxious lack of discipline.[8]

On the other hand, *Newsweek* found the film "a high class low comedy . . . thinking man's slapstick." Archer Winston predicted that "the fun is really there, but not if the name (of Hitler) triggers other emotions too strongly." Wanda Hale in the *Daily News* gave it a solid rave, adding that "anyone, from whose head came this fantasy with profound undertones, can be forgiven for occasional looseness in direction." After a private screening, actor Peter Sellers took out full-page ads in *Daily Variety* and *Hollywood Reporter* to extoll this "ultimate film. . . . Brilliantly written and directed by Mel Brooks, it is the essence of all great comedy combined in a single motion picture. Without any doubt Mel Brooks displays true genius in weaving together stage-comedy, comedy-tragedy, pity, fear, hysteria, schizophrenia, inspired madness and a largesse of lunacy with sheer magic."[9]

Brooks won the Oscar for Best Screenplay for *The Producers*—surprisingly, in view of the general sense of its structural anticlimax—over such solid competition (and strange bedfellows) as *The Battle of Algiers, Faces, Hot Millions,* and *2001*. Wilder was nominated for Best Supporting Actor but lost to Jack Albertson for *The Subject Was Roses*.

Chapter 7

The Twelve Chairs (1970)

THE PLOT IS SET in Russia in the 1920s. Once a nobleman, now a snivelling bureaucrat, Ippolit Vorobyaninov (Ron Moody) learns from his dying mother-in-law that when the Revolution broke out, she hid the family jewels in one of a set of twelve dining room chairs. Ippolit flings himself into the quest to retrieve—if not to recover—the chairs. But the priest who heard her confession, Father Fyodor (Dom DeLuise), has a head start. At the family's ancestral home, Ippolit is tricked into taking a partner, the smooth con man Ostap Bender (Frank Langella).

The first chair Ippolit has to wrestle away from Father Fyodor; it proves empty. Pretending to be a clerk in the Bureau of Housing, which took away the other eleven chairs, Ostap sends Fyodor off on a wild-goose chase to Siberia. Bent and bickering, our heroes track down the other chairs themselves, but all prove empty. They find four in a museum, then gut three more, which they joined a travelling acting company (The *Columbus* Repertory Theater!) to get to. Two others are bought from a thief in that company. To raise the money for that purchase, Ostap persuades Ippolit to overcome his pride and to pretend to be an epileptic begging alms. Ippolit steals the second-last chair from a circus, but as he struggles with Ostap over it, the chair is whisked off by Fyodor. Atop a mountain, Fyodor tears it open. Disappointed again and unable to find a way down, Fyodor is left stranded on the mountain. When Ostap and Ippolit pause for a free buffet lunch at a new recreation center for railroad workers, they find the last chair. But its jewels have already been found; they paid for the center. Defeated, Ostap says he cannot afford to support Ippolit any further and strikes out on his own. When he hears Ippolit swallow his pride and launch into his epileptic beggar act, Ostap happily rejoins him.

The film is rich with the usual Brooks slapstick. There is much fallabout and frantic comedy. Chases and fights are shown in speeded-up action. A traffic cop in Moscow directs the flow of pedestrians. When Fyodor opens the train window in Siberia, he finds a solid wall of ice. There is also a good deal of Brooks's verbal mugging. To Ippolit's "You're not worth spitting on," Father Fyodor replies, "Well, you are! PTUI!" Later Fyodor tries to pass himself off as Vorobyaninov's son, "His firstborn. He was like a father to me." So too, the con man tells his lady (of the moment) that he may not love her but, "I'm very much in lust with you." As the leader of the acting troupe performing a comedy, *The Rise and Fall of the Upper Classes*, Andreas Voutsinas plays a variation on his Carmen Giya role in *The Producers*, preening and casting off an airy "I hate people I dislike." He and Ostap literally struggle for oneupmanship on a staircase. When clerk Ippolit caresses his dying mother-in-law, he leaves a "CANCELLED" stamp on her cheek. The unreliability of social exchange is neatly satirized when the neighbor tells Ippolit in a loud voice the dying woman can hear, "She's doing splendidly. The doctor says she'll be on her feet in a week," then whispers somberly, "She'll be dead before morning. She looks terrible."

These gags notwithstanding, *The Twelve Chairs* has a different feel from Brooks's other works. Partly this is due to the location shooting in Yugoslavia, the local extras, the period setting, the straightforward narrative thrust, and the predominance of social satire over his characteristic reflections upon the medium and genre. Because this film does not spin back against its form, it seems to lack Brooks's usual excess. This may be what prompted Dilys Powell, in her *Sunday Times* review, to admit, "For once I find myself actually laughing at a Mel Brooks joke—not all the time, but at any rate some of it."[1] *The Twelve Chairs* is a film that people who don't like Mel Brooks films may actually like; conversely, it may disappoint his rabid enthusiasts.

Brooks himself considers the film a technical advance upon *The Producers*:

The shots are more beautiful and the whole ambience, look and texture of the film are more cinematic. But who cares about all that junk? It's really the spirit of the thing that counts. It's whether or not the performances smash across the screen into your heart or into your laugh-box and live with you, remain with you.

In 1976 he defended the film as "rather beautiful. And very funny. And very brave. And very rich." *The Twelve Chairs* is certainly conceived as a work of passionate indignation. Indeed, after the critics' cool response to *The Producers,* Brooks told Albert Goldman, "My comedy is based on rage. I'll show these cockamamie *Cahiers* critics. I'll make a movie that'll bend their bagels." That's *The Twelve Chairs*.[2]

Typical of Brooks's films, the characters here are subject to monomania. As Gavin Millar noted, all Brooks's characters "are in the grip of such simple, unrelenting passions," and in *The Twelve Chairs* "almost everyone in sight here is driven to distraction by appalling greed—a greed so acute, in fact, that it begins to betray the symptoms of lust."[3] In the early scenes, a preponderance of close-ups concentrates the character's burning selfishness and obsession with the jewels.

This is also the point of the broad acting styles. The mother-in-law and Ippolit both drift off into private reveries about the jewels. The two characters of highest social and cultural status, nobleman Ippolit and Father Fyodor, degenerate into animal growls and grunting. Often the cool Ostap must restrain Ippolit as if he were a wild dog straining against a leash. Ippolit continually goes for another thief's throat. But Fyodor retains the ability to pretend civilities. On his search after the wrong set of chairs, he follows an engineer from Siberia to Yalta, begging and badgering insanely: When the engineer asks him what he's doing, the priest explains, "Grovelling. I must grovel at your feet." "This is a Soviet household," the engineer's wife responds. "We do not not allow grovelling." When he is finally sold the chairs, the satisfied maniac resumes his decorum: "You shouldn't have done it." Brooks's vision is of a greed so basic it can shiver man's highest pretense to honor and dignity. In Brooks's own summary, "It's the story of a quest for all that you're told you can have—luck, diamonds, riches. Not fame."[4] This theme is its most obvious connection to *The Producers*.

He also admitted a political dimension to the film's satire upon greed; his target is "the common goal government. Everybody's the same: eternal need and eternal greed."[5] In Brooks's Communist saga, the most corrupt self-seekers exploit the slogans of socialist idealism. Both Ostap and Fyodor demand the chairs on the Soviet principle, "There is no personal property. . . . Everything belongs to the people." Father Fyodor adds, "The Church must keep up with the times," to justify his espousal of an atheist politics. The element of religious satire is implicit in Brooks's opening shot—a cross looms, authoritative but impotent, in the foreground while the greedy old lady dies behind. If Ippolit is safe from this particular hypocrisy, it is only because his growling lust is beneath words. In the same spirit, the chief in the acting company complains indignantly that another thief has stolen the chair *he* was planning to steal. The socialist society is presented as a world of cons and gulls.

Indeed it is in their highest virtue, their faith, that the gulls are vulnerable. Ostap originally begs while hiding an eye and a leg. He carries a sign, "I left an eye and a leg at the Winter Palace. Won't you leave something with me?" At the sight of a beautiful woman, he casts off his pretense and pursues her. But he pauses long enough to console a donor: "What can I say, little father? It's a miracle. I can see. I can walk. Let's rejoice." It may seem generous of Ostap to console his dupe, but the line shows that he is exploiting a whole system of values. In the same spirit, when the lady's husband returns home too soon, Ostap pretends to be reviving her from a faint with (genuinely) artificial respiration. He uses revolutionary terms: "Out goes the bad air, in goes the good air." Of course, when the husband performs the same task, it lacks Ostap's benefit: "Out goes the good air, in goes the bad air." Even in his illegitimate activity, Ostap is an enlivening, fresh, beneficent spirit, although he acts according to simplest self-interest.

Brooks's central point is man's need for adult community. *The Twelve Chairs*, again like *The Producers*, shows three variously childish and selfish men working out a relationship of generous and irregular fraternity. Furthermore, Brooks recalls that "there was also the love story between the two men, which seems to be one of my motifs. Maybe my heaviest. I mean I do love the fellowship of men. It's in all my pictures."[6] This theme accounts for all the major changes that Brooks made upon his source, a 1928

Russian satiric novel, *Drenadstat stuler (The Twelve Chairs)*, by Ilya Ilf (actually Fainzilberg) and Yevgenii Petrov (Katayev).

Brooks's gibes at Russian politics and life usually originate in the novel. Thus Ostap passes one sign naming Marx, Engels, Lenin, and Trotsky Street, but the Trotsky has been crossed out. The novel often jokes about street names following the vagaries of political fashion. Surprisingly, some of DeLuise's most manic moments actually occur in the novel, such as his licking and grovelling when he finds the (wrong) chairs. Brooks drops the novel's topical satire upon advertising and upon the irksome living conditions in Russia at the end of the New Economic Policy. But he keeps the general satire upon man's social, cultural, and political pretensions, because it serves his major theme, man's need to outgrow his obsessive selfishness. He also suggests the novel's satire upon bureaucracy (another universal aspect of the human condition). Ostap visits the Housing Ministry, with its separate bureaus for China and Silverware, Paintings and Tapestries, Lamps and Chandeliers, a Bureau for Bureaus, and a Bureau for Furniture Not Used in Other Bureaus. In a room stuffed with papers and files, someone has conspicuously printed on the wall, "Don't Waste Paper." The joke is a miniature of Brooks's larger point, that human folly persists despite the preaching of greater values.

Brooks underplays the novel's social and political satire because his concern is with human maturity and community. That involves deeper reform and fraternity than government or social movements can provide. So Brooks focuses on the individual growth of his three central figures. Ostap begins as an amoral loner, but develops affection and concern for his detestable partner, Ippolit. When Ippolit ruins their chance in the acting company, Ostap abandons him. But he relents, takes him aboard his rowboat and warms him with his coat. The humbled Ippolit admits that the con man is "a good soul."

For his part, Ippolit grows from an incompetent, arrogant, and helpless brute into someone who can and—more important—*will* do things for someone else. His first response to the news of his mother-in-law's dying betrays his childish self-concern: "Poor woman. Who is going to take care of me?" Indeed he seems at loose ends until joined by Ostap. In their first scene together, Ostap prophetically tells Ippolit, "Maybe if you weren't such a selfish pig we could do business." For most of the film Ippolit is helpless. He loses sight of one chair (which turns out to have been the one with the jewels) because he takes too literally Ostap's demand to "Sit there!" He carries the bench when he briefly follows the railway worker, but loses him in the steam at the station. Ippolit cannot perform roles. In one play he rehearses a simple line—"I am Cousin Michael from Kiev; all the Voro-byaninovs are dead"—which he proceeds to botch: "I am Cousin Kiev from Vorobyaninov; all the Michaels are dead." But Ippolit develops some spirit and ability. At one point he climbs up into a high-wire act and wrestles away the chair, his weakness over-whelmed by his greed.

Ippolit even grows out of his arrogance. He initially refused Ostap's "disgusting idea," that he fake an epileptic fit for alms: "There never was and there never will be a Vorobyaninov that begs!" At first he seems to be objecting to the bad taste of faking an ailment to exploit others' sympathy. But the question of taste proves secondary to the old nobleman's vain pride. Ostap, who has begged all his life, wheels upon him as a "disgusting, helpless, inept, bloodsucking parasite. . . . Pride is a luxury that neither you nor I can afford." To sustain their partnership, Ippolit relents. Significantly, they need the money at this point to buy the chairs that they lost access to when Ippolit failed to act the part of a nobleman in the company's play! Having failed to portray the nobleman he actually was, Ippolit now must sink to begging.

The audience is tempted to make the same facile judgment about taste as Ippolit did. Brooks bravely makes the character's moment of human fulfillment and maturity ambivalent. His character is healthiest when he fakes the epilepsy; he is most honest when he performs that con. This jars our habitual opposition to lies, tricks, and the exploitation of tragic disease. But Brooks always challenges our reflexes, especially those about taste.

This tension between our sympathy for the heroes and our revulsion at the idea of exploiting epilepsy is concentrated in the last shot. In an overhead view, we see Ippolit lying flat on the ground faking a fit. A circle of curious, sympathetic, and presum-ably generous onlookers gather around. In his thrashing Ippolit seems to be running, but of course he is flat on the ground, stationary.

This shot parallels an earlier gag, when Ippolit's drunken

servant, Tikon (Brooks) lies on his back, pumps his legs, cries "I'm coming, master," but gets nowhere. When Ippolit comes and stoops over him, Tikon says, "See, I'm here." In both shots, there is a distinction between the illusion of advance and stasis. Brooks's point in the parallel is that there may be advance where we don't see it, such as honesty within a con, or growth within a lapse. In both shots, too, Ippolit must stoop to prove his connection, his humanity, and to earn help.

As the camera draws further back on that last shot, the film audience is physically removed from the character and given the dilemma that Ippolit faced earlier: whether to remain aloof from that unattractive business or to embrace it as an index of common humanity and responsibility. We are directed to a choice when Ostap's voice-over summons both the audience in the image and that in the cinema to respond to Ippolit's ambivalent humanity. "Give, give," Ostap says warmly, in the last speech in the film, "from the bottom of your heart," for a victim of "the same disease that struck down our beloved Dostoyevsky." What seems to be another selfish con act is infused with a redeeming spirit of fellowship.

Finally, in reviving his partnership with Ostap, Ippolit goes a step further than merely stooping to beg. He accepts a new sense of himself. When he first performed the begging act, he told Ostap, "When this business is over, I never want to see you again." The implication is that he wants to forget his shame, and he loathes the man who caused it. But in that last shot, Ippolit goes beyond accepting Ostap—he accepts that his own noble past is invalid and that to survive he must address his essential human vulnerability. Because he can no longer aspire to his lost and hollow status, he flings away his last remnant of the family chair. Instead, he embraces human weakness, which even such greats as Dostoyevsky share. The last image expresses the community of mortal interdependence. As Brooks has observed "even though there's a tragic ending, it's a very happy ending—strange, marvelous thing."[7]

The ending also lends itself to a precisely Freudian interpretation. Vorobyaninov launched himself into the quest for the chairs when his mother-in-law died. His quest is unsatisfactory because it is misdirected. What he really craves is not the chairs but someone to care for him ("Poor woman—who will take care of me?"). So he finds what he craves in Ostap, although he loses the chairs. Thus when he flings away the last chair he is flinging away the substitute gratification he wrongheadedly sought. Brooks's happy ending is rooted in Freud:

> Happiness is the deferred fulfillment of a prehistoric wish. That is why wealth brings so little happiness; money is not an infantile wish.

In Ostap, Vorobyaninov finds the very satisfaction that Tikon found in him. As Brooks told Fred Robbins, the film says two basic things: "Governments change, people never. It also says that we seek what society tells us to seek, in the outside—and what we are really seeking is love."[8]

The developing fraternity between Ostap and Ippolit is contrasted with the solitary career of the greedy Father Fyodor. Once the spiritual leader, Fyodor isolates himself in his lust for jewels, until we last see him alone on a mountain. In the novel, he was eventually retrieved by the fire department and committed to an insane asylum (an institution then used for the insane, not the dissident). But Brooks prefers the image of high isolation. As in the original, the film Fyodor is an ecclesiastic who does not feel his religion deeply. In the novel, he is simply a materialist who joined the church to avoid conscription and who yearns for his own candle factory (a happy mix of religious rite and private gain). DeLuise's Fyodor has no such respectable objective. He just craves the jewels. His cherubic face and serpentine civilities accentuate his greed. Father Fyodor's greed dispels his religious nature completely. So he roughly pushes the neighbor into the dying woman's room: "It's in the hands of God now. All we can do is pray. Go to her, my child, and comfort her. She needs you." This religious instruction is solely intended to free Father Fyodor to pursue the jewels. His chase involves his utter secularization. Thus he almost castrates himself when, cassock hoisted, he tries to scissor over a picket fence. Thus corrupted, he arouses rather unreligious attitudes in his parishioner Vorobyaninov: "Oh, how I hate him! God, how I hate him." Another consequence is Fyodor's own despair: "I don't want to live!" he periodically wails, between flushes of greedy hope. Most important, he assumes that he has God's support in his quest. Throughout he conducts a comradely conversation with God. As he prepares to shave off his beard, for example, he prays: "Oh, Thou who knowest all—You know!" When by happy coincidence he finds a prayer answered, he gives God a brisk "Thank you." In his prayers Fyodor seems to speak to as well as for himself. Thus his cheer "C'mon, God!" parallels his earlier "C'mon, brain," when he struggles to think up a respectable reason for craving the engineer's chairs. Finally, atop his hopeless aerie, he wails: "Oh, Lord, you're so strict!" Father Fyodor's community with God is antithetical to the heroes' modest human fraternity.

Brooks makes this point in the resolution of the quest. When our heroes find the last chair, the wealth they sought lies all around them, in the posh clubhouse that the jewels have bought. Yet they remain focused on the (empty) chair. As in the novel, the wealth has been spent upon a useful symbol of human fraternity. But Brooks adds another level of reward. The famished Ippolit is revived (however animal-like his eating!) by the free buffet that attracted them to the center. So he has already benefited from the diamonds before he espies the chair. Moreover, in the film we learn that the jewels were accidentally found by a worker named Kaminsky, who delivered them up for the public good. As Kaminsky is Mel Brooks's real name, this act of generosity is a human form of intervention by the Maker. Where Father Fyodor corruptly prays for God's help and our heroes make no acknowledgment of higher powers, the resolution pivots upon an act of human generosity in the name of the maker. By involving his (the maker's) own name, Brooks gives the denouement an element of religious humanism. Man can know his Maker only through acts of human community and generosity.

Brooks implied this point earlier in a lyrical, wordless sequence, when Ostap and Ippolit return empty-handed and in despair from the isolated Fyodor. Our heroes walk separately. Shown at a distance, they appear dwarfed first by a skeletal autumn landscape, then by a community of beautiful trees. It is an image of man isolating himself in selfish pursuits, impervious to the potential of (God's?) natural bounty. In a parallel scene, Father Fyodor arranges the engineer's eleven chairs in a circle at a

Richard Thorndyke (Mel Brooks) comes clean in *High Anxiety*, while a *Psycho*-tic danger lurks without (or even with). Copyright © 1978, 20th Century-Fox.

In *The Producers*, Max Bialystock (Mostel) applies sweet reason to his accountant, Leo Bloom (Gene Wilder). Copyright © 1967, Embassy Pictures.

"When you got it, flaunt it!" The Producers hire a secretary (Lee Meredith). Copyright © 1967, Embassy Pictures.

Misfits find community. In *The Producers* Bialystock (Mostel), Liebkind (Kenneth Mars), and Bloom (Wilder) enjoy a sentimental journey. Copyright © 1967, Embassy Pictures.

Mel Brooks as the noble peasant Tikon in *The Twelve Chairs*.
Copyright © 1971, Sidney Glazier.

"Hello, boys. Have a good night's rest?" In *Blazing Saddles* Governor
LePetomane (Mel Brooks, *left*) is hard at work with secretary Miss
Stein (Robyn Hilton). Copyright © 1974, Warner Brothers.

"The next man makes a move, the nigger gets it!" In *Blazing Saddles* Sheriff Bart (Cleavon Little) holds himself hostage. Copyright © 1974, Warner Brothers.

Changing his mind. In *Young Frankenstein*, the faithful Igor (Marty Feldman) must settle for a second-string brain. Copyright © 1974, 20th Century-Fox.

"One giant step for mankind." Young Frankenstein teaches his brainchild to walk. Copyright © 1974, 20th Century-Fox.

Gene Wilder is a rather Rathboney Young Frankenstein, as he leads his lovely Inga (Terri Carr) down the obligatory secret passage. Copyright © 1974, 20th Century-Fox.

Grounds for hope. In *Silent Movie* the fallen Mel Funn (Brooks) is
revived by coffee with his friends, Dom Bell (Dom DeLuise), Vilma
Kaplan (Bernadette Peters), and Marty Eggs (Marty Feldman).
Copyright © 1976, 20th Century-Fox.

In *Silent Movie* the lovely seductress Vilma Kaplan (Bernadette Peters) makes eyes at lover Mel Funn (Brooks). Copyright © 1976, 20th Century-Fox.

The new head shrink, Richard Thorndyke (Brooks), meets his colleagues in the state of *High Anxiety*—the subdued Dick Van Patten, the sinister Harvey Korman, and the pointed Cloris Leachman. Copyright © 1977, 20th Century-Fox.

Funn (Brooks), The Studio Chief (Sid Caesar), and Dom Bell (Dom DeLuise) gather in front of the popcorn butterer at the preview of their *Silent Movie*. Copyright © 1976, 20th Century-Fox.

A therapy session in *High Anxiety*: Professor Lillolman (Howard Morris) treats Dr. Thorndyke (Brooks) while Dr. Montague (Harvey Korman) referees. Copyright © 1977, 20th Century-Fox.

"Look, ma. No *Vertigo!*" In *High Anxiety* the hero conquers his trauma, aided by his sweetheart, Victoria Brisbane (Madeline Kahn). Copyright © 1977, 20th Century-Fox.

The dashing hero. Mel Brooks in *High Anxiety*. Copyright © 1977, 20th Century-Fox.

beautiful seaside setting. To allay suspicion, he exults: "Fine day for a picnic. The others should be along any minute." When finally alone, he turns that idyllic picnic spot into an orgy of pointless destruction. These sequences catch both the indifference and the abundance of the natural world, as expressed in the last sentence of the novel: Ippolit emits "an insane, impassioned wild cry" that fades away, "rebuffed everywhere by the sound of the waking city," as it "sets off on its daily routine" on "a marvelous autumn morning."[9]

Brooks's ending is radically different from that of the novel. In the original, Ippolit ensures sole possession of the last chair by slitting Ostap's throat in his sleep. Brooks dropped this and stressed instead the celebration at the Moscow Railway Workers Communal House of Recreation. Whereas the original Ippolit "had developed determination and cruelty" when he "lost the air of smugness with which he had begun the search for the jewels," Brooks's Ippolit grows through aggressiveness to humility, from selfishness to fraternity. Where the novel traced the character's disintegration, the film develops his maturing and salvation. Brooks will not be as strict as his Father Fyodor found his God— and as the novel was, in propelling its central character toward murder. This softening demonstrates Brooks's overriding concern for his characters:

> When I am writing a script, I don't worry about plot as much as I do about people. I get to know the main characters—what they need, what they want, what they should do. That's what gets the story going. Like a child, I listen to the characters. "Oh, so *that's* what they want! I hope they get it! I love them!" You can't just have action, you've got to find out what the characters want. And then they must grow, they must go somewhere.

Ostap and Vorobyaninov—like Max and Leo before them and Bart and the Waco Kid after—grow by redefining what they think they want.[10]

Consistent with his interest in fraternity, Brooks also omitted all the relationships with women in the novel. There Fyodor had a long-suffering wife whom he abandoned and impoverished in his hunt. Ippolit met an aging former sweetheart, then humiliated himself and squandered the team's resources in pursuit of an idle, unhappy young wife. Ostap took another in a series of wives whom he weds for brief convenience. Dropping all these, Brooks allowed Ostap a single dalliance to establish his all-around conmanship. In these inflections, and in the faint effeminacy of DeLuise's performance as Father Fyodor, Brooks values male relationships, love based upon fraternity rather than romance or sex.

Brooks's optimism is also expressed in the song he wrote for the film, "Hope for the Best, Expect the Worst." Its ethic is "Live when you're alive, no one will survive." There is also a sense of accepting one's limitations: "You could be a Tolstoy or a Fannie Hurst/ So take your chances, there are no answers/ Hope for the best, expect the worst." The buoyant melody provides a lift against the lyrics of bleak realism: "Life is a stage. We're unrehearsed." (Brooks took the tune from Johannes Brahms: "I always wanted to work with Brahms. So it was a real thrill when he agreed to write the music. A nice man, too. A short man, in a wig, but nice.")[11]

All in all, *The Twelve Chairs* is a very personal, distinctive film for Brooks, however different it may feel from his other works. As he told Gene Siskel, *"The Twelve Chairs* for me was Russia. I'm a Russian Jew, and finally, I could bathe in everything Russian that's in me."[12] Anyway, as Brooks quipped on that David Susskind Show, "Chairs are Jewish to begin with. You come in, 'Take a seat.'"

When Brooks appeared in the film as Tikon, Ippolit's loving, faithful, and stupid servant, his accent was cut from the same gabardine as his two-thousand-year-old man. "Oh, I miss Rossia," Tikon moans, complaining that "everyone in the new Soviet Union is a *comrade.*" The fraternal term has been worn flat by overuse. Tikon wistfully recalls his cruel master: "I loved him. He hardly ever beat us." In Vorobyaninov's nostalgic fantasy, Tikon kisses his hand after every slap and croons "I love him; I love him." This emotion, rather than the lost wealth, is what Vorobyaninov really misses. Brooks's Tikon is a far cry from the characterless servant in the novel; he exaggerates the shibboleths of feudal fidelity and embodies the basic virtue in the film; fraternal love, heedless of class difference and punishment. Also, something of Brooks smacks through Tikon's description of what is happening in the old folks' home: "Mostly dying." The house is full of "werry old ladies" who "tippy-toe in, dey have a bowl of porridge and den dey—pphhffft!" Translation: They kick the bucket. The image and spirit recall Max Bialystock's pleasuring of unwary old ladies en route to the cemetery. Brooks's own robust spirit and joyous values augment Tikon's rueful sense of the passing of another generation and the secure, albeit oppressive, social order.

In addition to reviving a minor literary classic—which Brooks claims to have wanted to film since he read it at fifteen years of age—*The Twelve Chairs* revives a fading, remote period. From Ippolit's *moujik* cap to the ubiquitous samovar, the details of place, time, and custom resurrect a disappearing culture. This supports the ethical spirit of the film, which exhorts self-centered modern man to recover lost ideals of fraternal community. Behind the opening credits and later, in a key interlude between Fyodor's trip to Siberia and our heroes' to Moscow, Brooks cuts in montages of citizens going about their daily work and their warm family relationships. As well as being a record of the citizens' lives, these montages contrast the characters' rootless waste of life and spirit. This nostalgia contrasts with the vain egotism of Vorobyaninov's fond memory of his lost nobility and glory. In celebrating his own cultural roots, Brooks calls us back to an essential humanity that will most fully exploit our brief lives together.

BACKGROUND

Brooks made the film on a budget of only $1,400,000. He received $50,000 for writing, directing and acting in the film, a total of three years' work. But he was probably used to this. On an old *Your Show of Shows* skit, Professor Kurt von Closeup (Sid Caesar) was interviewed about his new book, *My Life As a Director, or How to Live on $22.50 a Week*.

The film was shot over four months along the Dalmatian Coast, in Subotica and Dubrovnik. Filming in Yugoslavia, Brooks recalls, was fine except that "on Saturday nights Tito had the car." Suitably warned against the water, the crew drank "Kieselavoda, which is a mild laxative." The food there was "either very good or very bad. One day we arrived on location late and starving and they served us fried chains." Meanwhile, back in their hotel rooms, "mosquitoes as big as George Foreman were waiting for us. They were sitting in armchairs with their legs crossed." The nightlife was disappointing "because all of Belgrade is lit by a ten-watt bulb." Still, Brooks fondly remembers those "Wonderful people! If they had another ten-watt bulb, I'd go there to live." [13]

The stars were largely unknown at the time, except for Ron Moody, who had played Fagin in the stage and screen version of *Oliver*. DeLuise was known only for his TV work. Frank Langella had established a reputation for his work on stage, including *A Cry of Players* opposite Anne Bancroft, but *Diary of a Mad Housewife* and *Dracula* lay well ahead. Brooks used the distinguished Yugoslavian cameraman Djorje Nilolic.

Oblivious of the film's thematic concerns, Pauline Kael argued that Brooks "still doesn't go beyond gag comedy," and the film "never quite recovers" from the loss of "fervid enthusiasm" and "comic tension" when his role as Tikon is over. She also complained about the excess of DeLuise, the restriction of Moody's character to "manic intensity" and Langella's narcissism, all of which, of course, are essential aspects of the film's themes. Vincent Canby quite blindly found the film "almost as joyless as the Soviet Union the film purposefully depicts," because Brooks's sense of humor is "expressed almost entirely in varying degrees of rudeness and cruelty, unrelieved by any comic vision of mankind, of the Soviet Union, or even of his characters." In contrast, Wanda Hale declared it "a gem, a bright and unique comedy with humor and heart." Derek Elley praised its "unac-customed warmth" and hailed its 1976 rerelease as "a genuine discovery in every way." To the *New Statesman*, the film was "an unjustified nonsense." [14]

The Twelve Chairs was filmed with an American setting as *It's in the Bag* in 1945, starring Fred Allen, Victor Moore, Jerry Colonna, Don Ameche, Jack Benny, and Robert Benchley. It was also the basis of a 1936 George Formby comedy, *Keep Your Seats Please*. As Brooks was filming his version in Yugoslavia, a Russian adaptation was being filmed in Malta by director Leonid Gayday.

In 1970 Brooks also tried to set up a film adaptation of the classic Goldsmith comedy, *She Stoops to Conquer*, a play he considers "Mozartean." His approach was to have been "madness. I am using the basic structure that Oliver Goldsmith has so beautifully designed and adding the antics that I am committed to . . .

Goldsmith and Brooks would look marvelous in lights."[15] After Albert Finney declined the starring role of Tony Lumpkin, Brooks considered doing it with Gene Wilder, but a number of agents, studios, and producers declined the project. Denied his Goldsmith, he made the next best thing—a Western.

Chapter 8

Blazing Saddles (1974)

IT's 1874. The new railroad is pushing civilization and its discontent and corruption westward. A black laborer, Bart (Cleavon Little), hits his racist foreman, Taggart (Slim Pickens), with a shovel and is sentenced to hang. Instead, he is appointed sheriff of Rock Ridge, because the villainous speculator Hedley Lamarr (Harvey Korman) wants to demoralize all its citizens. When they leave, Lamarr will profit from the railroad's plan to run its tracks through town.

Sherrif Bart is received coldly by the townsfolk. His only friend is the legendary quick-draw gunslinger, the Waco Kid (Gene Wilder), now a quivering alcoholic. Bart deputizes Waco; together they bring law'n'order to the dusty town. Bart wins over two agents of Lamarr, the behemoth Mongo (Alex Karras) and the saloon chantoosy, Lili von Shtupp (Madeline Kahn). Desperate, Lamarr recruits an army of desperadoes to clear the town. But Bart foils him again. The black and white citizens unite to build a completely detailed replica of Rock Ridge. When the bad guys attack the fake set, they are ambushed with dynamite.

The subsequent battle overflows the cardboard Rock Ridge into the western hills, then into the surrounding studio areas of modern Hollywood; thence to an adjacent Warner Brothers set, where Buddy Bizarre (Dom DeLuise) is rehearsing a musical spectacular. His objection is brushed aside by Taggart: "Piss on you. I'm working for Mel Brooks." As the riot sweeps through the studio, Bart rides into Mann's (née Grauman's) Chinese Theater to watch the happy ending of the movie *Blazing Saddles*. Hedley

Lamarr also comes to the cinema for safety, but Bart guns him down. Bart and Waco ride into the sunset together, but in the desert, they abandon their horses for a chauffeured limousine.

As this plot summary may suggest, *Blazing Saddles* plays against most of the conventions of the American Western. The church scenes, the building of the railroad, the rescue by lariat, the saloon, the climactic free-for-all—everything in the saga of Rock Ridge has roots in the Hollywood Western. So do the characters. The fallen Waco Kid wobbles in from the tradition of Thomas Mitchell's drunken doctor in *Stagecoach* and Dean Martin's gunslinger in *Rio Bravo*. As the cool outsider who saves the town, Bart is a hipster Shane. Madeline Kahn's torch singer parodies Marlene Dietrich's role in *Destry Rides Again* (with echoes of her Lola Lola from *The Blue Angel,* a popular target for Imogene Coca's parody on *Your Show of Shows*). As dumb henchman Taggart, Slim Pickens draws upon his iconic association with the Old West, developed over 130 films and already deployed ironically in *Dr. Strangelove* and elegiacally in *Pat Garrett and Billy the Kid*. The parody extends to formal elements as well. The titles—yellow wooden letters with flaming red tops, against a sagebrush backdrop—recall the credit style of the old Republic Westerns. In the manner of *The Gunfight at O.K. Corral*, Frankie Laine belts out an opening ballad—punctuated with the whip cracks from his hit, "Mule Train,"—about the hero:

> *He conquered fear and he conquered hate.*
> *He turned dark night into day.*
> *He made his blazing saddle*
> *A torch to light the way.*

That verse collapses under critical scrutiny. Like the other conventional Western material in the film, it is slightly askew.

As Brooks explained, he used "every Western cliché in the book in the hope that we'll kill them off in the process."[1] *Blazing Saddles* is a critique of the Western genre. Specifically, Brooks charges the Western with racism, with projecting false ideals of masculinity, and with lying, *i.e.*, with presenting as history an essentially fictitious fantasy. Brooks's Western is an anti-Western.

He renders extravagantly explicit those elements which are only implicit in the conventional Western; in effect, he brings to the foreground what Hollywood has contrived to hide.

To this end, many of his sight gags violate the surface familiarity of the shot. For example, in a hanging, the horse as well as the cowboy has his head in a noose. In Hedley's office, a picture shows the rear view of a marriage scene, quietly emblematic of the reverse exposure that characterizes the entire film. True to the tradition of the cowpuncher, Mongo punches out a horse.

Brooks's most striking device is the scatological inflection given much of the material. The very title undercuts the heroic notion of blazing guns with the rump comedy of the saddle. Brooks's cowboys shoot off their pants more than their guns. So too, Hedley instructs his colleagues, "Rest your sphincters." Brooks himself portrays the cross-eyed, lecherous, corrupt Governor LePetomane (French for "the farter") and is addressed by school-marm Harriet Van Johnson as "the leading asshole in the State."

In this regard, the key scene is the funniest. Around a familiar campfire, the familiar cowhands enjoy their familiar repast of beans. But Brooks adds the realistic offshoot of such a diet. His cowboys explode in a symphony of farts. Brooks describes the effect:

> With the first fart, a slight shudder goes through the crowd, and you can hear a gasp from the people who are just a little more sensitive. With the next series of three or four farts, titters begin to escape from mouths. The fifth or sixth fart evokes a flat-out laugh from a third of the audience. By the time the sixteenth fart rolls around, the entire audience is in a state of hysterical convulsion.[2]

This may have been the "miraculous" effect upon the first viewing of the film. In its reissues, the scene draws laughter more quickly, in anticipation.

Warner Bros. wanted to cut the scene, but Brooks stuck to his guns. It is vital because it concentrates his intentions of the film as a whole (so to speak). Brooks is reintroducing realism to a genre that sank into artifice and mythic unrealities: "I mean, you can't eat so many beans without some noise happening there." His realism has honorable precedent: "Shakespeare said hold the mirror up to life; I held it a little behind and below." This restored life to the artificial genre: "Wind was never broken across the prairie in a Ken Maynard picture." Brooks is amused that flatulence should arouse such indignation in a genre that is generally crude and violent:

> For 75 years these big, hairy brutes have been smashing their fists into each other's faces and blasting each other full of holes with six-guns, but in all that time, not one has had the courage to produce a fart. I think that's funny.

And for a pertinent sociological analogue:

> Farts are a repressed minority. The mouth gets to say all kinds of things, but the other place is supposed to keep quiet. But maybe our lower colons have something interesting to say. Maybe we should listen to them. Farts are human, more human than a lot of people I know. I think we should bring them out of the water closet and into the parlor.

As we shall see, Brooks's defense of the "repressed minority" was not limited to the low-born but eloquent fart. Brooks's bean scene blew human reality into a genre stultified by convention.[3]

By deflating the pretensions of the scene, Brooks's scatology works as a kind of bathos. So the cowboys' free-form farting can be related to the spitting and belching of bartender Anal [sic!] Johnson, whose noises are absorbed into the rhythms of "The Ballad of Rock Ridge":

> *The town saloon was always lively.*
> *There was nothing nasty or obscene.*

Both play against the dignity of the conventional American Western. So too, in the obligatory church scene, the citizens bemoan the town's immorality with a hymn that ends: "There's no avoiding this conclusion: Our town is turning into shit." Later, when the citizens rally against the villains, Reverend Johnson (Liam Dunn) concludes a prayer: "Oh, Lord, do we have the strength to do this mighty task in just one night, or are we just jerkin' off?" Brooks's bawdry and scatology shiver the conventional decorum. Similarly, the threat of dynamite inflects the minister's injunction that his congregation rise and "read from the book of Matthew, Mark, Luke and—Duck!"

The characters act as bathetically as they speak. A sweet little old lady, punched in the tummy by two toughs, asks the camera, "Have you ever seen such cruelty?" She later responds to the friendly sheriff with a curt "Up yours, nigger." In the climactic battle, she knocks out one bad guy, the reverend kicks others in the groin, and the town's Colorful Rustic, Gabby Johnson (Ennis Starrett Jr.), overpowers another by breathing on him. This is no Gene Autry skirmish.

Against the usual innocence of the genre, Brooks emphasizes sexual corruption. Bewailing the disorder in town, the minister reports people stampeded and cattle raped. That is to say, the generic as well as the natural order has been upset. Apparently cross-eyed from lust, Governor LePetomane slavers over his mistress-secretary's bulging breasts: "Hello, boys. Have a good night's rest? I missed you." In another confusion of genre, Hedley Lamarr chafes at being continually called Hedy. "What the hell are you worried about?" LePetomane advises him genially. "This is 1874. You can sue *her*."[4]

Despite his ambiguous title of "State Procurer," Hedley is a figure of arrested or diverted sexuality. He bathes with a ducky and a froggy. Worse, he is impervious to the charms of Lili von Shtupp. Even as he deploys her against Sheriff Bart, he misogynistically calls her a "Teutonic twat" (changed to "Teutonic twivit" in the film's reediting for TV). In a related gag, Hedley looks up his strategy in a manual for outlaws: "Land snatching. Land: see 'snatch.'" In the villains' manual, the only "snatch" that counts is that of land. This is not a healthy state.

For her part, Lili von Shtupp plays against the Hollywood genre's laundered libido. Her name combines the pretense to lily-whiteness with the generic function of the Shtupp (Yiddish for "push," with the colloquial meaning of "fuck"). "We almost called the picture *She Shtupps to Conquer*," Brooks reports, as if still rueing his failed Goldsmith project.[5] So too, her voice combines the sexuality of Dietrich with the lisp of Elmer Fudd. She's touched by Bart's gift of "a wovely wed wose." She even writes with a lisp: "I must see you wight away," she writes the black Bart. "Please come to my dwessing woom." To Dietrich's themes of world-weariness and moral lassitude in "Falling in Love Again" and "The Laziest Girl in Town," Lili adds impotence and sexual frustration. As the Teutonic Titwillow croons, "Who can satisfy [men's] lustful habit? I'm not a wabbit, I need a rest." And "I've had my fill of love/ From below and from above," what with all those men, "always coming and going and going and coming, and always too soon." As she puts it:

I've been with thousands of men again and again
And they always sing the same tune.
They start with Byron and Shelley ,then jump on your belly
And bust your balloon.

She concludes: "Everything below the waist is *kaput*." In addition to her dollop of Dietrich, there is also a pinch of Mae West: "Is that a ten-gallon hat or are you just enjoying the show?" In Lili's weary sexuality, Brooks rebuts the Hollywood genre's scrupulous concealment of the sexual reality through innocent saloon girls and coy, teasing song-and-dance. Lili's summary of her conquest by the sheriff is a girlish, "Oh, what a nice guy!"

Brooks also suggests that the Western creates a false and narrow sense of what constitutes proper manhood. The libidinous Le-Petomane and the celibate Hedley have opposite forms of sexual deviation, but are equals in greed and corruption. At the other extreme are the various male chorus lines. Taggart calls his dancing cowboys "a bunch of Kansas City faggots," but his own masculinity is a matter of tangled bluster; he plans to "make Rock Ridge think it's a chicken that got caught in a tractor's nuts!" The manly image of Lili's dancing corps of burly German soldiers is undercut by her song of frustration *cum* exhaustion. Meanwhile, back at the raunchy studio next door, Buddy Bizarre directs a chorus of gay men in "The French Mistake" ("Throw out your hands/ Stick out your tush/ Hands on your hips/ Give 'em a push . . ."). These dancers are rallied to the fight by a firm "Come on, girls." In this collision of genres, Brooks introduces alternative styles of manhood to the monistic Western.

He also raises the issue of homophilia that lurks implicit in the male bonding patterns of the traditional Western, from *The Outlaw* through *Butch Cassidy and the Sundance Kid*. The hulk Mongo, by his prowess (and the casting of footballer Alex Karras) the film's conventionally manliest figure, decides to stay with the heroes. "Mongo has deep feelings for Sheriff Bart," he explains with a boyish shuffle. When Waco teases Bart, Mongo adds "Naw, Mongo straight."

Mongo's nonsexual affection for Bart is amplified in the central love story between Bart and Waco. Brooks admits that the film "had to do with love more than anything else," but emphasizes Bart's heartbreaking rejection by the granny ("Up yours, nigger!") and the weak support from the town liberals. When Granny brings Bart a pie, in gratitude for besting Mongo, she immediately returns to advise, "I trust you'll have the good sense not to tell anyone I spoke to you." Brooks also admits his usual personal concern: "I guess maybe the story also has a little to do with me searching for my own father . . . in the picture, both Cleavon and Gene Wilder are searching for someone to believe in. When they find each other, it's a marriage made in heaven." The two men discover their instinctive community in their first conversation, when Sheriff Bart finds Waco awakening, literally hung over in his cell:

SHERIFF: Are we awake?
WACO: We're not sure. Are we—black?
SHERIFF: Yes we are.
WACO: Then we're awake. But very puzzled.

In that "we" the characters use a modern, not a Western, idiom. It confirms their common sense of being outsiders.[6]

In addition to the drunk and the black being social outcasts, their modern consciousness makes them outsiders from the Western genre. As Waco quite properly asks Bart, "What's a dazzling urbanite like you doin' in a rustic setting like this?" Moreover, both men refer to themselves as genre creatures. Waco introduces himself as "Jim, but most men call me—Jim" and "I must have killed more men than Cecil B. DeMille." Later Bart wins a reprieve by appealing to the citizens' faith in Randolph

Scott. A sense of modern knowing continually plays around the "I'm hip" Bart:

> They said you was hung.
> They was right.

Bart and Waco do not fit into their Western genre because they do not fit into the conventional white racist society. In the conventional Western, Black Bart would be a dumb villain, not the cool, modern virtuous hero he is here. (As a matter of fact, in one *Your Show of Shows* parody, "Tall, Dark and Strange," Carl Reiner played a villain named Black Bart, who lit cigarettes just to keep his nose warm.) By transcending their genre, Bart and Waco affirm their character and humanity against the genre's prejudices.

In one motif, Brooks jokes about the culture's sexual stereotypy of the black man. When Bart first rides into town, he throws the citizens into a panic (and one white woman into a faint) when he reaches into the front of his pants to "Whip this out." The "this" turns out to be his formal appointment as sheriff. Later Lili asks him, "Is it twue vot zey say about how you people are gifted? [Un-ZIP] OOh! It's twue! It's twue! It's twue!" In the editing, Brooks removed Bart's reply: "Excuse me, I don't mean to criticize your technique, and this may have been what you had in mind all the time, but you're sucking my arm."[7] In the film, Brooks opts for more subtlety; he cuts to the blissful Lili handing Bart a huge breakfast sausage. Again, Brooks is rendering explicit what lurks implicitly in the conventional Western, the white man's sexual dread of the colored savage, whether red or black.

The film opens with a joke about racism. Taggart orders his black laborers to sing a "good ole nigger worksong." Bart obliges with a cool Cole Porter, "I Get a Kick Out of You." At the crooner's "kick from cocaine," the foreman interrupts with an apt oath: "Hold it! Hold it! What the hell is that shit?" The white foreman's "shit" is nothing to sniff at but the modern Bart's is. The white bigots then demonstrate what they want—the religious submission of "Swing Low, Sweet Chariot" and the social resignation of "De Camptown Races." The white racists do a ludicrous cakewalk, chanting "Gwine to run all night/ Gwine to run all day."

This performance the blacks watch bemused. Again, where the whites are restricted to their genre, the blacks transcend the white bigots' myth.

Bart's very modernity ruffles the surface. His buckskin image is modified by his doubleknits and Gucci saddlebags. Later he shares a joint with Waco. The black stays cool, but the stoned Waco speaks in falsetto, his voice, like his nature, raised by hipness. Bart is also detached from the white's rhetoric when the background music at his introduction is shown to be provided by Count Basie and his orchestra, playing "April in Paris" on a desert bandstand. The number is later balanced by Buddy Bizarre's "The French Mistake." When the heroes switch from horse to limo at the end, they complete their transcendence of the genre and all its implicit biases.

Excepting Waco, all the whites are restricted to the bigotry of the Western. Its conventions represent the conventions of social tradition. LePetomane provides one example: "You can't make a nigger—no offense—the new sheriff of Rock Ridge!" Earlier, LePetomane blindly confides in Bart that the new sheriff is "a nig—." He catches himself in midslur. Then the church bells abbreviate Gabby Johnson's warning to the town that the new sheriff is "a nig." The governor's mistake becomes a convention of speech. Finally the word is completed when the welcoming official formally extends "a laurel and a hearty handshake to our new— nigger."

In the event, Bart succeeds by manipulating the whites' bigotry. When the townsfolk prepare to shoot him, Bart holds a pistol to his own head and yells "Hold it! The next man makes a move, the nigger gets it." Bart then assumes the voice of a stereotypical terrified black boy: "Oh, lawdy lawd! He's desperate. Do what he say, do what he say." By slipping into the silly character, Bart preempts the white folks' fury and overcomes their antagonism. He wins their sympathy by playing the role with which they are familiar and comfortable. "Isn't anybody going to help that poor man?" cries the lady who moments before cried for his blood. Safely holding himself hostage in the sheriff's office later, Bart congratulates himself: "Baby, you are so talented. And they are so dumb." In similar business, Bart bests Mongo by appearing as a

Western Union delivery boy with an exploding Candygram. When Bart and Waco infiltrate Hedley's desperadoes, they again "put on" white bigotry; they dress as Ku Klux Klansmen. To lure the whites, Bart reverts to stereotype: "Where de white wimmen at?" Exposed, he leaves with "My next impression—Jesse Owens."

In a related sight gag, Bart tells Waco that his family had to ride at the back of the wagon train when they moved West. Under Indian attack, Bart's family runs its own wagon in its own little circle: "The white folks didn't let us travel in their circles, so we made our own." Again Brooks satirizes both the social and the genre conventions. To the idealized frontier spirit he imputes the roots of modern racism; the back of the wagon train leads to the back-of-the-bus. Conversely, the film's representation of the West is not an historical image but a projection of the modern sensibility. In addition, Brooks satirizes the Western convention in which settlers draw their wagons into a circle, around which the Indians would foolishly ride until they were all killed. This image has no basis in history. Rather, it is a metaphor for the white community's defense of its inner circle against savage penetration.

The whites' racism is blatant from the first scene, where the foremen abuse the "chink" and "nigger" on the work crew. Rather than risk two horses, two blacks are sent to test for quicksand, then left to die while the whites save their four-hundred-dollar handcart instead. When the blacks save themselves, Taggart snaps: "Well, boys, the break is over. Don't just lay there gettin' a suntan. Ain't gonna do you no good nohow. Har! Har!" A later speech by Taggart focuses the racism: "Well, don't that beat all. Here we take the good time and trouble to slaughter every Indian in the West, and for what? So's they can appoint a sheriff that's darker than the Indians. To wit: a nigra. Well, I'm so depressed." The whites remain prejudiced even when they need the colored people's help against a common enemy: "We'll give some land to the niggers and chinks but we don't want the Irish," resolves Mayor Olsen Johnson (David Huddleston). Only when the minorities stick together do the whites relent. Brooks's vision of the bigoted frontier corrects the John Ford myth of an open-spirited, melting-pot America. Or, as Waco consoles Bart, "These people are simple farmers, people of the land, the common clay of the

New West. You know—morons." In the screenplay, the crowning epithet was "scumbags," but Brooks is ever a voice of moderation and taste.

In addition to citing the Chinese and Irish, Brooks broadens his treatment of racism with Yiddish jokes. When Brooks himself plays the Sioux chief, he speaks Yiddish. Amazed at the *"Schwartzes,"* the blacks, he orders his braves to let Bart's people go: *"Zeit nisht meshugge. Loz em gaien. . . . Abee gezint.* Take off." (Translation: "Don't be crazy. Let them go. . . So long as we're all healthy. *Aveck.")* In his two roles, Brooks portrays the opposite extremes of the social hierarchy. As Governor Le-Petomane, he is the rich archinsider, a corrupt power. As the Sioux chief, he is the archoutsider and victim, a warm and generous human being doomed to defeat in the white man's history and mythology alike. Because his humanity embraces all minorities—except perhaps Nazis and gays—the Indian chief speaks Yiddish. In the original screenplay, Brooks's role as LePetomane far outweighed his as Chief; "My whole performance was on the cutting-room floor" because it slowed down the last third of the film.[8] This proportion signified which character is dominant in society. Still, in the ads for the film, Brooks appears in profile as the Indian head on a coin, with "Hi, I'm Mel. Trust me" etched around the rim in place of "In God We Trust." Hebrew lettering on the headdress assures us that the feathers are kosher for Passover. The black cowboy rears up against the headdress feathers, as if a mental projection by Brooks's Indian, the victimized Everyman regardless of race, religion, color or creed (no offense). So even a white citizen can be included in this community: When Mongo smashes into the saloon, a panicky white speaks Yiddish: "Gottenew!" (an anguished "Oh, God!").

Nevertheless, Brooks's Yiddish jokes were attacked rather than understood in the film's first reviews. Pauline Kael complained that they "aren't even jokes anymore but just an assertion of Jewishness—as if that were always good for a laugh." (With similar insight she declared that Madeline Kahn's role as Lili "isn't worthy of her—and I didn't enjoy hearing her insulted.") Rather more understanding was Robert Fulford:

Like most Jewish comedians, he sees something inherently funny in

Jewishness itself—its language, conventions, etc. And he finds Germans, in all their attitudes, loathsome. All these things he crams into his movie, pushing stereotype against stereotype, myth against myth.

But Brooks's Yiddish jokes have a more serious function in *Blazing Saddles*. They affirm the character and humanity that are excluded from America's racist mythology. They are a key element in the film's intention: As the ads quipped, "Never give a saga an even break." So Brooks was frankly surprised at the film's success with the average middle American: "What would a guy who talks about white bread, white Ford station wagon and vanilla milkshakes on a Friday night see in that *meshugas* [Yiddish for "craziness"]?" But the Warren Blands lapped it up.[9]

Brooks elaborates upon the racism of the Western when Hedley and Taggart sign up their horde of desperadoes. These henchmen run the gamut of historical and generic rowdies, for Hedley is "An Equal Opportunity Employer." So there are Mexican revolutionaries, German soldiers, a motorcycle gang, Bedouins, and Klansmen. Less visible types are named in Hedley's order: "rustlers, cutthroats, murderers, bull dykes, mugs, pugs, thugs, nitwits, half-wits, dimwits, vipers, snipers, muggers, buggerers, bank robbers, train robbers, horse thieves, hornswogglers, bushwackers, ass kickers, shit kickers, and Methodists." (At the end of this Swiftian catalogue of Americana, Taggart finally finds a pencil: "Could you repeat that, sir?") Escaping the bias of the traditional Western, Brooks roots his humanism in the Jewish Indian as a universal victim, and provides an international, anachronistic roll call of evil. Brooks declares the Western to be racist for celebrating the dubious triumph of the white-man's civilization over colored personifications of savagery.

Brooks makes these points exclusively through gags. Le-Petomane buys 200,000 acres of prime Cheyenne land for a box of toy paddles. His pretense to paternal power is shattered when he shows he can't handle the toy himself. When Taggart proposes that the citizens of Rock Ridge might be subdued by "killing the first male child of each household," Hedley considers, then concludes, "Too Jewish." The apparently principled act of appointing a black sheriff is clearly motivated by Hedley's greed and LePetomane's presidential aspirations. His catch-phrase "no offense" shows a formal attempt to make bigotry decorous: "Good luck, nigger—no offense"; "They'll kill that nigger—no offense, son—stone-cold dead on his first day on the job." (These examples from the screenplay were edited out of the film.) And the victimized white community of Rock Ridge is no better. The minister is a vicious, hypocritical, impotent coward: "The time has come to act and act fast. I'm leaving."

In addition to the anachronistic characters of Bart and Waco, there are abundant allusions to the modern media and popular culture, such as Taggart's "What in the Wide World of Sports is goin' on here?" and the hanging of a man in a wheelchair for "the Dr. Gillespie killing" (an allusion to Dr. Kildare movies). When the Gabby Hayes type sputters a nonsensical tirade, he is applauded both for his courage and for supplying "authentic frontier gibberish." Later Hedley exhorts his henchmen to "go do the voodoo that you do so well." He is risking not just his life but his Oscar hopes for Best Supporting Actor. The hulk was named Mongo solely to set up the frightened citizen's cry, "Mongo! Santa Maria!" in playful homage to the great bongo player Mongo Santamaria. The welcoming committee's "laurel and a hearty handshake" is a play on Laurel and Hardy. "No more Mr. Goodbar," resolves the turning-worm Hedley, and then, "Head them off at the pass? I hate that cliché." These jokes remind us that the Western film itself is just a fabrication of popular culture. For all its historical pretenses, it is a modern artifice. This is also the point of the gags in which characters address the camera (*i.e.*, the cinema audience) directly, as in Granny's "Have you ever seen such cruelty?" and Hedley's meditation, "Where would I find such a man? Why am I asking you?"

In a transparent historical pretense, Brooks fills Rock Ridge with members of the Johnson family, as if his mythic setting were the direct forerunner of Lyndon Johnson's America. We find Howard Johnson (John Hillerman) with his orange-roofed Conestoga and his auspicious one-flavor ice-cream parlor, Mayor Olsen Johnson (anticipating the comedy team from whom Brooks took his model for formal coherence), the grizzled Gabby Johnson, schoolmarm Harriet Van Johnson (Carol Arthur), and even Dr. Sam Johnson (Richard Collier), who is the medic in a town of feverish lexicography. These names establish the setting as a projection of the modern awareness, rather than as a historical image of the past. They also acknowledge the spiritual debt of President Johnson's style and image to the mythology of Hollywood's West.

Brooks's film does not, as one critic suggests, "assert that the Western is an exhausted artifact of our cinematic culture, worthy only of put-on and put-down."[10] On the contrary, there is always an element of affection in Brooks's choice of what to parody. In this case, he luxuriates in the space, the rhetoric, and the energy of the Western. He only reminds us that it is a myth, with dangerous assumptions and biases, and that it is a modern system of thought, not a fixed historical entity. As a modern system, it proves inexhaustible in the range of character and incident that it can support.

In this reading, there are even logic and point to the section of the film that bore the most critical attack, the ending. *Variety* dismissed "the last fifteen minutes of film-within-a-film nonsense." *Time* reviewer Richard Schickel claimed, "The whole raveled sequence is the work of men desperate for an ending." Even Brooks's supportive biographer William Holtzman declared the ending "the one inescapable indulgence . . . breaking the thread of believability upon which the film's comic anachronism dangles." In contrast, Robert Fulford argued that the film is about Westerns, about Hollywood, but "also about the clash between different perceptions of reality," thus justifying the ending. As Brooks recalls, because *Blazing Saddles* was "a breakthrough comedy" taking audiences into new kinds of satire and vulgarity, "some critics felt confused and disoriented. So they thought that because *they* were confused, *we* were confused. We weren't."[11]

Brooks's wild ending makes perfect sense. The seeming chaos brings us to the heart of the film's purpose, because it exposes the Western rhetoric to be arbitrary modern projection. First, the marauding villains are slowed in their attack across the wide-open space by the erection of a paltry toll booth. While the wild men wait, someone rides back for change so that the gang may continue on the nonexistent LePetomane Throughway. That is, even the wildest Western villains unquestionably obey the restrictions of the modern sensibility.

The townspeople's subsequent ploy is a parallel to the myth-making process by which Hollywood has reinvented the historical West. They erect a flat, false image of their town, then populate it with flat images of themselves. Both the Western myth and the cardboard town are flat projections, false images devised to evade the forces of villainy (in the film) or guilt (in the historical reality, for having murdered, stolen, and lied to create the foothold of "civilization"). At both levels, the aim is to preserve the community's sense of security and innocence. As Brooks's citizens blow up their fabrication, Brooks's film explodes the myths of the Western.

After the relatively realistic fight between the settlers and the villains, the camera pans back to expose the scene as a studio set. Then it reveals the modern cityscape beyond. The exposure continues when the fight spills over into the antithetical genre, the musical (an urban fantasy of predominantly feminine values, in contrast to the rural, masculine spirit of the Western). In this device, Brooks's point is the essentially arbitrary choice of language for a world view. The musical, the Western, any Hollywood type, provides only one of several alternative visions and value systems; none monopolizes truth or history.

The self-reflective theme culminates when Hedley, then Bart, arrive at the premiere of *Blazing Saddles*. With the art and reality continuous, the film is clearly stated to be about itself. As befits characters of opposite morality, the two men come there for different reasons. Hedley seeks refuge: "Drive me off this picture," he tells the cabbie. Bart arrives to ensure that justice is done. Here Brooks warns against the escapist use of a popular art and alerts us to its political and social uses (as he did in *The Producers*).

Finally, Hedley dies in double agony. Mortally shot in the groin, he utters his last words in bitter envy: How could Douglas Fairbanks "do such fantastic stunts with such little feet?" For the villain, Hollywood's mythic world brought impotence and impossible aspirations. So he aptly dies at the feet of the Hollywood mythology, the stars' imprints in the sidewalk. In contrast, Waco and Bart ride away from Hollywood, having enjoyed its opportunities and diversions, to resume their real, modern lives.

Brooks's multi-genre conclusion is the logical climax for a drama that opens with sly anachronisms, the modern sensibility persistently intruding into the mythic past, and that closes with the camera itself demonstrating the need for a widening, more embracing perspective. Brooks uses the Western's conventions to define the narrowness and limitations of Hollywood's vision. So the film really is what he claims, "a surrealist epic," a Cubist exercise in shifting perspective. "The official movie portrait of the West was simply a lie," he told Kenneth Tynan. "What I did when the gunfight spilled over onto the Busby Berkeley set with fifty dancers was what Picasso did when he painted two eyes on the same side of the head." He obeyed the single most revolutionary tenet of modern art—escape from the limitations of a single, fixed perspective—and of modern social philosophy—humanist relativism. *Blazing Saddles* reminds us of the arbitrary and willful nature of any set of conventions by which we choose to live or to perceive, whether in art or in life.[12]

In tone, *Blazing Saddles* has all the rage and passion of the great literary tradition of satire. Because Brooks figured that his career as a filmmaker was finished anyway, he "wrote berserk, heartfelt stuff about white corruption and racism and Bible-thumping bigotry. We used dirty language on the screen for the first time, and to me the whole thing was like a big psychoanalytic session. I just got everything out of me—all my furor, my frenzy, my insanity, my love of life and hatred of death."[13] Yet for all that load of pain and passion, the work remains a hilarious comedy.

BACKGROUND

In view of the rich, free form of *Blazing Saddles*, it is surprising to see what Brooks chose to drop from the screenplay. Some of his omissions sharpen the point of the joke. Gone is Mongo's response to the explosion in the Candygram: "No card?" Gone too are a host of specific references to other movies. There was a parody of the *Stagecoach* journey. One scene, in which little boys play beat-up-the-sheriff, was a rather sentimental parody of *The Gunfighter*. Gone too is Lili von Shtupp's Germanic manservant, modelled after Eric von Stroheim's roles in *La Grande Illusion* and *Sunset Boulevard*. Brooks cut out Tony Martin singing "Tenement Symphony," which lumped together Cohens and Kellys with Thompsons and Vermicellis, Benson Fongs and Huey Longs.

Gone too is a reference to "that Disney feller . . . building like crazy out there" in Anaheim. The screenplay had the Jolly Green Giant add his colorful hand to the multicolored cooperative building project at the end.

Some changes were made to temper our impression of Bart. In the screenplay, the sheriff paints white the dark jockey figure on the jail's ashtray. When he beat Waco at chess, he did a little braggadocio dance, as if he were some jive-ass footballer celebrating a touchdown! Gone too is Bart's scrapping of a Wanted poster about another black. ("He's got enough trouble without a bunch of honkies chasing his ass from here to Mexico.")

And of all things, some of Brooks's deletions seem to have been made in the interests of good taste. One example is Bart's explanation for claiming Dutch ancestry: His grandmother "was always hanging around with a lot of dykes." When LePetomane mumbles through Harriet Van Johnson's telegram, he concludes, "mmmph . . . rmph . . . ASSHOLE!" at which his secretary obediently rolls over: "Sure, Bill, anything you say." When Bart and Waco overpower two Klansmen for their uniforms, Bart (in the screenplay) inserted a cactus in one rectum. In the fight between the cowboys and the dancers at the end, a cowboy punched out a friendly dancer with "you miserable little fruit" and another shot his pistol with "OK, pansies, start dancin'." Instead, Brooks has one cowboy go off with a male dancer, as if to draw Andy Warhol's *Lonesome Cowboys* into his range of reference.

But generally the omissions were in the interest of narrative efficiency. So as not to overdo scenes, Brooks cut the number of granny-punchers instructed to attack her down to two people, not three. He dropped a trick lasso act at the quicksand scene. Gone from the outlaws' revelry is a bad man's tying a boy's pet snake into a running bowline. At the sheriff's swearing-in, Brooks dropped a few twists in the routine in which Bart holds himself hostage (*e.g.*, Reverend Johnson advises, "Go along with him, son. There'll be another time for you."). Taken all in all, the volume and nature of Brooks's trimming of the screenplay further attest to the discipline and formal order in the final film.

The original story for *Blazing Saddles* was written by film scholar Andrew Bergman, author of *We're in the Money*. Warner Brothers' story editor Judy Feiffer (then wife of cartoonist Jules) found Bergman's screenplay, *Tex X*, which placed a modern hip black sheriff amid the Western clichés. Warner Brothers hired Brooks for $50,000 to assemble and head a group of writers to rework Bergman's script. Brooks gathered Norman Steinberg, Alan Uger, Richard Pryor, and (in something of a departure from usual studio practice) Andrew Bergman. (As Brooks recalls, "They said, 'Why do you want the original writer when we have his script?' and I said, I'm sure there's more in his head since we liked his idea so much.")[14] Four months of brainstorming produced a 412-page script, which was pared down to 275 in three more months. Brooks was hired for $100,000 to direct the film, which took ten weeks to shoot and nine months to edit.

Dan Dailey, whose musical associations would have been an important aspect of his role, was originally cast as the Waco Kid but he withdrew from the project. So did a substitute. As a last-minute replacement, Brooks cast friend Gene Wilder, who had to have Stanley Donen rearrange his shooting schedule for *The Little Prince*. Now, of course, anyone but Wilder in the role seems inconceivable.

Brooks wanted Richard Pryor for the role of the black sheriff. Warner Brothers refused, explaining that he lacked the box-office stature. But when the role was given to the lesser-known Cleavon Little, the producers' explanation was suspect. The choice was likelier due to Pryor's unpredictability.[15] While his wild, inspired antics were just what the writing staff needed, there may have been some reluctance to risk the production schedule on him. The film would doubtless have been improved by Pryor's performance. At the insistence of the Screenwriters Guild, Pryor was given a writing credit on the film.

In other casting, Anne Bancroft and Mrs. DeLuise appear as extras in the church scene. Madeline Kahn had appeared as the uptight fiancée in *What's Up, Doc?* and as the loser Trixie Delight in *Paper Moon*. Afficionadoes also recall her fine performance in a university short parodying Bergman, *The Dove*. *Blazing Saddles* was Harvey Korman's first major film role, after bits in *Three Bites of an Apple*, *Lord Love a Duck*, and *The April Fools*. He was best known for his work on the *Carol Burnett Show*. Cleavon Little was a Tony-winner on Broadway, and he played a guest burglar on *All in the Family*, but his film exposure was negligible: *What's So Bad about Feeling Good?*, *Cotton Comes to Harlem,* and *Vanishing Point.* Pryor was far better known as an antic wit.

Brooks plausibly claims, "Every scene and damn near every line in the film were in the script. Even the farts were in the script. It was calculated chaos." Yet Gary Arnold attacked the film as "slapdash . . . a messy and antiquated gag machine," with Brooks "acting outrageous about a moribund, irrelevant subject." Holtzman found the film "nearly amorphous." Pauline Kael complained that Brooks "doesn't have the controlling vision that a director needs . . . he's not a planner . . . [though] he's a genius at spontaneous repartee . . . he seems to fear subtlety as if it were the enemy of all he holds dear—as if it were gentility itself." All in all, she called *Blazing Saddles* "just dirty TV." If Brooks did "fear subtlety," it would be because Kael and her type of subjective, once-over-lightly reviewer rarely respond to anything subtle, such as Brooks's patterning of gags and his overall structure.[16]

More shrewdly, Peter Schjeldahl found the film "about movies and show business on one level, but it is also a movie about racism and about human nastiness in general . . . its comic catalogue of meanness and depravities has a cumulative, purging effect."[17] Schjeldahl proved a rarity—a reviewer who responded to the work's character and intentions unhindered by his own predispositions.

Although *Blazing Saddles* was voted the funniest film of 1974 by the American Academy of Humor, there was one tragic misunderstanding about the film. In the March 31, 1974, issue of the *New York Times,* the parent of a retarded child wrote a letter to the editor attacking Brooks's use of Mongo. The writer took the character's name to be Mongol, and was "appalled at the return of the 'village idiot' as a source of humor." Shaken by this letter, Brooks replied in the June 2, 1974, *Times.* He agreed that it would be "cruel, heartless and unthinking" to seek comic effect from Downs Syndrome. The name of his "Mongo" was a homage to the bongo star, and his character was a loving homage to the late Dan Blocker's character on *Bonanza,* Hoss Cartwright, the kindly strongman. "I cannot tell you how truly heartsick everyone connected with the film feels," Brooks concluded. "I must tell you, in all candor, reading that letter and the endorsement of it in the *Mental Retardation News* was one of the unhappiest moments of my life."

But let's end on a brighter note. Brooks's brilliant gag of Bart holding himself hostage is based upon an absurd incident in Brooks's childhood. Young Mel was once caught trying to steal a cap pistol. He wheeled upon the store manager, pointed the toy gun and shouted, "Stand back or I'll blow your head off!" The boy escaped with the gun. "Those idiots! They *knew* it was a cap gun, and still they backed up!"[18]

Chapter 9

Young Frankenstein (1974)

F REDERICK FRANKENSTEIN (Gene Wilder), grandson of the notorious Baron Frankenstein of the Mary Shelley novel and the ensuing mythology, is a modern Baltimore brain surgeon. To dissociate himself from his family, he insists on being called "Fronkensteen" and denies any interest in his grandfather's work. Frederick is summoned to the ancestral castle in Transylvania to claim his inheritance—the estate and all its secrets. Nocturnal violin music, played by the inherited housekeeper Frau Blücher (Cloris Leachman), leads Frederick to the hidden library, where he decides to resume the notorious attempt to create life out of dead matter.

Frederick is aided by Igor (Marty Feldman), the hunchbacked descendant of the baron's faithful servant, and by a pretty servant girl, Inga (Terri Garr). Igor is sent out for a brilliant, saintly man's brain, but smashes it in sudden fright. So he brings the abnormal brain of a murderer. This is installed in Frederick's monster (Peter Boyle). A massive electricity charge brings the corpse to life. After an accidental fright, he breaks loose. He plays with a little peasant girl, teeter-tottering unevenly. Then he suffers through a painful encounter with a well-meaning but clumsy blind hermit (Gene Hackman). Although the monster can be soothed and drawn home by a violin melody, he arouses the fear and murderous hatred of the villagers, led by Inspector Kemp (Kenneth Mars), who wears a wooden arm to replace the one the original monster plucked out in the inspector's boyhood.

Taking his cue from the monster's susceptibility to music, Frederick lavishes love and admiration upon him. With this new

120

self-esteem, the monster is cultivated to the point that he and the doctor can perform a song-and-dance duet, "Puttin' on the Ritz," before the Bucharest Academy of Science (who bring along rotten fruit and vegetables, in case they dislike the lecture). When a footlight accidentally explodes, the monster is frightened by the flame and goes beserk. Imprisoned, then tormented by his jailers, the monster breaks loose again. He carries off and—to her delight—ravishes Frederick's frigid fiancée, Elizabeth (Madeline Kahn). Frederick draws him back with the violin music.

Since he originally intended his monster to have the brains of a scientist, Frederick engineers a partial exchange of power between the monster and himself. The invading mob of villagers threatens this operation, but it is completed. The touchingly eloquent monster wins the villagers' acceptance, and Kemp's wooden handshake. At the end, Elizabeth is happily married to her monster, who lies in bed reading the *Wall Street Journal*. Inga is similarly delighted with the improved sexual prowess for which her husband, Frankenstein, swapped some of his intellect.

Brooks considers this film "a case of satire and homage, a valentine to the horror movie."[1] Consequently, it is not as critical of its genre as *Blazing Saddles* was of the Western. Indeed, technically the film is a loving re-creation of the classic horror film style and mood. Brooks revived the old 1:85 frame proportion and such archaic optical devices as iris-outs, wipes, spins, and stings. There are several set pieces in the film, such as the obligatory laboratory lecture, the grave-robbing, the Gothic castle in all its shadowy, cobwebbed glory, the secret passageways, the steamy train station, the cobbled streets, the pastoral idyll, the torch-lit mob shot in slavering close-up.

Brooks insisted on reviving the old back-lit black-and-white photographic period, which proved no simple task. For one thing, the film laboratory had not processed a black-and-white film in over six years, because the film industry (for its TV afterlife) focuses on color. In addition, the lighting had to be ingeniously managed to give the effect of candles and encroaching shadows yet not lose the visibility of the actors' slightest comic gesture or expression. Brooks sought the tone of the old movies, "bathed in antique radiance."[2] In a stroke of rare fortune, he was able to use the same laboratory set that Dr. Frankenstein used in the original

James Whale *Frankenstein* (1931). Designer Kenneth Strickfaden, now seventy-eight years old, had the original set in his garage. He also devised new tricks and machinery for Brooks. As the young Dr. Frankenstein returned to his family's obsession with reanimating dead life, Brooks's film revived an aged rhetoric with apparent affection.

The first shot catches this sentiment: The familiar hilltop castle is illuminated by a lightning bolt in a storm. The film springs to life as the monster will later, revived by a bolt of lightning. As Brooks pans across the shadowy interior, the clock strikes midnight—but with thirteen chimes (as it is a Brooks movie, some excess is obligatory). His first visual gag—the unearthed skeleton refuses to release the secret notebook from its bony clutch—establishes another theme: the unyielding hold that the past has on the present. That shot foreshadows Frankenstein's submission, into following his grandfather's muddy footsteps.

Brooks drew his characters and plot line from beyond the original Whale film. The Dr. Pretorius who summons Frankenstein home is a reformed version of the evil scientist in Whale's sequel, *The Bride of Frankenstein* (1935). This film supplied the monster's abduction of Frankenstein's fiancée. Whale's monster holds her hostage until Frankenstein creates for him his own female monster; here he simply claims this woman (the direct approach). The brain-transplant operation derives from *The Ghost of Frankenstein* (1942). The scientist assumes a new name, Dr. Stein, in *The Revenge of Frankenstein* (1958). The monster's riot in the theater derives from *King Kong*. The Igor here supplants the Whale Frankenstein's Fritz with the Igor that Bela Lugosi played in Rowland Lee's *The Son of Frankenstein* (1939), which also supplied the wooden-armed Inspector Krogh (Lionel Atwill). As Lugosi's Igor and Atwill's Krogh played against Lon Chaney Jr.'s Monster in *The Ghost of Frankenstein* and *Frankenstein Meets the Wolf Man* (1943), the tradition outweighs the original. Madeline Kahn's Elizabeth is a mixture of Mae Clarke, Valerie Hobson, Elsa Lanchester, Jeanette MacDonald, and Trixie Delight! Cloris Leachman's Frau Blücher evokes Judith Anderson's Mrs. Danvers in Hitchcock's *Rebecca*. Gene Wilder has the facial features, clothing, flowing hair, and glinting eyes of Basil

Rathbone's doctor in *Son of Frankenstein* (1939), rather than the Colin Clive original.

Peter Boyle's monster recalls the Boris Karloff prototype, a towering, stiff, ugly character who still expresses pathos through his caked features. He was given a green makeup, which comes through as a sickly gray tone in the black-and-white photography. Finally, he is distinguished by a Courreges zipper on his neck! Not just the latest thing, this touch, but a rather sensible way for the doctor to get at his creature's internals for repairs or a tune-up without having to open another wound. All in all, Brooks played fast, loose, but faithfully with the vast range of Frankenstein conventions.

As Brooks's subject is not just the basic story but the entire myth, his characters are aware of the Frankenstein legend and its conventions of plot and setting. Indeed, here as in *Blazing Saddles,* one measure of the character's intelligence is his awareness that he is living in a conventional fiction. That is, self-awareness in a Brooks film is not just a matter of a character knowing what he is as a human being, but knowing that he is a character in a fiction.

We find such awareness in Frau Blücher's tired resignation to the neighing of the horses whenever her name is mentioned. She seems to operate on a more elemental level of existence than everyone else. For one thing, her melody plays at the beginning and end of the film, lures Frankenstein to the secret library, and soothes and summons the monster. Coming at such key points, the tune is "a continual reminder of the redeeming power of love," in Martin Tropp's words. Also, though Frau Blücher seems young enough to be Frederick's older sister, his grandfather was—"Yes! Say it! Say it! He was—he was—MY BOYFRIEND!" Not like the other girls, Frau Blücher seems a preternatural force. She virtually personifies the preserving power of fertile love. Hence the softening in her sinister tone when she first meets Frederick and offers him successive temptations: brandy, coffee, Ovaltine. Though her name arouses the eternal neigh-sayers, she represents an eternal, ennobling passion. And she seems aware of her otherworldly existence.

The monster has one scene of such extraordinary understanding. Having dropped a flower down the well, piece by piece, the little peasant girl innocently asks him, "Oh dear, what shall we throw in now?" The monster smiles to his film audience; he knows his part in this legend. But because he has this knowing, the character can supersede his role and safely catapult her into bed.

On a lesser level, a shoeshine boy plays into the fiction of a popular song:

FREDERICK: Is this the Transylvania Station?
BOY: Ya. Track 29. Oh, can I give you a shine?

There's a modern knowing in the sign on the door of the Brain Depository: "After 5:00 P.M. slip brains through slot in door." The luscious Inga plays into the tradition of naive and sexually open native girls when she invites Frederick to join her for "a roll in the hay," and when she takes as a compliment his remark about the castle door's "big knockers." Here clichés or old phrasings are revived. Similarly, Frankenstein seeks the hidden passage in the library because "there's always a device." The trick door that subsequently slams him around seems a metaphor for the mechanics of the form and the machinations of his "Destiny" (to which he surrenders in a nightmare).

In this respect, the most aware character is Igor, so he best transcends his genre. Igor continually shifts in and out of character, even outside the myth, and into styles and tones strange even to a modern Transylvanian. Hence his song-and-dance routines. When he suddenly appears as a head in a row of skulls, Igor sings "I ain't got no body, and nobody cares for me." When he tells Frankenstein to "walk this way," he knows the gag about a limping man meaning the phrase literally, but rejects it. Another conversation turns into the film convention for the grave-robbing scene:

FREDERICK: What a filthy job.
IGOR: Could be worse.
FREDERICK: How?
IGOR: It could be raining.

That brings on a familiar cloudburst. Later, when Frankenstein says, "All we need now is a magnificent brain. You know what to do?" Igor shows his acquaintance with the plot: "I have a pretty good idea." Though he serves this Frankenstein as his ancestors did theirs, "of course, the rates have gone up." Igor is also prone to madcap jokes. When he overhears Frankenstein say "were-wolf," he obliges: "There wolf." Asked to give a "hand with the bags," Igor reaches for Elizabeth and says Groucho-ly: "Certainly, you take the blonde and I'll take the one in the turban." More significantly is his new name, "Eye-gore," instead of the tradi-tional "Ee-gore." The emphasis on the "eye" can be taken as the character's acknowledgment of actor Marty Feldman's bulging, wayward eyes. So, too, his "too late!" when Frankenstein says, "Damn your eyes!" Alternatively, Igor adopts "Eye-gore" in retaliation to Frankenstein's change to "Fronkensteen":

Frankenstein?
Fronkensteen.
You're putting me on.
No, that's the way it's pronounced. Fronkensteen.
And do you also say Fro-derick?

I am Eye-gore.
Isn't that Ee-gore?
Not anymore. Now, it's Eye-gore.

Igor's name change satirizes his master's. The young Frankenstein lacks Igor's self-knowledge and acceptance. Igor can flaunt, shift, ignore or omit the hump on his back. And even joke about it. After making a guess, he quips over his shoulder, "Call it a hunch." Igor's multiple self-awareness provides Frankenstein with a model as well as an aide.

As the title suggests, the film is about Frankenstein's growth, his maturing from naive young man to self-aware adult. (In a comic pointer to the dangers of self-unawareness, Igor drops the healthy brain when he is frightened by his own sudden appearance in a mirror.) Specifically, Frankenstein outgrows his self-denial. To start with, he must come to terms with his family name. Significantly, he first proclaims that he is a Frankenstein after his speech of love and affection to his monster. That is, his self-acceptance begins with his acceptance of the monster.

In the Frankenstein tradition, the monster is the embodiment of the creator's suppressed nature. In Jungian terms, the monster is the shadow, the hidden, repressed and shameful aspect of the conscious personality. As the ego contains unfavorable or destructive qualities, so the shadow also has good qualities—normal instincts and creative impulses. Traditionally, Frankenstein must accept his monster in order to accept himself and his own dark nature. Brooks's Frankenstein, after creating the monster in order to fulfill his own role both in his family tradition and in the film genre, must then embrace the monstrous self: "Love is the only thing that can save this poor creature, and I am going to convince him that he is loved, even at the cost of my own life." He makes his colleagues promise not to let him out of the room in which he locks himself with the monster.

Without weakening the point, Frankenstein's ensuing panic deflates the pompousness of this explanation. As the monster looms over him, Frankenstein pounds the door, wails for release, then stoops to his most helpless cry: "Mommy!" This recovery of his own childish helplessness, expressing naked terror, shows him his course to his monster. He lavishes upon the brute a mother's unquestioning affection:

> Look at that face—that boyish face. The sweet mouth. Want to talk about strength? Sheer physical power? Want to talk about power? I'm putting my cards on the table, boy! You got it! You are a god!

In this pivotal speech, the creator grants his creature godhead; in the tradition it is the doctor who claims godhead by his unnatural creation of life. When his affection reduces the monster to tears, Frankenstein cradles him maternally:

> This is a *good* boy! This is a nice boy. This is a mother's angel. I want the world to know this boy is a lamb! I shout it to the heavens! I say it without shame! We *love* this boy!

Although this gush of maternal sentiment overcomes the monster's savagery and alienation, Frankenstein's own maturity is not yet complete. He must overcome his selfish interest in this monster. This is prefigured in his first words about his creature: "He's beautiful. And—he—is—mine!"

In effect, Frankenstein's maternal sentiment has turned him into a show-biz mother. The climax of his expression of newfound devotion is, "I'm going to make you a star!" When Frankenstein introduces his monster to the academy, he is only showing off himself. He gloats over his own ability to turn a once-inarticulate mass of tissue into "a cultured, sophisticated man-about-town." But the monster can only yowl phonetically in approximation to the tune. Unable to speak, he is still an inarticulate child. Frankenstein is still condescending to his creature, still egocentric and still harsh:

> Here's your cue again, for God's sake! Are you trying to make me look like a fool! Sing, you amateur—sing! . . . I will not let you destroy my work! As your master, as your creator, I command you— Go back!

Far from being the loving parent, Frankenstein is still exploiting his creature in order to fulfill his own frustrated desire for a show-biz career. This is foreshadowed in his opening lecture, when he introduces a patient with a show-biz turn of phrase: "Mr. Hilltop here, with whom I have never worked or given any prior instructions." There is a similarly callous touch in his number with the monster. Frankenstein slips him a cookie now and then as a reward, treating his child like a trained animal. So it's not just "the Ritz" that Frankenstein is "putting on" in their duet, but the pretense of parental love, self-sacrifice, and self-knowledge.

Frankenstein's maturity is completed when he sacrifices himself in the operation to give his creature intelligence. As Brooks explains, "This creator loves his creature so much that he risks his sanity and his life to help his brain child survive. In our picture, Dr. Frankenstein starts out like Yahweh and winds up like Christ."[3] In other words, the harsh demanding god/parent turns forgiving, self-sacrificing, and loving. In addition, when Frankenstein exchanges some of his intellect in return for sexual enhancement, he enacts Brooks's warning that modern man's excessive intellectuality can endanger his intuitive and emotional capacity.

Here again Brooks points to an important element in the Frankenstein legend. When his doctor swaps mental power for phallic, he accepts man's sexual nature. In the horror tradition, the various monsters embody the sexual and physical potential that civilized man dreads unleashed. The double marriage in Brooks's version overcomes the fear of the monster's sexuality, and grants both the monster and the maker a normalized sexual freedom. Brooks gives the monster a new place, peace, and balance. In this version, the primitive energies that the monster embodies can be embraced and accepted into society. So love, humility, openness, tolerance, and joy at the "ah, sweet mystery of life," replace the arrogance, fear, and repression that demand the sacrifice of the monster throughout the tradition of the tale—and that inhibit the young Frankenstein.

Consistent with the hero's maturing, the film develops the distinction between merely existing and being fully alive. This existential concern is expressed in contrasts between the sentient and the unfeeling. In Frankenstein's opening lecture to his class, he distinguishes between man's voluntary and his reflexive impulses, between man's conscious actions and his instinctive ones. This distinguishes the conscious creator from his creature, who is at first limited to instinctive response. In his lecture, Frankenstein affirms the primacy of the conscious over the unconscious. But in the final operation, Brooks's point is that the human condition requres balance between these polar opposites; either extreme is dangerous. Where the grandfather (in a purely scientific context) merely switched the poles, "from plus to minus and from minus to plus," Brooks's resolution is more subtle, mixing the strengths at both poles, the instinctual and the rational.

Furthermore, young Frankenstein's demonstration upon poor Mr. Hilltop is a parallel to his grandfather's work, "the reanimation of dead tissues." Young Frankenstein demonstrates that if his victim's nerve center is shut off, he will not be able instinctively to avoid a knee in the groin or feel its pain—until the nerve center is reopened. Hilltop's subsequent agony disproves Frankenstein's claim that "dead is dead." Even as the young doctor denies his family's obsession, his own work is on that very subject. His "Hilltop" is a domestication of the Frankensteins' Gothic mountain retreat. His family tradition—like the truths of human nature—is inescapable. In addition, the Hilltop demonstration is paralleled by Frankenstein's attempt to speak while the monster is throttling him. His aides slip into a game of charades, but we see the doctor suffering what he earlier imposed upon his patient—

and what he will later save his monster from—the frustration of being unable to communicate.

Inspector Kemp and the hermit also develop this metaphor. Kemp is a creature of various forms of insentience. One-eyed, he wears a monocle over his eye patch, as if to deny that socket's total lack of vision. In addition, Kemp continually has to repeat himself because even the local villagers cannot understand his impenetrable accent. In both these running gags, Kemp is shut off by genre conventions from full experience and expression. Of course, his wooden arm is his primary image of insensitive humanity.

In two scenes, Frankenstein relates to Kemp's lumbering insensitivity. In the first, Frankenstein loses his composure in denying the family science. Childishly, he calls his grandfather's work "doo-doo" and his voice cracks when he calls him a "kook." At the height of this tirade, he stabs his leg with a scalpel, but he does not let on that he is hurt. He espouses insensitivity in denying both his family and his pain. His stoic bearing of the scalpel wound aligns him with Kemp's woodenness. In the second, when the two men play with darts, Kemp painlessly sticks them into his wooden arm (in contrast to Frankenstein's jabbed leg). Kemp throws the darts with mechanical but cheating precision. (In the original screenplay, Kemp threw as erratically as Frankenstein.) In this situation, Frankenstein is too nervous and sensitive to sustain Kemp's crooked calm. So Frankenstein's darts break a vase, flatten the car tires outside, and evoke a squawk from a cat (actually performed by Brooks off camera, repeating a line he once emitted on *Your Show of Shows*). Kemp embodies man's temptation to prefer cold insentience over vulnerable liveliness.

Like Kemp, the hermit is another example of the insensitivity from which young Frankenstein must mature. In Mary Shelley's novel, the monster engages a blind old man in a brief friendship, which ends when the man's family is alarmed by him. In *Bride of Frankenstein,* the monster has a more rewarding experience. He enjoys a cigar, wine, and music. Under the blind old hermit's beneficence, he speaks his first words: "Smoke. Good." The monster flees when a hunter stops to ask directions. In the confusion the cottage burns down, but the blind hermit is led away to safety. The entire episode is couched in emotions both religious (the meal of bread and wine and the hermit's monkish robe) and sentimental (a tear rolls down the monster's cheek when the hermit puts him to bed).

But Brooks plays his hermit scene for laughs, not sentimentality. The harmony in the James Whale scene is replaced by the slapstick chaos that results from the hermit's every move. He pours hot soup in the monster's lap (with the line, "We tend to forget the simple pleasures that are the basis for true friendship"), hits his head with his cane, smashes his goblet in a toast, and lights the monster's thumb instead of his cigar. A logic underlies this hilarity. In a drama about man's coming to recognize his ambivalent nature and accepting his shadow self, blindness is a threat, not a sentimental virtue. Man needs vision. The blundering hermit is a failure at self-sufficiency, and a caution (Hackman's hermit is a caution!) against trying to live either blind to reality or in solitude.

In addition, Brooks's hermit has a faint suggestion of homosexuality:

> Don't say a word! Just let me find you, let me touch you, let me feel you, let me hold you, let me smell you. . . . You *are* a big one, aren't you? . . . My name is Harold. I live here all alone. What's your name? . . . Look how Heaven plans. Me, a poor blind man, and you, a—an incredibly big mute. Are you hungry? . . . Oh, yes, you're right, this is going to be a fun night. . . . Wait! Come back! I was going to make expresso!

This hermit speaks too colloquially to be innocent as he flutters about the big stranger. His repressed homosexuality is another alternative to the sexuality to which young Frankenstein and the monster will mature.

Finally, Brooks plays against the hermit's association with religion. To this end there is a precise echo of the scene in *The Twelve Chairs*, in which Father Fyodor (DeLuise) prays to God for help, then says "thank you" after Vorobyaninov (Moody) runs by with a chair. Here hermit Harold prays for company to relieve his solitude. At that moment the monster breaks through the door. "Thank you, Lord, thank you," says Harold. In both gags, a blind(ed) character thinks that an infernal coincidence is God's answer to his prayers. In both the moral is the same: man must seek his salvation in human fraternity, not in hope of divine intervention.

Frankenstein's two women also dramatize the importance of an instinctive and sentient life. At the outset, Frankenstein is engaged to the frigid and remote Elizabeth. Lacquered and unyielding, she and the doctor rub elbows good-bye at the train station, so as not to disturb her lips, hair, taffeta, and nails. She speaks in pulp cliché: "Hurry now, before I make a fool of myself." We are grateful when the train's smoke and soot destroy her pristine pretense. Later, when she gives her fiancé a passionate good-night kiss, she warns, "No tongues." Though she acts frigid, she has not yet been excited to sexuality. The monster succeeds where her docile Frederick fails. When the monster unzips, the cowering maiden overcomes her qualms: "Oh, my God! Woof!" Of course, Igor sensed her lusty nature at first sight. But only the monster brings it out. Under his effect, she explodes in a chorus of "Ah, Sweet Mystery of Life." Brooks confirms this reading: "The men she knew just weren't worth it to her." Also, "it's a little bit of a female fantasy to have a big, dumb, almost animal lover."[4] After her abduction by the monster, Elizabeth's entire appearance changes. Instead of a tightly turbaned hairdo, an index of her expression, she wears a towering hairdo that is streaked like the one Elsa Lanchester wore as the Bride of Frankenstein. Paradoxically, as Elizabeth becomes fulfilled as a woman, she acquires the image of her place in the film genre; again Brooks treats genre-awareness as an index to his character's self-awareness. Moreover, at the very moment that she becomes a film allusion, she becomes more recognizably human. Hence her rather cynical *aubade* to her departing lover:

Oh, you men are all alike. Seven or eight quick ones and you're off with the boys to boast and brag. Well, YOU BETTER KEEP YOUR MOUTH SHUT!

But once her "old zipper-neck" has gone, she softens: "Oh, I think I love him."

Happily, the monster was also detraumatized and humanized by his sexual experience with her. When he lights up the two postcoital cigarettes, he too slips into a behavior pattern from film convention. Incidentally, he also shows that he has conquered his primal fear of fire. "Fire is our friend," quoth hermit Harold, but his fires are inferior to those the monster enjoys with Elizabeth.

But Elizabeth does not offer Frederick Frankenstein the sexuality she gives the monster. On her first night in the castle, she sends her aroused Frederick back to his room, grunting stiffly. In the original screenplay, he went off to Inga, but in the film this scene is replaced with a significant segue. From Frankenstein's groaning exit, Brooks cuts (Yes, a lap dissolve would have been excessive!) to the grunting, climbing monster. This transition parallels the one in *The Bride of Frankenstein,* where the scientist's new wife speaks to her husband but is answered by the monster. By this juxtaposition, the monster becomes a personification of the doctor's sensuality. In Brooks's film, as the monster approaches her, Elizabeth sits at her vanity, singing, "His truth is marching in."

Young Frankenstein's alternative to teasing denial by Elizabeth is the frisky, open acceptance by Inga. Though played as a comic-romantic ingenue, Inga is an instinctive and openly sexual delight. Even in her confusions she is a lifegiving force; when Frederick pounds the inert corpse in anger, she presciently warns, "Stop it. You'll kill him." Her warmth and intuitive wisdom contrast to Frankenstein's infantile tantrums, which belie his pretenses to maturity:

> If science teaches us anything, it teaches us to accept our failures as well as our successes with quiet dignity and grace. . . . Sonofabitch bastard! Why did you do this to me? I don't want to live! . . . Momma!

When Inga warmly observes that the disappointed Frederick has not touched his food, he childishly plunges his hands into it: "There. I've touched it." Inga has a maturity beyond the more learned Frederick, and much of it is a matter of her sexual acceptance. She responds to the prospect of the monster's size with a matter-of-fact "He would have an enormous *schvantz-stucker*" (tail for sticking). "That would go without saying," the doctor replies, and it does. "He's going to be very popular," Igor predicts. Later Inga kisses Frankenstein's fingers, murmuring that she wishes she could help him somehow, to relieve his tension and give him (ambiguously) "a little peace." His order to raise the platform, "Elevate me," she mistakes to be a sexual invitation ("Now? Right here? . . . Oh, the platform!"). In passing from Elizabeth to Inga, Frankenstein matures from a childish, asexual and repressive relationship to one of mature and open sexuality. He moves from a mother figure to an adult, sexual responsibility.

Brooks's treatment of this romantic triangle points to the sexual drama at the heart of the Frankenstein legend. Frankenstein attempts to create a child without the natural process of sexuality. On one level, this represents man's presuming to the function of God; Mary Shelley's subtitle identified her hero as a modern Prometheus, stealing God's secret and being condemned for so overreaching the mortal limit. Brooks's doctor too vows "to hurl the gauntlet of Science into the frightful face of Death!" In the James Whale *Frankenstein,* the emphasis is instead on the solitary egotism and sterility of the scientist's creative act. He retreats from his impending marriage, to an act of reproduction by his own hand, by implication onanistic. While his father drinks hopeful toasts to "a son for the house of Frankenstein," the scientist goes off by himself, bent upon creating his satisfaction "with these hands." That phrase rings through the film like a chorus.

Brooks picks up the tune. *Young Frankenstein* abounds with jokes about hands. At one extreme, there is the wooden arm of Kemp and the flaming finger bestowed by hermit Harold; these are sterile and destructive images of the hand. Alternatively, we have Inga kissing Frankenstein's fingers. As in the Whale original, the monster shows his first sign of life by moving his fingers. In the laboratory lecture, as Frankenstein dissociates himself from his grandfather's science, he literally washes his hands of the whole thing. Later, in order to fool the policeman, Frankenstein pretends that the stolen corpse's dead hand is his own. He plays with it, picks its nails, uses it to shake hands with the constable—yet another instance of the reanimation of dead tissue. The policeman's "Need a hand?" is more resonant than he realizes; so too are his parting words: "If you have everything in hand, then, I'll say goodnight, sir."

The creation of the monster is also in sexual terms. It is brought about by lightning, which Frankenstein explained to Inga as "an atmospheric discharge." He speaks of penetrating to the very womb of nature. The lightning is aimed directly at the corpse's groin by a phallic coil. But Brooks's Frankenstein is saved from the masturbatory creation in Whale's by the sexual intervention of his Inga.

Still, Brooks picks up on Whale's implications of masturbation. On Frederick's train trip to Transylvania, three couples, in different languages, discuss their sons' suspicious habits:

> Harry, he was at it again.
> What do you want me to do about it?
> Every day?
> Let him. Let him.

(In the original script, the doctor was instead hounded by passengers wanting free professional advice, whatever profession he claimed.) The same implication plays around Igor's nostalgic memory of what his "dear old Dad" used to say: "What the hell are you doing in the bathroom day and night? Why don't you get out of there and give someone else a chance?" The hump, of course, is in folk traditions one of the effects of masturbation. And bathrooms are where Brooks envisions the typical *Playboy* readers, "sitting on the toilet with the centerfold open, doing God knows what?"[5]

More generally, Brooks develops the sexual significance of Mary Shelley's novel. In his reading, the theme of the novel is "womb envy. Most men get even with women for being able to have children by saying 'I can paint, I can write,' and women say, 'You're full of shit. Look—a baby.' And of course, she's the winner." Brooks finds Shelley's novel exploring the male's attempt to evade this female advantage. To Brooks, a secondary theme in the film is the eternal suspicion that the ignorant have for the intelligent: "Watergate proves how serious gullibility is. Always mistrusting the intellectual. . . . The story of Dr. Frankenstein addresses itself to the fear quotient. The monster is just symbolic of his mind, and the mob hates his mind, they hate his imagination." Again Brooks's film makes explicit a theme that is implicit in the legend.[6]

In a political reading of the story, Frankenstein signifies the aristocracy and his monster the working class, harnessed but threatening to break free. Both of Whale's Frankenstein films are clearly political allegories. The scientist is the figure of intellect and authority; the monster is the victim, a sleeping destructive power. Awakened, its rage threatens all of society. The 1935 *Bride of Frankenstein* adds a specific reference to Nazi eugenics with the authoritarian Dr. Pretorius's toast, "To a new world of gods and monsters!" and in his breeding and control of homunculi. So when Brooks has Frankenstein and his monster "puttin' on the Ritz," the aristocrat is teasing the crudely dressed monster with the uniform, but not the reality, of a power and grace that are denied him. In ultimately reading the *Wall Street Journal,* the monster shows that he has grown into this song-and-dance image.

In one respect, the film works contrary to the novel. (As the credits declare, it is only "based on the characters," not an adaptation.) In the original there is something dark and sinister in the baron's turning away from normal sexuality to create his own monster. But Brooks's scientist learns to act out of love and generosity. And as we have observed, his creation remains within the context of romance and sexual love.

More importantly, in the Frankenstein legend the creator remains at odds with his creature. As R. W. Dillard points out, Shelley's monster "dies a Romantic hero, morally superior to Frankenstein in his suffering and his refusal to yield his identity and his life while his creator still lived." Whale's monster "dies in a moment of total despair, rejected by even a creature of his own kind (the bride), driven to destroy not only himself but everything he is. . . . The monster of the films is the ultimate victim, the final image of lost and suffering man, all illusions stripped away, naked in his own damnation."[7]

But Brooks's Frankenstein story breaks away from death. At the end, as in the well scene, the character's knowledge of the context and his new, mature self-acceptance prevent death. At first the young Frankenstein, in denying his grandfather's work, claimed, "I'm not interested in death. There's only one thing that concerns me, and that's the preservation of *life!*" But in undertaking his grandfather's project, young Frankenstein confronts death:

From that fateful day when stinking bits of slime first crawled from the sea and shouted to the cold stars—I am man!—our great dread has been the knowledge of our own mortality! But tonight we will hurl the gauntlet Science into the frightful face of Death! Tonight we shall ascend into the heavens. We shall mock the earthquake. We shall command the thunders and penetrate into the very womb of impervious Nature herself.

Frankenstein's loving creation of life out of dead matter becomes a passionate opposition to death. In his personal life, too, Frankenstein comes to embrace his sexual, impulsive being. Through the joint emotional expansions by the monster and by Inga, Brooks's Frankenstein matures into a creature who is both fuller and healthier. So there is a psychoanalytic aspect to Frankenstein's intellectual exchange with his monster, from which the hulk rises with "a calm brain—and a slightly more sophisticated way of expressing myself," and the blithering doctor learns passion. No longer the offshoot either of Promethean ambition or of masturbatory retreat, Brooks's creature frees his creator to have the capacity to feel, to love, that is, to be fully human.

The film's ads point to this balance between the imperfect halves of the individual psyche. In the middle, over a cemetery, looms the mountain with the Frankenstein castle sucking a lightning bolt from the sky. On either side, the two male leads face away from each other, as if to deny their essential unity. But they are joined by the mountain between them and by the sunlike orb that enrings them. On the left, Dr. Frankenstein, the ostensibly civilized intellect, rails maniacally, eyes ablaze, brow furrowed, mane blowing in the breeze. On the right is the monster, ostensibly the insentient brute, but in his "Ritz" suit, tipping his silk top hat in salute, with a beatific calm on his zippered mug. The maker and his monster, the creator and the creature, exchanged trust, mind, and senses and found a unity and maturity that neither could have had alone.

This makes *Young Frankenstein* Brooks's ultimate love story. It accommodates man's bond with woman as well as his bond with men, for its subject is the integrated psyche. In this respect, Brooks's version, for all its divagations in plot and emphasis, is faithful to Shelley's. Shelley intended her novel to warn against man's icy heart, so she closes with Frankenstein chasing his monster into the frozen North. In Brooks's translation, variously juvenile souls are transformed from cold solitudes into the warm, sweet mystery of life. The lesson is the same. *Young Frankenstein* is a noble addition to the Frankenstein myth, with its power and purpose, as R. W. Dillard summarizes, "the power to inspire love for the untouchable, feeling for the violent and murderous beast, love and fear involved as they seldom are but always should be. The Frankenstein myth teaches us how fallen we are and, at the same time, how we must love one another."[8] So Brooks's monster has an extremely touching speech, when he uses his fresh gift of language to protect his maker from the mob:

> For as long as I can remember, people have hated me. They looked at my body and my face and ran away in horror. . . . I decided that if I could not inspire love, which was my deepest hope, I would instead cause fear. I live now because this poor, half-crazed genius held an image of me in his mind as something beautiful.

This defense recalls Leo Bloom's paean to Max Bialystock at the end of *The Producers*, the developing interdependence between Ostap and Ippolit in *The Twelve Chairs*, and the unconventional relationship between the fallen Waco and the black sheriff in *Blazing Saddles*. In *Young Frankenstein*, the scientist, as well as the monster, is an insentient creature brought to new life by the animation of the heart in illumination and fire.

BACKGROUND

Gene Wilder originated the idea of a *Frankenstein* parody and drafted a 150-page screenplay while Brooks was finishing *Blazing Saddles*. Brooks joined him for the rewrite, which brought the script down to 123 pages. As Wilder recalls, "My job was to make him more subtle. His job was to make me more broad. I would say, 'I don't want this to be *Blazing Frankenstein*,' and he'd answer, 'I don't want an art film that only fourteen people see.'"[9] The Screenwriters Guild objected to a rather lopsided Brooks credit and won Wilder an equal writing acknowledgment.

Brooks asked for a budget of $2,200,000 but Columbia balked and offered only $1,700,000. Twentieth Century-Fox president Gordon Stulberg read the script and eagerly offered to produce it on a budget of $2,800,000—giving Brooks the right of final cut. The film's success earned Brooks a three-feature pact and a luxurious office suite in West Los Angeles. The film was shot in fifty-four days. Brooks spent six months editing it, with Wilder in attendance, preparing for his own directorial debut.

In editing, Brooks cut over a third of the three-hour footage. Primarily what he dropped were "literary jokes, not cinematic," including much brilliant comedy. As he explained to Digby Diehl, "You can't be self-indulgent—often you cut out the stuff you love first." [10]

To judge by Gilbert Pearlman's novelization, Brooks also trimmed to make the plot more direct. For example, he dropped a lengthy introductory scene in which young Frankenstein's relatives attend the reading of the will. The baron left his will on a phonograph record, which sticks at an inopportune point:

> For the path to salvation must be climbed up the barren mountain of my soul, and not up yours—up yours—up yours—up yours. . . .

In the original, the young doctor was captivated by the Transylvanian lullaby from the outset; Brooks makes its enchanting hold the result of the exchange with the monster. The omission of the doctor's earlier entrancement by the tune simplifies his character. Brooks dropped a cheer-song for Destiny ("Give me a D. Give me an E.") in the doctor's dream that prepares him to resume his grandfather's work. Gone too is some of the black comedy involving the parents of the monster's playmate:

> No, Mama, don't be frightened. Don't tink about monsters.
> Who's tinking about monsters?
> I am!

The grave-diggers sang of a well-hung murderer, "'E's swingin' in the rain." Brooks dropped the monster's encounter with highwayman Jack Sprat, a scene in which Frankenstein jocularly reads his grandfather's notebook, Frau Blücher holding off his aides at gunpoint, and their attempts to teach the monster to walk like Inga and to play various musical instruments. Omitting these training scenes better set off the surprise duet of "Puttin' on the Ritz."[11]

In its scrupulous details of setting and tone, *Young Frankenstein* is something of a reply to the critics of *Blazing Saddles*. It's as if Brooks set out to demonstrate that the sprawling nature of the previous film was a matter of calculated choice and not due to any inability. So too, the later film's straightforward plot, free from the overflow of self-reflection. Perhaps as a consequence, *Young Frankenstein* won Brooks his best reviews. Sören Fischer called *Young Frankenstein* Brooks's "best movie . . . his most controlled work, more fluent, simpler in set-up and marginally less vulgar, frenzied and indulgent than *Blazing Saddles*."[12]

Pauline Kael attacked the film by faint praise. She recommended it for "when your rhythm is slowed down and you're too tired to think. You can't bring anything to it (Brooks's timing is too obvious for that); you have to let it do everything for you, because that's the only way it works." Conversely, two *Frankenstein* specialists who brought their knowledge and stayed awake, felt happily rewarded. Radu Florescu found it a "brilliant satire on the series as a whole." Martin Tropp noted, "The film sets out quite deliberately to remake the entire myth and bring it to a comic conclusion. . . . infused by a genuine love for the old Monsters and faith in human nature, Mel Brooks tries, once and for all, to transform the horror tale into a fairy tale, and let maker and monster live happily ever after." As Brooks put it, "In all those old films [the monster] was the only one who never came out well. And I decided to rectify that injustice." John Simon called it the best comedy of the year (over *The Fortune, Love and Death* and *Return of the Pink Panther*); it brought "to the surface things latent in the genre that have not dared to become conscious: the intense sexuality masquerading as horror, and the secret double identity of the only superficially monstrous monster as object of our lust as well as of our repressed empathy."[13]

On the other hand, Colin L. Westerbeck Jr. condemned its pastiche as "a comedy of production errors." Judith Hess found it "a silly, pointless film complete with underlying viciousness. . . . [Brooks] creates a world in which nothing has moral or social significance, a world in which racism, sexism, and cruelty evoke titters rather than indignation." Hess declared both *Blazing Saddles* and *Young Frankenstein* "repellent" because Brooks "portrays people as absurd and degraded" and his "protagonists rely on an amoral cleverness."[14]

Brooks claimed not to mind if his audience did not fully comprehend the work. "If they never understand womb envy, that's fine, that's very private stuff in my own mind. If they want to join in that celebration, it's fine. But if they pay three dollars to forget about their problems and just want to laugh, that's fine too."[15]

Creator Brooks makes two subtle appearances in the film: His name is hidden in that of the intended source of the monster's brain, Hans Del*bruck*, "Scientist and Saint"; and Brooks's face appears as a gargoyle aghastly grimacing when the monster escapes from the laboratory.

Chapter 10

Silent Movie (1976)

In *Silent Movie*, Brooks returned to the self-reflexive ironies of *Blazing Saddles*. It's a comedy about its own making. Mel Funn (Brooks) is a washed-up, reformed-alcoholic director, trying to make a silent film in this day of modern sound extravaganzas. In addition to reviving his own career, this film would save the bankrupt Big Picture Studios ("If it's a big one, it was made here") from takeover by the monster conglomerate Engulf and Devour. Funn is aided by sidekicks Marty Eggs (Marty Feldman) and Dom Bell (Dom DeLuise).

The trio woo and win the cooperation of Burt Reynolds and James Caan. Wearing suits of armor, our heroes then corner Liza Minnelli in the studio commissary and enlist her, too. At a posh nightclub, they meet and sign Anne Bancroft. From the hospital room of the studio boss (Sid Caesar), they phone Marcel Marceau long-distance to enlist him, but he declines. Paul Newman agrees to a role in the film, but only after a motorized wheelchair chase.

Meanwhile, Engulf and Devour ("Our fingers are in everything") have not been idling on their laurels. To seduce and betray Funn, they hire the voluptuous seductress Vilma Kaplan (Bernadette Peters) of the Rio Bomba club. The plot works. The heartbroken Mel hits The (giant-sized) Bottle the night before shooting is to commence on the film. Happily, Vilma relents and helps Eggs and Dom sober Mel up in time. (The final film omits some slapstick sequences about the zany shooting of Mel Funn's film that were in the script.)

But all is not yet won. Minutes before the premiere of *Silent Movie*, it is discovered that some reels are missing. While Eggs unwinds the reels that they do have, the others rush off and snatch the missing reels from the Engulf and Devour fireplace. Meanwhile, to stall for time, Vilma performs tirelessly for the cinema audience. The heroes ward off the villains by firing Coke cans from a vending machine. Eventually, *Silent Movie* proves to be a hit. At least, within Brooks's *Silent Movie*, Funn's *Silent Movie* is a hit.

It may seem perverse for such a gifted verbalist as Brooks to make a wordless film. However, he is on record as preferring "visuality." "I've no patience for dialogue in cinema. Dialogue should be on the stage: action should be on the screen . . . people running around, slipping, falling, banging into each other. I like chases." In addition to being his own predilection, he finds that physical comedy appeals to the largest audience: "It cuts across every class and it is international." *Silent Movie* attempts to recover the international language of silent comedy, before the Talkies erected language barriers.[1]

Although the film is modern in its setting, characters, color and knowing humor, there are important touches of archaic cinema. Its zoom shots are wobbly, as in the good old days, before sophisticated machinery allowed for slickness. Moreover, much of the comedy involves the falseness of silent-film conventions. In the opening scene, for instance, there is a discrepancy between a long, angry speech and the curt title that represents it. The obviously mouthed "disgusting son of a bitch" becomes "you're a bad boy." The filmmaker seems to be showing off his power when he changes Burt Reynolds's "No way" to "I'll do it," and tempers a long Mel Funn tirade into a discreet "Maybe you're right." Other titles allow sounds the cultural differences of language. So the French telephone goes "Sonnez—sonnez," in contrast to the American doorbell's "ding dong." In the same spirit, for Vilma's musical number, when she is peeled out of a banana, we are given the rather superfluous titles, "Brrrrrr" and "Ba—ba—looooo."

Other jokes revive classic conventions of narrative. In one running gag, our heroes' successes are chronicled in a series of newspaper headlines. Extending this tradition, the newspaper bundles are hurled upon the frail newsy (Liam Dunn) with increasing force and destructiveness. His eventual disappearance is reported in the very paper that buries him. This is a miniature of the film's general process—a sound film completes the replacement of the silent film by making an ostensibly silent film. That is to say, the burier reports the burial; the report *is* the burial. Perhaps because of redundancy, Brooks dropped another scripted gag that involved the familiar image of a spinning issue of *Variety*. It stops too quickly so the letters of the headline fly off the paper and out of the frame, to be hastily replaced by awkward, nervous hands.

Brooks also indulges in topical humor. Reflecting the turmoil in the American film industry, an ominous door sign identifies the office of the "Current Studio Chief." In addition to suggesting the insecurity of the profession, the joke may also express Brooks's sympathy for David Begelman, a staunch Brooks supporter-in-need, who was at the time under siege and cloud as the deposed head of Columbia Pictures. Engulf and Devour are obviously a satiric jab at the Gulf & Western Corporation. "Pure coincidence," Brooks claims, turning his other tongue-in-cheek in the film press book. But he has also bemoaned the industry's shift of power away from the film people and onto corporate industrialists, who have neither love for nor interest in film. Brooks's villainous conglomerate is by its name a swallowing, ravenous monster.

In addition, Brooks satirizes the corporate mentality as laughable yes-men and buck-passers. In a ribald extension of their group-think, when the board members (so to speak) are shown a picture of their agent Vilma, their appreciation is registered in the uniform rising of their table. In broader satire, board chairman Engulf (Harold Gould) rants and raves himself into a lather like a rabid dog. Morning prayers are said to the dollar sign: "Oh Almighty Dollar we pray to thee, for without thee, we are in the crapper." Speaking of which, executive washrooms are distinguished by patrician graffiti—"Yea for the rich" and "poverty sucks"—and there is a formal slogan in the marble wall: "Our toilets are nicer than most people's homes." In heroic contrast to this threat from the new moguls, when Funn's film opens, studio chief Sid Caesar appears lionlike in the mock MGM logo; his studio's motto is *"Ars est Pecunia."* These gibes at the industry recall Brooks's jokes about his own low earnings on his early films. He once quipped that one studio's motto, emblazoned in Hebrew on an office wall, is "We make the money. You try and find it."[2]

Other gags satirize the absurdity of life—especially in Los

Angeles. One man leaves his tailor's wearing a piecemeal suit model, missing one sleeve, the serge and burlap lapels and the buckram showing. Another leaves his acupuncturist's with a backful of spears. A Szechuan restaurant seems infernal from its hot dishes.

The satire in the chief's hospital is more biting. A receptionist reads her pulp novel (discreetly titled *My Filthy Dreams*) while the TV monitors behind her reveal her patients in various disasters. The studio chief's life hangs in the balance while Dom and Marty play electronic Ping-Pong with his life-support systems. This scene gains poignancy from the fact that the suffering, neglected chief is played by Sid Caesar, whose long absence from film and TV comedy is rued by many. "I'm all right," the chief tells his friends, "except for the constant pain." Shades of the great mime's glory are revived in one close-up, in which he impersonates a computer.

Other gags revive classic comic traditions. In this vein, Funn battles with a recalcitrant Murphy bed. A fruit pie hits a traffic cop. A fumbling valet ends up trapped in the jacket he is helping his master put on. Charlie Callas figures in a sick joke: a blind man's seeing-eye dog is mistakenly switched with someone else's aggressive pet German shepherd, to the inconvenience of both masters. Henny Youngman complains about a (giant) fly in his soup. Gas pumps are used to butter the huge popcorn containers at the movie. Feldman has one frenetic routine with unsympathetic elevators and another that involves offending beautiful girls. Some jokes are visual puns. People literally sneak into a sneak preview. At good news, the heroes really do flip. Other gags recall the absurdity of the animated cartoon. Thus DeLuise suffers a grotesquely elongated shoe when a door is slammed on his foot. Another gag suggests that a character has been flattened and stretched thin by a passing steamroller. Brooks leaves no comic turn unstoned in his rush for comedy.

As if in summary, Caesar says, "Don't you know slapstick is dead?" His indignation propels him over his desk, across the room, headlong into the wall. He rises with a steadfast "Who ordered the veal cutlet?" This quip may not be the total nonsequitur that it seems. According to Brooks, the screenplay was hashed over by the idea's originator, Ron Clark, with Rudy

DeLuca, Barry Levinson, and Brooks, over meals at a delicatessen. So among the intrusions of real life into the screenplay, some came from the menu. The veal cutlet is part of the real world in which the absurdity of slapstick has survived longer than it has in film. In the original screenplay, Caesar's pratfall was to culminate in his setting off a projector showing a scene from *Mother Wore Tights*; in the filming, Brooks worked the joke around to reality instead of film life.

Brooks claims the writing team pursued two objectives. One was nonverbal comedy that was also contemporary. "We cannot go back to any old silent movie techniques; we must create our own with the given technology of the moment." The second was to "write a strong story and make a comment." About what? Well, Brooks told one reviewer that the film deals with his strong feelings about multinational companies and conglomerates "moving into an art form and I hate them for it." But this would account for only the odd fifth of the film that deals with Engulf and Devour.[3]

Brooks also admits a personal expression in the film. He regards the Feldman and DeLuise characters as surrogates for his own three loved and missed brothers, Irving (a chemical company executive), Benny (a war hero), and Bernie (a fast-food franchise operator): "So I love my sidekicks in the picture. I love their innocence, their lack of guile."[4]

If we take the public satire and the personal nostalgia together, Brooks's two given motives make sense of the entire film. *Silent Movie* is a meditation on the remoteness of the past, the impossibility of returning to an antiquated rhetoric, art form, or state of innocence. Both personally and culturally, the film details the desire and the impossibility of retrieving a lost innocence and simplicity. As he predicted to Kathleen Tynan, this new film "won't be meat and potatoes. It will be pure strawberries and cream. It will condemn nothing and no one. It will simply celebrate the joy of being alive." In its pervasive nostalgia, it logically follows *Young Frankenstein*, the making of which allowed Brooks "to relive my whole life as a child," watching horror movies.[5]

But *Silent Movie* most resembles *The Producers* because it parodies the musical genre. One of its best jokes is musical: over an establishing shot of the New York skyline, we hear "San Francisco, Open Your Golden Gate," which is hastily corrected to "I'll take Manhattan." Its last image is a shot familiar from films about stage musicals: the five central figures march arm in arm, saluting their own success, in happy harmony with the audience around them and with us. Familiar too are the several dance-line routines: the three heroes walk along in unison; the Engulf and Devour board members slap each other in rhythmic routine; there is a dance in a geriatric lounge; our heroes have a slinky tango with the even slinkier Ms. Bancroft.

Brooks plays against the romantic tradition. At Funn's first sight of Vilma Kaplan his throbbing heart turns out to be a live frog under his jacket. Beneath his traditional passion lurks a modern awareness: "She's incredible. I hope to God she's not a female impersonator." When the lovers frolic on a merry-go-round, her horse excretes loud cubes. Funn and Kaplan enjoy the obligatory slow-motion romp through the verdure, but the tone gradually changes: The lovers strip and fall into a hurdle race, which Vilma wins. The scene makes explicit the competitive tension that is common in musical romances ("Anything You Can Do," from *Annie Get Your Gun* is the apotheosis). At the peak of their bliss, Funn fantasizes an elegant dance atop a wedding cake, of Astaire-y lightness in foot and elegance, but it all collapses in goo and guck. In romantic tradition, the hero suffers a shattering disillusionment. He finds her $50,000 check "for pretending to have fun with Mel Funn." The creaking plot devices creak all the louder. So too, his decline at the Hotel Sleez. Its ad—"Murphy Beds, charming to the unsophisticated"—evokes the tradition of slapstick comedy films as well as the riches-to-rags rhetoric.

Beyond these incidental parodies, the film adopts the genre's suspicion of the rich and its democratic celebration of the struggling, penurious performer. The entire Engulf and Devour plot line works to this effect. This was also the point of the film's most lavish sight gag, which was cut after sneak-preview audiences failed to respond to it. In a posh restaurant called Chez Lobster, a huge lobster in a maître d's tuxedo and a white-jacketed lobster waiter guide two lobsters in evening dress to a giant tank, from which they select from among several chubby human beings swimming nervously but appetizingly around. And, in the finished

film, Vilma's abandonment of her wealthy employers and her
heroic performance at Mel's premiere place her in the noble
tradition of plucky hoofers who dance and sing their virtuous little
hearts out (Debbie Reynolds by any other name). Vilma will get
her just dessert. "If this show is a hit," Mel vows, "I'm going to
marry you and you'll never have to take your clothes off again." On
the other hand, the film enjoys the glamor of the wealthy, even as
it is satirized. As an alternative to the company's corrupt wealth,
Anne Bancroft is characterized as generous and warm. She tips the
maître d'—whose obeisance turns into push-ups—with her dia-
mond bracelet and dances freely with Funn and Eggs.

Consistent with the genre parody, the characterizations are
based upon film conventions rather than on any plausible human
realism. Composer John Morris's score enhances the stylization by
providing each character with a distinctive theme, at once
parodying and illustrating the most basic convention of film music.
Moreover, in their respective images, the three male stars are
different Hollywood clichés. Funn wears a yachtsman's cap and a
natty suit, pretending to an affluence that he has long since lost
(but must pretend to, if he is to recover it). Feldman's Eggs is
dressed as a flying ace. Even his tux is a one-piece jumpsuit
painted to look like a tux. However, he continually proves his
incompetence with either women or machinery (such as spiteful
elevators). DeLuise's Bell is a fey gourmand in a cashmere coat.
The three register on three levels. As the characters carry the
actors' first names, they register as extensions of their supposedly
real nature. They also register as different types of familiar
Hollywood hero. Finally, as a threesome they pay implicit homage
to the tradition of comic trios, such as the Ritz Brothers (Harry
appears in the tailor skit), the Marx Brothers (sans Zeppo), the
Three Stooges, even Dean Martin and the schizoid Jerry Lewis!

In the same vein, the guest stars appear ostensibly as themselves but actually portray classic Hollywood types of glamor. Burt
Reynolds self-deprecatingly pretends to be a colossal, preening
narcissist. He lives in a castle with his name and face emblazoned
on huge signs; he blows kisses to himself in his shower mirror.
There is even a trace of religious self-worship in his Siva image,
when our heroes materialize in his shower and are first seen as
additional hands reaching up to soap and scrub him. When they

next approach him, they are arrayed as a three-man giant "with a gland problem." Both gags allude to Reynolds's extravagant sex appeal.

James Caan appears as a slow-witted athletic star whose trailer home suggests his mobility and spartan life. It is so precariously balanced that a plate of melon balls must be nibbled strategically lest the trailer's weight be shifted. DeLuise's sneeze disrupts all. Here the gag plays upon the tradition of a tough-guy hero whose essential strength is tempered by delicacy and balance. Moreover, the masculinity of the type is undercut in a running gag that has two spinsters mistake the men's tumble as a homosexual orgy. Alternatively, Brooks's target may be the popular tendency to speculate about manly stars' sexual proclivities. (In the screenplay, Caan appeared in a suave white outfit. The food-balancing scene was to be played with corncobs, meatballs, lemonade, careful emulation, and with a small burp, instead of a loud sneeze, upsetting the balance.) Caan's persona is of a tough guy, short on intellect and understanding but long on pluck and perseverance. He is a polar opposite to the brash cunning and savvy of the Reynolds persona. The characters they portray here respond to these differences.

The two female guest stars represent basic types of Hollywood actress. The first is the wholesome, girl-next-door type, Liza Minnelli. Before such innocence, our heroes feel awkward and stiff, hence their chaotic routine in armor. They also carry a fugitive (though excessive) reminder of the Tin Man from Minnelli's mother's classic, *The Wizard of Oz*. The second is the supersophisticated woman of the world, played by Anne Bancroft. She enters the posh nightclub wearing a fire-red satin gown and trailing a white feather boa and four handsome young studs. As the waiflike Minnelli brought out the men's awkwardness, the glamorous Bancroft feeds their style. In their tango, she follows Feldman so completely that she even crosses her eyes to match his. And then some: her eyeballs move side to side, then separate, then cross (a schoolgirl talent that her stage and film career has allowed all too infrequent opportunity to exploit). While she tangos with caballeros Marty and Funn, the lone, heavy Dom stomps a table into the ground with his fat flamenco. Of course, Bancroft's glamorous image and high life style here are quite different from her real life with "the real" Mel Brooks. Through lover Reynolds, fighter Cann, gamin Minnelli, and vamp Bancroft, Brooks surveys Hollywood's basic star types and their remoteness from the actors' real natures.

The last star appearances play upon their personae, the public images that run through all their work. In a scene omitted in the final version, Dean Martin was to appear underneath a pile of drunks through which Marty and Dom were rummaging in search of the lapsed Mel. In the finished film, Marcel Marceau is phoned in France. Made up as his famous Bip, as he crosses his windy room to the phone, he performs his famous mime of walking into a stiff wind. This interlude recalls the tradition of specialty acts woven into the old musical-variety films. Then Marceau violates his persona—and the speechless nature of the entire film—by speaking the only word heard in *Silent Movie*: *"Non!"* Marceau is the only star who refuses to participate in Funn's project; of course, he makes his appearance in the act of refusing to appear, much as the obliterated newsy appeared in (and under) the newspaper that announced his disappearance. In a verbal correlative, Marceau performs his familiar mime routine in order to speak, yet his assertion of speech denies the movie both his presentation and its own silent character. In this moment, Brooks's self-reflexive games and ironies are at their most concentrated. Of course, such are the barriers of language that Funn (considerately) tells the chief that he can't understand Marceau's *"Non!"* Again paradoxically, the film's faith in the power of silent film peaks in the moment when we hear speech. Despite the familiarity of Marceau's word, the point of the scene remains the limitation of language in contrast to the international accessibility of Marceau's mime.

The last guest, Paul Newman, appears in a wheelchair, recovering from a broken leg suffered in his (real-life) hobby of racing cars. Newman leads our heroes through the kind of fast, dangerous, and spectacular chase that we expect of a Paul Newman character, from Hud to Butch Cassidy (and with a nod to the grinding chariot wheels of *Ben Hur*). The chase climaxes in Newman's escape in a spectacular leap across a chasm, leaving his pursuers behind. Having escaped them, however, he asks to join their film! Newman obviously fled them for the sheer pleasure of the evasion itself, for the thrill of the chase, not to avoid the invitation. Newman dramatizes the Hollywood adventure star's existential thirst for the test, the challenge, the experience for its own sake.

By the end of *Silent Movie*, we have enjoyed an abundance of gags. Some are good and new. The old are paid homage. It takes Brooksian cheek (translation: *chutzpah*) to dig out such old jokes whether for homage or for laughs. Moreover, his film reaffirms two lost kinds of innocence—Hollywood's silent-film tradition and Brooks's fraternal affections—in the antipathetic world of Engulf and Devour. The very re-creation of the old style and old characters reminds us of their remoteness—and effects their limited recovery.

BACKGROUND

Silent Movie appeared amid a flood of Hollywood nostalgia films: *W. C. Fields and Me, Won-Ton-Ton: The Dog that Saved Hollywood, Valentino, The Last Tycoon, Hearts of the West, Nickelodeon, Gable and Lombard*. It looks even better in this company. As usual, it met mixed reviews. David Wilson thought its best joke is that "it must be the noisiest film since *Earthquake*. Gavin Millar especially praised the encounter with Liza Minnelli:

> The sheer perseverance of the armored three is taking. They have gone beyond the point of lunacy. If their original intention was to entice by tact, guile and diplomacy, the starry Miss Minnelli, that moment has long passed. But they go on, and on, senselessly trying to establish an equilibrium, hoping they'll somehow, by repetition, fit themselves back into ordinary life.

Millar appreciates the witty use of noise in that scene, with its clash and tinkle of armor, formica, and stainless steel, and in Caesar's hospital scene, with its ominous "thunk" of the life-support Ping-Pong. But in Russell Davies's view, that very scene with Minnelli "might have gained still more if left rigorously soundless—and I have an idea the whole soundtrack could have been profitably lopped."[6]

The moral: Trust the art, not the critics (present company excepted). Still, *Silent Movie* remains a slight work, as if Brooks needed a calming period in which to retrench after his effusions in *Blazing Saddles* and *Young Frankenstein*. He returned to form and complexity in *High Anxiety*.

Chapter 11

High Anxiety (1977)

A TERRIFIED Dr. Richard H. Thorndyke (Brooks) arrives by plane to assume his duties as head of the Psycho-Neurotic Institute for the Very, *Very* Nervous. His "driver and sidekick" Brophy (Ron Carey) drops broad hints that the previous "head shrink" may have been murdered, and that Thorndyke's appointment is bitterly resented by the assistant director, Dr. Montague (Harvey Korman). Montague enjoys a sado-masochistic affair with the militaristic head nurse, Charlotte Diesel (Cloris Leachman). She rules with an iron fist—and what seem to be iron cones where her breasts ought to be.

On the more attractive side, Thorndyke finds that his old mentor is at the clinic. Professor Lilloman (Howard Morris, Brooks's favorite mugging victim), undertakes to treat Thorndyke's fear of heights, acrophobia, here renamed "high anxiety." When Thorndyke tours the clinic, he meets two unusual patients. A man who thinks he's a cocker spaniel (Charlie Callas), and relieves himself accordingly, is introduced as Arthur Brisbane. The other patient, Zachary Cartwright (Ron Clark) believes himself to be cured of his paranoid visions, but some covert attacks by Dr. Montague extend Cartwright's stay in the expensive clinic. As Dr. Montague computes it on his pocket calculator, the clinic's rate of recovery is "once in a blue moon."

When Thorndyke goes to a psychiatric conference in San Francisco, Montague and Diesel deploy a tin-toothed panting sadist (Rudy DeLuca) after him. Meanwhile, Thorndyke is accosted by a mysterious, sexy blonde, Victoria Brisbane (Madeline Kahn), who is worried about her father at the clinic. Thorndyke's suspicion is also aroused when he discovers that her father is not the man who was presented to him as Brisbane, the "cocker spaniel." Then the sadist, disguised as Thorndyke, murders a man in the hotel lobby. This places Thorndyke in the classic Hitchcock situation: He must flee the police, who suspect him of murder; he must flee the real murderer; and he must solve the mystery of the seductive, cool blonde with whom he is falling in love.

Brophy establishes Thorndyke's innocence by enlarging his coincidental snapshot of the murder, but he is captured by Diesel and Montague. To evade the airport guards, Thorndyke and Victoria pretend to be loud, quirky, vulgar old Jews. They return to the clinic, rescue Brophy and Brisbane, and even overcome Thorndyke's trauma. During the climactic chase up a tower, Lilloman forces Thorndyke to confront the origin of his high anxiety: As an infant, he fell from his high chair during a quarrel between his parents.

High Anxiety is a loving salute to Alfred Hitchcock, the witty master of suspense films about guilt and complacency. The film abounds with Hitchcock touches and allusions. The institute is a cross between the sanitarium in *Spellbound* and the Mount Carmel convent in *Vertigo*. One scene was actually shot on a *Vertigo* location, Fort Point, under the Golden Gate Bridge. From *Vertigo* too come the San Francisco locale and the hero's fear of heights, the insecurity that Hitchcock has consistently explored since *Downhill* (1927). From *Spellbound* comes the general plotline of a psychiatrist solving the murder of a colleague. On a minor note, when Nurse Diesel impales Montague's cuff with a fork, there is the echo of a fork-induced trance at a dinner in *Spellbound*.

The only Hitchcock title actually named in the film is *North by Northwest*, the direction where Victoria is to meet Thorndyke. But that film also supplies the hero's framing with a public murder, and the scene in which the strange blonde suddenly embraces and kisses the hero, in order to avert discovery. Similarly, the threat of death by falling derives from *Blackmail, Saboteur, Foreign Correspondent, North by Northwest,* and *Vertigo*.

There are more subtle Hitchcock allusions, too. Several scenes are dominated by gray metallic decor, in line with the master's scrupulous control of color scheme, especially with the colors of *Torn Curtain*. Brooks uses Hitchcock's favorite 1.85:1 frame ratio. John Morris's score has the tightening pressure of Bernard Herrimann's strings in *Psycho* and *The Birds*. The weblike shadows that play behind the victims recall *Suspicion*. In the opening sequence, Brooks depicts anxiety by using Hitchcock's montage of many short shots and by alternating objective and subjective perspectives. Thorndyke's middle initial—H for Harpo—plays on Hitchcock's disengagement from his work and parallels Roger O. (O for nothing, but making him ROT) Thornhill, in *North by Northwest*.

The murder of Dr. Wentworth for trying to leave the clinic conspiracy recalls the loose-lipped Nazi's death in *Notorious*. The doctored car also occurs in *North by Northwest* and *Family Plot*. Wentworth's death by music parodies the planned "orchestration" of the murder in Hitchcock's two versions of *The Man Who Knew Too Much*. Similarly, Thorndyke's performance of the title song recalls Doris Day's musical turn in the latter version.

A down-shot of a cell evokes *The Wrong Man* The stylized insert of vertiginous spiralling in Thorndyke's dream (of dropping forever down "a womb or a waterspout, I'm not sure which," Brooks explains Freudianly),[1] coheres with the vertiginous inserts in *The Ring*, *Spellbound*, and *Vertigo*, and the red suffusions in *Marnie*. The dangerous broken step comes from *Shadow of a Doubt*. A Mr. MacGuffin changes Thorndyke's hotel reservation to a high floor from a low; the MacGuffin is Hitchcock's term for a trivial device that sets the plot under way. The hero is summoned by a flashing light across the courtyard, à la *Rear Window*. When Victoria ultimately unites her father and her lover, the shot recalls the end of *Young and Innocent*.

The characters also originate in Hitchcock. Thorndyke is a Hitchcock hero; suave, elegant, and forced to mature by overcoming his complacency. Madeline Kahn's sexy, mysterious blonde is in the classic mold of Hitchcock heroines, from Amy Ondra through Madeleine Carroll, Eva Marie Saint, Grace Kelly, and Tippi Hedren. She even wears Kim Novak's style of gray suit from *Vertigo*. And she has the Hitchcock heroine's sexual candor (via Brooks: "I'm so close to my menstrual cycle that I could just scream."). When Thorndyke is being strangled as he talks to her on the phone, she takes him to be a stranger making an obscene phone call, and gradually succumbs to his appeal. (Thorndyke fails to notice her kinky inclination.) Ron Carey's incapacitated photographer (Brophy) is a comic version of the James Stewart hero in *Rear Window*, with a nodding homage to Antonioni's *Blow Up*. Nurse Diesel has the points and pressures of the Nazi mother-in-law in *Notorious* (with echoes of Mrs. Danvers in *Rebecca*). Professor Lilloman, whom Thorndyke first calls "li'l ol' man," is the obligatory father figure, a kindly, elderly, usually short gent, like Edmund Gwenn or Leo G. Carroll, common in Hitchcock's work.

Of course, the key scenes derive from Hitchcock's most famous work. Nurse Diesel's demise recalls the Novak character's drop at the end of *Vertigo*, even in its apparent artifice. When Thorndyke phones Victoria, behind him we notice an ominous gathering of loaded birds. (For the squeamish: The ensuing white deluge was a mixture of mayonnaise and chopped spinach.) So too, the ominous shower that Thorndyke takes, parodying the famous murder of the Janet Leigh character in *Psycho*. Among precise formal parallels, the major change is the nude Mel Brooks replacing Janet Leigh (not an inconsiderable difference). Ink washes down the drain the way the blood did in the earlier, black-and-white film, and there is a parallel drawing back from the victim's blank eye. Brooks reports that the film's biggest laugh comes at the start of the shower scene, when Brooks slowly shucks his robe: "They are saluting the intention of the scene."[2] Like Hitchcock, Brooks assumes the complicity of his audience at the most scandalous moments.

I may have missed some, but you get the idea: *High Anxiety* is a fairly wide-ranging anthology of Hitchcock touches. And what was the old master's response to being thus raked over the funny bones? He sent Brooks a case of magnums of Haut-Brion '61. Hitchcock took everything with the proper spirits.

But *High Anxiety* is something more than a collection of Hitchcock jokes. For one thing, it avoids the danger of bitsiness by possessing Brooks's most direct narrative and consistent characterization since *The Twelve Chairs*. Brooks realized that "logic is everything. A film has to have a center to hold it together." However impressive the individual gags in *High Anxiety* may be, "there are no space fillers. Every moment is significant because we were dealing with the elements found in every Hitchcock suspense thriller: will the hero solve his problems and will the villains get him before he does?" True to Hitchcock, too, "the plot is crazy and angular rather than being in a straight line. You have to pay attention to know what's going on."[3]

In addition, the jokes establish some consistent patterns or motifs. One minor example is the running line of digs at the commercialization of psychoanalysis. "The most important lesson" Professor Lilloman taught his pupil was "No personal cheques." Over the dais at the psychiatrists' convention are the towering portraits of the pantheon: Freud, Rank, Adler, Jung—and Joyce Brothers. The culmination of Thorndyke's summary of their legacy is "a nice living." Later he explains to Victoria that he once considered a singing career but "the big bucks are in psychiatry. I mean, it's so much more emotionally involving." Brooks identified his major targets in this film as "two things I love desperately: Alfred Hitchcock and Psychiatry." Of course, "in every spoof I make real love to the things I am spoofing."[4]

On a more serious level, Brooks deals with the theme of projection. For example, Thorndyke warns Brophy that working in an asylum may be conducive to fantasy and paranoia. When Brophy means to say he's a camera buff, he says "I'm very photogenic." He confuses the object of sight with the process of perception. To put it another way, Brooks emphasizes the process by which our perception alters our sense of what we see. In this respect, the film is about a key element in Hitchcock's art. Hitchcock frequently explored the moral issues in the act of intrusive viewing and the involving powers of subjective cinema.

Consequently, the characters in *High Anxiety* often experience not just the events in the plot, but the Hitchcockian rhetoric in which these events are depicted. The rhetoric of communication becomes part of the content of the shot; indeed it is often its very subject. For example, after Thorndyke passes through a number of strange encounters in the airport, all heightened by a melodramatic musical score, he remarks, "What a dramatic airport!" Later, just as Brophy expresses his suspicion of "foul play" there is a burst of symphonic music. But this is not the usual background score, without source in the scene of action. The next shot reveals the Los Angeles Symphony playing the music as they pass by in a bus. In a related device, background music becomes an active element in the scene when Dr. Wentworth is killed by the music on his car radio. As in Count Basie's appearance in *Blazing Saddles*, these out-of-content intrusions of synchronous music show Brooks to be concerned with the rhetoric of the genre, its artifices and devices. Both films share this Cubist spirit; they analyze their own process of perception and expression, as well as the subject of their view.

There is a similar effect in two dinner scenes. In the first, Brooks tracks in on a formal dinner, in a demonstration of Hitchcock's fluid camera movement and his common device of making his audience a voyeuristic intruder. Like the swooping start to *Psycho* and our sharing of Norman Bates's peephole in that film, and like the predatory zoom in on the incriminating eyes of the drummer in *Young and Innocent*, Brooks's camera action seems to swing us into the characters' lives from the outside. But Brooks draws attention to our intrusion: His camera breaks the glass door and the dinner guests turn to stare at us reproachfully. This shot is reversed at the end of the film. As Thorndyke and Victoria prepare for their wedding night at the Honeymoon City Motel, Brooks's camera makes an awkward retreat. It smashes through the brick wall, as it attempts to leave the lovers discreetly. "Keep going," we hear one crew member say, "Maybe no one will notice."

In both scenes, Brooks emphasizes our presence as voyeuristic intruders in the action. In the second case especially, a scene which we are smugly used to witness as nonpresent observers, he defines the erotic rights of marriage to be a private moment at which we are, in effect, peeping toms. In these scenes, Hitchcock is not being echoed but analyzed. Brooks enacts a dominant Hitchcock theme: the film-viewer's implication in what he chooses to witness and accept. For Hitchcock, his hero's moral lapses are a demonstration of the audience's moral vulnerability. In film after film, from *The Manxman* on, his audience is sympathetically involved in the hero's morally suspect situation. In our witness and in our sympathy, we become involved in the Hitchcock hero's exposure. Brooks's loud, intrusive camera movements enact this insight.

The other relevant dinner scene is the coffee conversation at which Diesel and Montague plot against Thorndyke. Brooks shoots the entire chat from under their glass-topped coffee table. The camera continually scuttles about in order to peer past the added impediments—the cups, coffee, cookies, and all-obliterating strudel. Again Brooks renders explicitly what is usually implicit. He makes the process of viewing the real subject of the shot. His point is our snooping, our spying upon the villains—and by implication, our complicity with the plotters. The viewer's complicity by passive acceptance is a theme Hitchcock developed throughout his career, but it is especially prominent in *Blackmail*, *Murder!*, *Rope*, *Under Capricorn*, *The Trouble with Harry*, *Psycho*, *Marnie*, and *Rear Window*.

This major Hitchock concern is the subject of these striking and graceful gags. Strangely enough, John Simon cites the latter example as one of those (in his view) successful moments when Brooks "forgets Hitchcock altogether." On the contrary, the scene is pure and crucial Hitchcock. In giving the audience a subjective experience of a morally incriminating conversation, it implicates the viewer in the exposure of the action. Brooks does physically what Hitchcock does morally: makes the film's viewer an actual party to the villain's scheme and guilt. In addition, in all three examples, Brooks's deliberate clumsiness in drawing attention to his act of filming is a compliment to the grace and fluidity of Hitchcock's camera and editing. One recalls Brooks's preference for a cinema that subordinates technology to humanity. As he told Jane Shapiro, his editing of *Blazing Saddles* was "far superior" to the award-winning *Bullitt*, "because it was *proper*. You can't crash in, you have to eavesdrop on their lives." (In the same breath, Brooks responded to a young filmmaker's question about using the eclair: "Naw, use a camera instead; an eclair is soft and mushy and sweet, you take two bites, you don't want anymore. But I digress.")[5]

The other major Hitchcock theme in *High Anxiety* is man's traumatic fixation upon his past. In addition to the hero's fear rooted in childhood, there is the infantilism of Brophy and the bellboy. The sado-masochist romance between Nurse Diesel and Dr. Montague is childish discipline and spite. Montague calls her "Mommy" and she taunts him with her fruit cup after withholding his, as punishment for lateness.

Typical of a Hitchcock work, the central characters have problems with their parents or with parent surrogates. Victoria is healthiest in her quest for her father because she alone is conscious of her need. Professor Lilloman is childish—he forgets his hanky when he blows his nose—but is Thorndyke's father figure. The resolution of the hero's trauma is foreshadowed when a therapy session turns into a boxing match with Lilloman, refereed by Montague. Here a repressed antagonism is exposed within the affectionate relationship between the hero and his elderly mentor.

In the climax, Brooks appears as the baby Richard, in his high chair, squawling in fright at his parents' tiff. "It's not height I'm afraid of," he concludes, "it's parents!" This is a fair verdict on most of Hitchcock's characters! There's a moment of Hitchcockian illumination when Lilloman heralds the hero's breakthrough: "So climb, you sonofabitch, climb!" (the filial oath is apt). An adult reaches self-awareness and moral responsibility by finally recognizing and overcoming his dependence upon oppressive parents. By recognizing his parents' traumatic effect on him, Thorndyke escapes the conventional sentimentalizing of the parent-child relationship that he slipped into his song at the nightclub: "And remember, folks, be good to your parents. They've been good to you." Again, Brooks catches a delicious moment of Hitchcockian irony and mischief. He sets up one of our sentimental reflexes, then undercuts it.

The film's focus upon trauma is played out in a minor pattern of gags in which the characters react to pain some time after they have suffered it. Cases in point are Montague's spanked bottom, Lilloman's sore jaw, Brophy's mouth when the tape has been torn off, and the bellboy's simmering resentment of Thorndyke. Then, too, Thorndyke's lecture to the convention is on a related topic, the effects of toilet training upon later sexuality. He claims there is none, but the entire film demonstrates the adult's traumatization by an incident in infancy.

In perhaps the film's wittiest scene, Thorndyke regresses into infantile language during his lecture to an audience of learned psychiatrists. We have had some indication that the adult Thorndyke still has much of the child in him. For example, when he brushes his teeth, he recites the instructions that he obviously learned as a child. Under hypnosis he calls for his mother. These jokes prepared us for the flashback, in which the adult appears as the baby. But in the lecture to his learned colleagues, we have the gradual transformation of a knowledgeable adult into a baby-talking neurotic.

The change is due to Thorndyke's becoming self-conscious when one member of the audience arrives with his two daughters, aged about ten or twelve. Immediately, the speaker loses his confidence and openness. He shifts from "penis envy" to "pee-pee envy." Instead of "breasts" he says "balloons." "Womb" becomes "woo-woo." He even redefines his topic: "Toilet training is a vast area. Are we talking about Number One or cocky-doody?" This leads him ultimately to a rather ambiguous conclusion: "I would have to say that going potty has very little to do with future sexual development." In "going potty," euphemism causes imprecision.

In this routine there are several ironies. First, the audience appreciates and understands their lecturer's regression. By the end, all the savants have reverted to baby talk. Second, Thorndyke's ploy is illogical. If he means to save the children from embarrassment, he would do better were he to stick to the clinical terms. In regressing to baby talk, he exposes the children to the very things from which he is trying to shield them. Third, while all the adults around them grow embarrassed and flustered, the two girls take the entire experience in stride. Indeed, they exchange a look as if to say "Can you believe these ass-holes?!" Finally, Brooks makes a general point about euphemism. He satirizes verbal decorum and the adult's fastidiousness about proper subject and tone in public discussion.

Paradoxically, the squeamish Thorndyke's qualms lead to a litany of scatological jokes, with such words as "cocky-doody" and "wee-wee." The episode can be taken as a defense of Brooks's own scatological spirit. In *High Anxiety*, it animates the scene involving the self-styled cocker spaniel, who lifts a leg to wet Montague but lavishes more erotic attention upon Thorndyke. That particular dog sets up Lilloman's line, "Dis is da cocker's daughter?" His Jewish accent makes "cocker" sound like "cacker," which is Yiddish for "defecator." Through all this, the children seem to have a natural, healthy, open spirit. Victoria has only to overcome her shame at being excited by an obscene phone-caller. In contrast, the adult males' euphemism reveals their sexual hang-ups.

Hitchcock's themes of childish fixation seem to have registered upon the reviewers of *High Anxiety*, but only subconsciously. Most of the reviewers complained about the childishness of the film, instead of working out the significance of childishness *in* the film. Pauline Kael attacked Brooks for his "child's idea of satire: imitation, with a funny hat and a leer." More temperately, Robert Fulford distinguished between Woody Allen's "persistently adolescent" style and Brooks's "intentionally childish" one: "In almost every scene of *High Anxiety*, as in the famous farting scene in *Blazing Saddles*, we can see the nine-year-old that Brooks must have been, the smart little kid who saw that those around him were phony and only he had the nerve to speak it." Though he understands Brooks's candor, Fulford concludes that "any serious intention he may have is undone by the childish pleasure he takes in his gags." The most sensitive response was Herbert Gold's: Brooks's "metabolism is driven by a heart which defies the loss of his father, the loss of childhood, by insisting on childhood everywhere." More to the immediate point: Brooks luxuriates in the wildness, the mischief, the license, and the energy of the child, because his work is a struggle to come to terms with his losses and his needs. The adult's traumatic shaping by his childhood is the central theme of *High Anxiety*. It makes the film one of Brooks's most personal and revealing works, despite its form as a Hitchcock pastiche.[6]

In a second level of intense personal involvement, Brooks reconciles his ethnic past to the image of the modern American. This is also an element of his Hitchcock homage, for Hitchcock always gave his viewer a handsome, elegant, sophisticated hero with whom to identify (and by whose ambivalence to be exposed). So Brooks relishes the chance to play Cary Grant:

> I've always wanted to be the character I'm playing . . . I mean, I like a hat that comes down on both sides. I like a Phi Beta Kappa key. I like a grey suit. I mean, there it is, a dream come true: I'm a Nobel Prize-winning psychiatrist in an Alfred Hitchcock picture. That's a kid's fantasy, especially a kid who loved *The 39 Steps* and *The Lady Vanishes*.[7]

Or even *Torn Curtain*, where Paul Newman played Cary Grant as Hud. Here Brooks admits to the personal wish-fulfillment behind his starring role—which explains Hitchcock's use of popular romantic stars as his leads. Brooks shared this pleasure by giving roles to his coauthors of the screenplay, Ron Clark (Zachary Cartwright) and Rudy DeLuca (the killer), and to Albert Whitlock (Arthur Brisbane), who was Hitchcock's special-effects director. Brooks shared his (Hitchcockian) chance to live out a fantasy through a film.

Only one reviewer seems to have twigged this aspect of the film. Gene Lees suggests that Thorndyke "aspires to be a romantic figure . . . and is impeded in his aspirations to derring-do by his preposterous and pathetic acrophobia." Lees takes this theme to be "a far more important factor than the Hitchcock parody."[8] True enough, but the theme of the viewer's vicarious identification with a romantic hero, which operates between us and Brooks on one level, and between Brooks and his heroic self-conception on another, is essential Hitchcock. But where Hitchcock persistently involves his daydreaming viewer in the guilt of the hero, Brooks has too joyful and celebratory a spirit for that. So he pronounces the charm of the free spirit and draws laughter, not unresolved anxiety, from the viewer's involvement in the character's life.

This is also the very Hitchcockian yet Brooksian function of the two scenes that seem most to obtrude from the surface of *High Anxiety*. The first is when Thorndyke is having a drink with Victoria at a piano bar. When the pianist invites him to sing, Thorndyke modestly demurs, but after minimal coaxing steps forward. "Do you know 'High Anxiety'?" "You've got it." And he has. Before our eyes, he metamorphoses from Mel Brooks into something rather like Sinatra. After an initial awkwardness with the microphone, he orders a B-flat opening and bursts into ballad. The lyrics express the writer's and the character's buoyancy:

> *My heart's afraid to fly.*
> *It's crashed before.*
> *But then you take my hand,*
> *My heart's ready to soar.*

But the style is even more telling than the words. Brooks sings with Sinatran fluency, grace, and ease. He banters with the audience and snaps his mike cord like a whip (exciting Victoria the way the obscene phone call will later). Suddenly Brooks is a Hitchcock hero, suave like Robert Donat, Bob Cummings, Jimmy Stewart, Cary Grant, and capable of public grace. Like his tango in *Silent Movie*, this song recalls Brooks's claim on the David Susskind Show: He implausibly described himself as a "marvelous amalgam" of Anthony Eden and Fred Astaire ("I'm putting on my white tie. I'm putting on my black tie. I'm putting on my *yarmulke*"—Kick!). But in *High Anxiety* Brooks's romantic self-projection points to the hero-identification and vicarious wish-fulfillment that is crucial to Hitchcock's casting and romance. Curiously, Pauline Kael singled out this singing scene as the film's "most buoyant sequence" but she complained that it "has no connection with Hitchcock." She argued that the satirist should "take something we've seen and show us that he had seen something more in it," but that "all Brooks does is let us know he has seen some of the same movies we have." In addition to confusing satire and parody here, Kael misses the fact that Brooks does the very thing she requires in the scene she finds jarring.[9]

In the second obtrusive scene, Victoria and Thorndyke dress up in Salvation Army clothes to pass the vigilant airport police. The lovers pretend to be cranky, bickering old Jews, quarrelling over the celery she's taking along in case the stewardess serves Bloody Marys, then over whether Murray Weintraub is dead or alive, and then over how Murray Weintraub and Morris Turtletaub actually limped. At first sight, this may seem to be more of Brooks's documentary realism than a Hitchcock insight. But Hitchcock's heroes often hide or protect themselves by being loud in a public place. The best defense is offensiveness. So Robert Donat gave an election speech in *The 39 Steps*, Cary Grant disrupted an auction in *North by Northwest* and Bob Cummings started one in *Sabotage*, and Paul Newman broke up a ballet in *Torn Curtain*. As Thorndyke explains, "If you're loud and annoying, psychologically people don't notice you."

Of course, this scene also allows Brooks to affirm his own ethnic roots, in counterpoise to his character's suave Sinatra and slick psychiatrist image, and the romantic lead that Brooks plays. To this reading we're directed by the Coke sign behind the loud couple: "Here's the real thing." Further, Brooks's reference to the Jewish stereotype parallels his character's recovery of his own infancy at the root of his anxiety. It's an affirmation of origin, of shameless self, and of quirky individualism.

Like the genre parodies before it, then, *High Anxiety* is a shrewd analysis of Hitchcock's characteristic themes, devices, and effects. John Simon was simply wrong to claim that Brooks lacked the "mental acumen . . . to perceive deeper ideological flaws on which mordant satire feeds." But then Simon thought that Thorndyke's song was merely a "send-up" of the silly title songs that "gum up the movies in which they appear without the slightest connection."[10] Seeing Brooks sing is too surprising and gratifying for the scene to register merely as a delay. It is an illumination, a flash of the private Brooks. From his encounter with Alfred Hitchcock's witty explorations in guilt and complicity, comes another personal, revealing work. As in his earlier genre parodies, Brooks expresses his intimate self through his encounter with a specific rhetoric of film.

Conclusion

M EL BROOKS'S COMEDY is a full-scale dramatization of the Freudian view of human nature. As Brooks has pointed out, Bialystock and Bloom in *The Producers* personify the Freudian id and ego respectively. There is a Freudian aspect in Brooks's central preoccupation with what his characters want. Moreover, these desires are usually framed in an understanding of Freud. Even the character who has conquered mortality, the two-thousand-year-old man, strives to sustain his quirky individuality, not to blur away into the generality of the species ("You walk by a fruit stand, you get hot. What the hell is that? That's no way to live!"). The two-hour-old baby anticipates his comfortable life with his mother; but once he contemplates the joys with his father, he becomes traumatized and collapses into normal helplessness.

Brooks extends this Oedipal drama in *Young Frankenstein*. At first the hero desires a character and fame that are independent of his family name and tradition. But as for all Brooks's heroes, fulfillment requires recognition of emotional bonds. Then young Frankenstein creates his monster, but still out of his selfish vanity, what Freud called "parental narcissism." Only when the doctor exchanges powers with his creature and grants him independence of thought and speech does young Frankenstein fully mature, as a parent, scientist, and lover. The society that then accepts both the monster and the Promethean scientist is healthier and more secure than the community in traditional versions of the Frankenstein myth, which remains repressive, terrified of its own force that it has only temporarily subdued.

Brooks's films trace the maturing of childish adults. His central characters begin as self-seeking, narcissistic whimperers, but

165

mature into responsible fraternal community. This is the drama in *The Producers, The Twelve Chairs,* and *Blazing Saddles.* In the later films this development extends beyond adolescent male camaraderie to embrace the challenges and rewards of heterosexual romance: *Young Frankenstein, Silent Movie, High Anxiety.* Even as a group, Brooks's heroes demonstrate Freud's view of sexual maturing. Curiously, there are few children in Brooks's films. The only ones are the two preteen girls who visit the lecture in *High Anxiety.* Their poised presence contrasts with the infantilism to which the adults are driven by ludicrous decorum and squeamishness. Brooks doesn't use children because his central concern is with adults who have not matured past childish dependencies (Leo Bloom with his security blanket, the helpless Ippolit, and so on through to the traumatized Drs. Montague and Thorndyke).

Further consistent with Freud, Brooks's characters are often misdirected in what they think they want. Wealth is the false lure in *The Producers* and *The Twelve Chairs* for characters who really crave companionship. Hedley Lamarr pursues wealth ravenously in *Blazing Saddles* but his real desire, unrecognized until his moment of death, is to live up to the heroic prowess of Hollywood legends.

In his most explicitly Freudian feature, *High Anxiety,* Brooks suggests that man is debilitated by his own anxiety, not by any outside forces. This coheres with Freud's ultimate view, that anxiety is the cause, not the result, of repression. Brooks shares with Freud (and his cinematic master Hitchcock) the optimism that man is not powerless before external forces of repression and traumatic inhibition. Rather, these projections from within are reducible by the understanding and the will. Indeed, Will Tabefree may prove as effective a doctor as the two-thousand-year-old man's Will Talive. The negative associations of the title phrase, "high anxiety," give way to a completely positive, exuberant, romantic aspect when Brooks breaks into his romantic ballad. When the trauma grows into the lyrical effusion of a love song, the anxiety becomes a high. For Brooks as for Hitchcock, this transformation is the function of art.

There is also a Freudian point to Brooks's basic penchant for parodies of popular genres. According to psychoanalytic theory, culture is a set of projections from man's repressed unconscious. The tensions that have been prohibited open expression find their way forth in defused and domesticated imagery, through jokes, dreams, art, social conventions, and societal structures. Like Freudian analysis of an individual psyche, Brooks's genre parodies psychoanalyze the culture for which these genres express unresolved tensions. They expose to the conscious mind the suppressions of the subconscious. In this light, *Springtime for Hitler*—both as Liebkind writes it and as DeBris and L.S.D. present it—demonstrates the dangers of repressive fantasy, by which the viewer evades reality and is deluded. *Blazing Saddles* exposes the racism, mythopoeia, sexuality, and callousness that lurk behind the conventions of the ostensibly "innocent" and "historical" Western. In *Young Frankenstein*, Brooks opposes the basic traditions of the myth by allowing his scientist and his creature reconciliation, equality, and both a social and a sexual normalization. *Silent Movie* is a pure exercise in nostalgia—both in its genre and in its personal spirit—but it openly declares itself as such. For Brooks, the conventions of a genre are not to be mechanically repeated, but questioned, evaluated from a humane perspective, then freely transcended. Conventional genre works are what Freud calls "substitute gratifications," indirect expressions of repressed tensions. Brooks probes behind the conventions to define what the genre at once expresses and conceals (e.g., the racism of the Western or the sexuality in the Frankenstein myth). By inferring what the fictions hide, Brooks translates the illusions into their sublimated reality.

Consistent with Freud's view of art, Brooks manages to remain extremely playful even at his most serious and profound. Comedy is to Brooks what play is to Freud; the pattern of energetic activity, freed from the serious business of life and the harsh, repressive judgments of the reality principle. To Brooks, man is most adult, mature, noble, and wise when he is afrolic. Hence Brooks's magnificent wildness and vulgarity. And his characters are often most self-aware and most fully humane at the instants they acknowledge that they are part of a fiction (*i.e.*, when they admit that their lives are play).

With his art of energy, openness and exuberance, Brooks values freedom more than discipline, outburst more than restraint, and

emotion more than abstemious craft. Energy and present out-
weigh control and the future. Wild, even vulgar, valor is the
better part of discretion. This director was a compulsive, open
humanist even before he discovered his medium:

> I was a born director. I would put warm water on two dogs making
> it. I *knew*. Cold water, they'd bite some kid the next day to get
> even. Hot water, they'd never screw again. Why give them a
> trauma?[1]

Yeah, why? Brooks's comedy continues his one-madcap crusade
against traumas, for all God's creatures, from cling peach to pet to
man (and even to such man-made glories as Frankenstein's
monster and the unsung Saran Wrap and nectarine!). But Brooks
is too open-eyed and open-hearted to moon about "Love Power"
(as L.S.D. did in *The Producers*). Rather, Brooks vents his entire
range of emotions:

> All right, I *am* often brash, rude and brutally direct. Someday I'm
> going to die and I don't have time to toe-dance around the periphery
> of hatred.[2]

Constantly Brooks explains his liveliness as his counterattack upon
mortality.

As early as his cartoon, *The Critic*, Brooks preferred a Freudian
openness over the cerebral suppressions and sublimations. There
the inner film, Ernest Pintoff's visuals, meet Freud's definition of
the dream—private, asocial, psychical and unintelligble—as op-
posed to art, which is social, communicative, and harmonizing. As
this inner film breeds confusion in the viewer and division in the
community, its effect is frustration. When Brooks adds his critic's
commentary, the total experience meets Freud's criteria for wit
and art: A conscious, controlled expression brings its audience (us)
to a common experience, illuminating, and understanding. Although it remains complex and ambiguous, the film is a harmonizing force. In addition, the abstraction in the inner film denies
man's fleshly nature and his individual experience. But Brooks's
quirky old Jewish commentator restores the hard grain of humanity in all its profane, ignorant, belligerent, but mortal glory.

Against such bloodless abstractions Brooks elsewhere unleashes his bawdry, scatology, Yiddish, and physical slapstick athwart the Warren Blands of modern civilization and its discontents.

So Brooks's robust vulgarity is central to his moral and psychological purposes. For he rejects the decorous abstractions and gentilities of cerebral art, those devices of suppression and sublimation by which cowboys have been fed innumerable cans of beans with nary a ruffle of the calm campfire air. From his soapbox, Brooks puts on farts not airs. He extolls the more sublime rigor and honesty of the freed and open energy, that will confront man in all his weakness and embarrassment, that will follow through the consequences of man's consumption, whether culinary or cultural. For Brooks as for Freud, comedy is man's highest defense because it openly confronts ideas that are generally deemed shameful or painful. Hence the *Blazing Saddles* ad: "Never give a saga an even break." Brooks means never give a sublimation an even break. Never give a succor an evil brake.

But Brooks shows himself as much as he shows his Freudian understanding. Time and again we find the same intense concerns: the pain from his loss of his father, the consequent hunger for male fellowship, an unattractive man's dream of beauty, the immigrant's clumsy embarrassment amid suave sophistication, and the need to be one's natural, unrespectable self. Mel Brooks's comedy is as revealing a personal statement as any American artist has given us.

We can even define his touch in a film that he did not direct himself, but that he "discovered" and went on to produce—the film about the nineteenth-century freak John Merrick. *The Elephant Man* differs from Bernard Pomerance's play of the same title and subject in just those particulars that define Brooks's concerns.

In the play, Pomerance uses Merrick to demonstrate two points. One is that man's poetic imagination enables him to transcend coarse physical nature. The other is that sexual repression in Victorian society made its Puritanism more monstrous than man's instinctive sexuality. The hero's relationship with the actress Mrs. Kendal builds to a climax of sexual engagement and the horrified, abusive response of the hero's guardian. But in the film these points are ignored. Its Elephant Man is simply a sensitive soul, not a poet. His plight is to have an abused self-image, a shame through which he has been inhibited and exploited. In the film, his relationship with the actress climaxes when he is given an ovation at the theater. Like the theme of abusive shame, the idea of finding public acceptance through the community of art is a rather Brooksian notion.

In addition, the film treats Merrick as a harbinger of our twentieth century. His misshapen body foreshadows the more monstrous society born out of the Industrial Revolution. Hence the intercut shots of hissing, pounding, infernal factories, and the hero's exploitation and abuse by the liberated masses, the desentimentalized working class, unbridled and inhumane. The hero's hungry fantasies of his lost mother are a Brooksian refuge of parental warmth from the cold, dehumanizing "progress" of modern society. Casting Anne Bancroft as the Beauty who befriends the Beast may be Brooks's most explicit input into the film. But the themes of repressed monstrousness, exploitative greed and hypocrisy, fading humanity, and a child reaching back helplessly for a last parent, show Brooks's involvement in the film. In addition, his sentimentality distinguishes this film from *Eraserhead*, the brilliant previous work by the director, David Lynch.

Mel Brooks's art is a varied body of comedy with distinctive emotional power, formal energy, and moral purpose. Whether the result of extended calculation (his films) or the flash of his improvisational genius (his quips and interviews), his comedy draws deeper than laughter. It invites us to face and to warm our essential nature. It challenges the myths and restrictions with which we have been afflicted and subdued. Most importantly, it bares a lively heart and soul—that of the wacko but wise Melvin Kaminsky. Ages have fed into his formation. Ages more may well be moved and nourished by his wild, warm wit.

Epilogue

As we go to press, the world (or at least Sweden and points West) waits with baited breath for Mel Brooks's new feature, *History of the World, Part I*. Brooks wrote, produced, and directed the film. In addition, he plays five roles. As in his double appearance in *Blazing Saddles*, Brooks here again plays humanity high and low. The high figures are historical: Moses, Torquemada the Grand Inquisitor, and France's King Louis XVI. The low are humble Everymen: Comicus, a stand-up comic-philosopher during the reign of Nero, and Jacques, a French lavatory attendant thrust into power in a Revolutionary intrigue.

Not having seen the film, this reviewer is reluctant to analyze it in any detail. But its historical sweep and apparent energy and irreverence recall Brooks's classic 2,000-Year-Old Man act. As well, the variety of periods covered in the film suggests that Brooks is once again basing his comedy upon the parody of familiar Hollywood genres, from the run of DeMille Biblical spectaculars to the dashing adventure in epics of the French Revolution.

The film promises to be a breakthrough film for Brooks by its immense budget and scale. Advance stills suggest finely realized historical settings and Brooks's usual close attention to arresting faces in the supporting cast. He also has a stellar stable of stars. Dom DeLuise plays Nero. As his wife, the insatiable Empress Nympho, Madeline Kahn extends her Brooksian persona of luscious lubriciousness from *Blazing Saddles* and *Young Frankenstein*. In the French Revolution episode, Harvey Korman is the evil Count de Monet and Cloris Leachman the famous knitter, Madame Defarge. The bit players should also grab the attention. Sid Caesar plays the chief caveman; Shecky Greene, Marcus

Vindictus; Howard Morris, a court spokesman. The Roman Empire story features TV's Maude, Bea Arthur, along with Charlie Callas, Paul Mazursky, Jack Riley, and Henny Youngman. John Hurt plays Jesus; Pat McCormick, a plumbing salesman; and Hugh Hefner, an entrepreneur. A gaggle of *Playboy* playmates and models appear as vestal virgins, but their vested interest was probably to protect Hefner from exploitation in his first against-type film-role.

In the other episodes we can look for such familiar faces as Jackie Mason, Ronny Graham, Jack Carter, Jan Murray, John Hillerman, Fiona Richmond, and the brilliant Spike Milligan as Monsieur Rimbaud.

For all this wealth of comic talent, however, Brooks's new feature may well prove to be his most scathing work of social satire to date. For his sense of human cruelty, that wonderful indifference to one's fellow man, is never far from the grin in a Mel Brooks frolic. With a large budget and a sparkling cast, we can expect Brooks to have been equally generous with his impassioned call for a revived humanity and a fired vigilance against the forces that freeze and erode the human heart.

Of course, I'm guessing. Buy this book and sell your friends on it. Then the publishers will insist upon a revised edition, and *Method in Madness, Book II*, will properly attend to Mel Brooks's *History of the World, Part I*. As the 2,000 year-old man might well tell us, "Stay out of small Italian cars." And watch this space.

Notes

Introduction
1. Charles Young, "Seven Revelations about Mel Brooks," *Rolling Stone*, February 9, 1978, p. 33.
2. *Playboy*, February 1975, p. 60.
3. Pauline Kael, *Reeling* (Boston: Atlantic-Little, Brown, 1976); p. 380.
   Young, p. 33.
   Playboy, 1975, p. 48.
   Gordon Gow, "Fond Salute and Naked Hate," *Films and Filming*, July 1975, p. 14.
4. *Variety*, January 9, 1980, pp. 24 ff.
   Robert Rivlin, "Mel Brooks on *High Anxiety*," *Millimeter*, December 1977, p. 20.
   Digby Diehl, "Mel Brooks," *Action*, X:i (January-February 1975), p. 22.
5. Bill Adler and Jeffrey Feinman, *Mel Brooks: The Irreverent Funnyman*, (Chicago: Playboy Press, 1976), p. 186.
   Time, January 13, 1975, p. 38.
6. *Playboy*, 1975, pp. 63, 68.
   Bill Adler, p. 90.
   Charles Young, p. 33.
7. Bill Adler, p. 98.
   Silent Movie pressbook.
8. Robert Rivlin, p. 20.
   Bill Adler, p. 90.
9. *Playboy*, 1975, p. 61.
10. Philip Fleishman, "Interview with Mel Brooks," *Maclean's*, April 17, 1978, p. 6.
    Playboy, 1975, pp. 48, 66, 62.

PART ONE: BACKGROUND

Chapter One: The Creed
1. Robert Rivlin, "Mel Brooks on *High Anxiety*," p. 20.
   Bill Adler and Jeffrey Feinman, *Mel Brooks: The Irreverent Funnyman*, p. 162.

2. William Holtzman, *Seesaw: A Dual Biography of Anne Bancroft and Mel Brooks* (New York: Doubleday, 1979), p. 273.
   Gordon Gow, "Fond Salutes and Naked Hate," p. 12.
   Gene Lees, "The Mel Brooks Memoes," *American Film*, October 1977, p. 16.
3. Kenneth Tynan, "Frolics and Detours of a Short Hebrew Man," *The New Yorker*, October 30, 1978, p. 54.
4. Philip Fleishman, "Interview with Mel Brooks," p. 10.
   High Anxiety pressbook.
   Gene Lees, p. 16.
5. Charles Young, "Seven Revelations about Mel Brooks," p. 35.
   Time, January 13, 1975, p. 38.
6. Gene Lees, p. 16.
   Charles Young, p. 34.
   Philip Fleishman, p. 10.
7. Gene Lees, p. 17.
8. *Playboy*, 1975, p. 61.
   Kenneth Tynan, p. 130.
9. Kenneth Tynan, p. 74.
10. Larry Wilde, *How the Great Comedy Writers Create Laughter*, paper ed. (Chicago: Nelson-Hall, 1977), p. 47.
11. Gordon Gow, p. 14.
12. *Playboy*, 1975, p. 68.
13. "The Mel Brooks 6 Rules of Dining Etiquette," *Feature*, April 1979, p. 28.
    High Anxiety pressbook.
14. Herbert Gold, "Funny Is Money," *The New York Times Magazine*, March 30, 1975, p. 21.
15. Charles Young, p. 35.
    Playboy, 1975, p. 52.
16. Lawrence Weschler, "Is Mel Brooks Going Crazy?" *The Village Voice*, December 26, 1977, p. 38.
17. Gordon Gow, p. 31.
    Lawrence Weschler, p. 38.
    Kenneth Tynan, p. 54.
18. Jacoba Atlas, "Mel Brooks: The Film Director as Fruitcake," *Film Comment*, XI:ii (March-April, 1975), p. 56.
    Charles Young, p. 35.
19. Charles Young, pp. 35, 36.
20. *Playboy*, 1975, p. 68.
21. *Playboy*, 1975, pp. 61–62.
22. Kenneth Tynan, p. 56.
    Charles Young, p. 33.
    William Holtzman, p. 273.
    Andrew Sarris, "Picking the Funny Bone," *The Village Voice*, March 14, 1974, pp. 71, 74.
    Stuart Byron and Elizabeth Weis, eds., *The National Society of Film Critics*

on *Movie Comedy*, (New York: Grossman Publishers, 1977), pp. 133–37.
Kenneth Tynan, p. 58.
23. *Playboy*, October 1966, p. 76.
Playboy, 1975, p. 48.
Mel Brooks, "Confessions of an Auteur," *Action*, November-December 1971, p. 14.
Playboy, 1975, p. 49.
24. Herbert Gold, p. 28.

Chapter Two: The Life
1. *Playboy*, 1975, p. 49. Unless otherwise noted, all the quotations in this chapter are from this interview.
2. *Playboy*, 1966, p. 80.
Philip Fleishman, "Interview with Mel Brooks," p. 8.
3. Larry Wilde, *How the Great Comedy Writers Create Laughter*, pp. 53–54.
4. Larry Wilde, p. 42.
5. William Holtzman, *Seesaw*, p. 12.
6. Bill Adler and Jeffrey Feinman, *Mel Brooks: The Irreverent Funnyman*, p. 19.
7. Ted Sennett, *Your Show of Shows* (New York: Collier Books, 1977).
Jay Cocks and David Denby, eds., *Film: 1973–74* (New York: Bobbs-Merrill, 1974), pp. 257–64.
8. Philip Fleishman, p. 10.
Charles Young, "Seven Revelations about Mel Brooks," p. 33.
9. Charles Young, p. 33.
Dick Stelzer, *The Star Treatment* (New York: Bobbs-Merrill, 1977), p. 8.
10. *Time*, April 25, 1957, p. 90.
William Holtzman, p. 127.
Theatre Arts, January 1957, pp. 15–16.
Brooks Atkinson, "*Shinbone Alley*," *New York Times*, April 15, 1957, p. 23.
Brooks Atkinson, "*Shinbone Alley*," *New York Times*, April 28, 1957, Section 2, Part I, p. 1.
11. *Playboy*, 1966, p. 76.
12. Josh Logan, *Movie Stars, Real People, and Me* (New York: Dell, 1979), pp. 259–67.
Playboy, 1966, p. 78.
13. John Simon, "*All-American*," *Theatre Arts*, May 1962, p. 58.
Time, March 30, 1962, p. 46.
William Holtzman, p. 194.
14. Gordon Gow, "Fond Salutes and Naked Hate," p. 12.

PART TWO: THE EARLY WORKS
Chapter Three: The Television
1. Ted Sennett, *Your Show of Shows* (New York: Collier Books, 1977.) Unless otherwise noted, the quotations from *Your Show of Shows* are taken from this book.

2. Charles Young, "Seven Revelations about Mel Brooks," p. 33.
   Gordon Gow, "Fond Salutes and Naked Hate," p. 11.
3. Jay Cocks and David Denby, eds., *Film: 1973–74*, pp. 260–61.
4. Mark Evanier and Jim Brochu, "Sid Caesar: The *Comedy* Interview," *Comedy*, I:i (Summer, 1980), p. 18.
5. Jay Cocks, p. 262.
6. Bill Adler and Jeffrey Feinman, *Mel Brooks: The Irreverent Funnyman*, p. 72.
   William Holtzman, *Seesaw*, p. 223.
   Playboy, 1966, p. 78.
7. *Playboy*, 1966, p. 76.
8. William Holtzman, p. 223.
9. Bill Adler, p. 166.

Chapter Four: The Recordings
1. Larry Wilde, *How the Great Comedy Writers Create Laughter*, p. 47.
   Kenneth Tynan, "Frolics and Detours of a Short Hebrew Man," p. 47. Tynan is the source of much of the pre-recorded comedy quoted in this chapter.
2. *Playboy*, 1975, p. 55.
3. *Time*, January 13, 1975, p. 38.
4. Kenneth Tynan, pp. 92–93.
   Playboy, 1966, p. 76.
5. *Playboy*, 1966, p. 80.

Chapter Five: Mel Brooks, All-American
1. *Playboy*, 1975, p. 54.
2. All references are from the acting text of *All-American* (Chicago: Dramatic Publishing Company, 1972).
3. *Playboy*, 1966, p. 78.
4. Kenneth Tynan, "Frolics and Detours of a Short Hebrew Man," pp. 106, 104.
5. *Playboy*, 1975, p. 64.
   Bill Adler and Jeffrey Feinman, *Mel Brooks: The Irreverent Funnyman*, p. 96.
6. Bill Adler, p. 65.

PART THREE: THE FEATURE FILMS
Chapter Six: The Producers
1. Gene Siskel, "Interview with Mel Brooks."
   Gene Lees, "The Mel Brooks Memoes." p. 16.
   Kenneth Tynan, "Frolics and Detours of a Short Hebrew Man," p. 114.
2. Kenneth Tynan, p. 108.
3. Philip Fleishman, "Interview with Mel Brooks," p. 8.
4. Kenneth Tynan, p. 115.
5. Larry Wilde, *How the Great Comedy Writers Create Laughter*, p. 49.

6. Ralph Rosenblum and Robert Karen, *When the Shooting Stops—the Cutting Begins* (New York: Viking Press, 1979).

7. Lillian Ross and Helen Ross, *The Player: A Profile of an Art* (New York: Simon and Schuster, 1961), pp. 64–65.

8. Stuart Byron and Elizabeth Weis, eds., *The National Society of Film Critics on Movie Comedy*, pp. 116–18.
   Renata Adler, *A Year in the Dark* (New York: Berkeley, 1971), pp. 108–10.
   Pauline Kael, *Going Steady* (New York: Bantam, 1971), pp. 79–82.
   Stuart Byron, pp. 116–18.

9. William Holtzman, *Seesaw*, p. 249.
   Bill Adler and Jeffrey Feinman, *Mel Brooks: The Irrevent Funnyman*, pp. 64–65.

Chapter Seven: The Twelve Chairs

1. Dilys Powell, *"The Twelve Chairs," Sunday Times*, October 1975.

2. Mel Brooks, "Confessions of an Auteur," *Action*, November-December 1971, p. 16.
   Jane Shapiro, "Mel Brooks: 'How Do You Like Me So Far?'" *The Village Voice*, July 19, 1976, p. 73.
   William Holtzman, *Seesaw*, p. 254.

3. Gavin Millar, "Uneasy Chairs," *The Listener*, October 9, 1975.

4. *Twelve Chairs* pressbook.

5. Bill Adler, *Mel Brooks: The Irreverent Funnyman*, pp. 90–91.

6. Gene Siskel, "Interview with Mel Brooks."

7. Fred Robbins, "What Makes Mel Brooks Run?" *Show*, September 17, 1970, pp. 12–15.

8. Sigmund Freud, *The Origins of Psycho-Analysis: Letters to Wilhelm Fliess, Drafts and Notes: 1877–1902*, ed. M. Bonaparte, A. Freud and E. Kris (New York: Basic Books, 1954), p. 244.
   Fred Robbins, pp. 12–15.

9. Ilf and Petrov, *The Twelve Chairs*, trans. John H. C. Richardson (New York: Random House, 1961), p. 394.

10. Ilf and Petrov, pp. 243, 386.
    Playboy, 1975, p. 66.

11. Bill Adler, p. 92.

12. Gene Siskel, "Interview with Mel Brooks."

13. *Playboy*, 1975, p. 64.

14. Pauline Kael, *Deeper into Movies* (Boston: Atlantic-Little, Brown, 1973), p. 180.
    Bill Adler, p. 92.
    Derek Elley, *"The Twelve Chairs," Films and Filming*, March 1976, p. 39.
    The New Statesman, October 3, 1975.

15. Mel Brooks, p. 16.

Chapter Eight: Blazing Saddles

1. Bill Adler and Jeffrey Feinman, *Mel Brooks: The Irreverent Funnyman*, p. 101.

2. Philip Fleishman, "Interview with Mel Brooks," p. 8.
3. Philip Fleishman, p. 8.
   Playboy, 1975, p. 64.
4. By strange coincidence, in 1980 Hedy Lamarr filed a $10,000,000 libel suit against a newspaper who ran a story about a two-headed goat that had been named Hedy Lamarr.
5. *Playboy*, 1975, p. 65.
6. Gene Siskel, "Interview with Mel Brooks."
7. Quotations from the screenplay are from *Blazing Saddles* (the novelization) by Tad Richards (New York: Warner, 1974).
8. Jacoba Atlas, "Mel Brooks: The Film Director as Fruitcake," *Film Comment*, March-April 1975, p. 56.
9. Pauline Kael, *Reeling*, pp. 378–81.
   Robert Fulford (as "Marshall Delaney"), *"Blazing Saddles," Saturday Night*, May 1974.
   Playboy, 1975, p. 64.
10. Daniel Golden, *"Blazing Saddles:* Heading 'em off at the cliché," *Jump Cut*, No. 3 (September-October 1974), pp. 3–4.
11. Stuart Byron and Elizabeth Weis, eds., *The National Society of Film Critics on Movie Comedy*, pp. 118–20.
    William Holtzman, *Seesaw*, p. 265.
    Robert Fulford, p. 64.
    Playboy, 1975, pp. 64–65.
12. Kenneth Tynan, "Frolics and Detours of a Short Hebrew Man," *The New Yorker*, October 30, 1978, p. 120.
    Charles Young, "Seven Revelations about Mel Brooks," *Rolling Stone*, February 9, 1978, p. 33.
13. Kenneth Tynan, p. 120.
14. Jacoba Atlas, p. 55.
15. Phil Berger, *The Last Laugh*, paper ed. (New York: Ballantine, 1976), pp. 187–88.
16. *Playboy*, 1975, p. 64.
    Stuart Byron, pp. 118–20.
    William Holtzman, p. 269.
    Pauline Kael, *Reeling*, pp. 378–81.
    Pauline Kael, *When the Lights Go Down* (New York: Holt, Rinehart and Winston, 1980), p. 375.
17. Peter Schjeldahl, *"Blazing Saddles," The New York Times*, March 17, 1974.
18. *Playboy*, 1975, p. 52.

Chapter Nine: Young Frankenstein

1. Herbert Gold, "Funny Is Money," p. 19.
2. *Playboy*, 1975, p. 66.
   Gerald Hirschfield, "The Story Behind the Filming of *Young Frankenstein*," *American Cinematographer*, July 1974, pp. 802–5, 840–2, 844.
3. *Playboy*, 1975, p. 66.

4. Jacoba Atlas, "Mel Brooks: The Film Director as Fruitcake,"p. 57.

5. *Playboy*, 1975, p. 49.

6. Jacoba Atlas, p. 57.

7. R. W. Dillard, "Even a Man Who Is Pure at Heart: Poetry and Danger in the Horror Film," in *Man and the Movies*, W. R. Robinson, ed. (New York: Penguin Books, 1969), pp. 84–86.

8. R. W. Dillard, p. 90.

9. Bill Adler and Jeffrey Feinman, *Mel Brooks: The Irreverent Funnyman*, p. 124.

10. Digby Diehl, "Mel Brooks," p. 20.

11. Screenplay references are from *Young Frankenstein* (the novelization) by Gilbert Pearlman (New York: Ballantine, 1974).

12. Sören Fischer, *National Film Theatre Program Notes*, British Film Institute, April, 1975.

13. Pauline Kael, *Reeling*, pp. 535–58.
    Radu Florescu, *In Search of Frankenstein* (New York: Warner, 1975), p. 283.
    Martin Tropp, *Mary Shelley's Monster*, (Boston: Houghton Mifflin, 1976), p. 150.
    Digby Diehl, p. 21.
    Bill Adler, p. 142.

14. Stuart Byron and Elizabeth Weis, eds., *The National Society of Film Critics on Movie Comedy*, pp. 121–23.
    Judith Hess, "*Young Frankenstein:* Some Things Just Aren't Funny," *Jump Cut*, No. 6 (March-April 1975), p. 12.

15. Bill Adler, p. 57.

Chapter Ten: Silent Movie

1. Gordon Gow, "Fond Salutes and Naked Hate," p. 10.
   Mel Brooks, "Confession of an Auteur," p. 16.

2. *Playboy*, 1975, p. 64.

3. Al Aronowitz, "Mel Brooks Talks Up *Silent Movie*," *The New York Times*, July 18, 1976, Section D, Part I, p. 11.
   Gene Siskel, "Interview with Mel Brooks."

4. Gene Siskel.

5. Kathleen Tynan, "Success Is a Great Big Spoof," *Evening Standard*, April 11, 1975.
   Gene Siskel.

6. David Wilson, "Sounds Funny," *New Statesman*, January 21, 1977.
   Gavin Millar, "Beyond Lunacy," *The Listener*, January 27, 1977.
   Russell Davies, "Comic Cuts," *The Observer*, January 23, 1977.

Chapter Eleven: High Anxiety

1. Robert Rivlin, "Mel Brooks on *High Anxiety*," p. 20.

2. Charles Young, "Seven Revelations about Mel Brooks," p. 33.

3. Robert Rivlin, p. 17.

4. *High Anxiety* pressbook.

5. John Simon, "Parodies Lost," *Maclean's*, February 6, 1978, p. 60.
   Jane Shapiro, "Mel Brooks: 'How Do You Like Me So Far?'" *The Village Voice*, July 19, 1976, pp. 73–74.
6. Pauline Kael, *When the Lights Go Down*, pp. 371–76.
   Robert Fulford (as "Marshall Delaney"), "The Juvenile Fixations of Woody and Mel," *Saturday Night*, April 1978, p. 8.
7. Herbert Gold, "Funny Is Money," pp. 16–31.
8. Gene Siskel, "Interview with Mel Brooks."
9. Gene Lees, "The Mel Brooks Memoes," p. 15.
10. Pauline Kael, pp. 371–76.
11. John Simon, p. 60.

Conclusion
1. *Playboy*, 1975, p. 64.
2. *Playboy*, 1966, p. 80.

Bibliography

Adler, Bill, and Jeffrey Feinman. *Mel Brooks: The Irreverent Funnyman*. Chicago: Playboy Press, 1976.

Adler, Renata. *A Year in the Dark*. New York: Random House, 1969; Berkeley: Berkeley Medallion, 1971.

Aronowitz, Al. "Mel Brooks Talks Up *Silent Movie*." *The New York Times*, July 18, 1976.

Atkinson, Brooks. "*Shinbone Alley*." *The New York Times*, April 15, 1957.

———. "*Shinbone Alley*." *The New York Times*, April 28, 1957.

Atlas, Jacoba. "Mel Brooks: The Film Director as Fruitcake." *Film Comment*, XI:ii (March-April 1975), pp. 54–57.

Bates, Dan. "*The Producers*." *Film Quarterly*, Summer, 1968, p. 60.

Berger, Phil. *The Last Laugh*. New York: William Morrow, 1975; Ballantine, 1976.

Brooks, Mel. "Interview," *Playboy*, October, 1966, pp. 71–80.

———. "Confessions of an Auteur." *Action*, VI:i (November-December 1971), pp. 14–17.

———. *All-American*. Chicago: Dramatic Publishing Company, 1972.

———. "Interview." *Playboy*, February, 1975, pp. 47–68.

———, with Ron Clark, Rudy DeLuca, and Barry Levinson. *Silent Movie*. New York: Ballantine Books, 1976.

———. "The Mel Brooks 6 Rules of Dining Etiquette," *Feature*, April 1979, p. 28.

Byron, Stuart, and Elizabeth Weis, eds. *The National Society of Film Critics on Movie Comedy*. New York: Grossman Publishers, 1977; Penguin, 1977.

Christmas, Linda. "Man with Another Kind of High Anxiety." *The Guardian*, September 11, 1979.

Cocks, Jay, and David Denby, eds. *Film: 1973–74*. New York: Bobbs-Merrill, 1974.

Davies, Russell. "Comic Cuts." *The Observer*, January 23, 1977.

Diehl, Digby. "Mel Brooks." *Action*, X:i (January-February 1975), pp. 18–22.

Dillard, R.H.W. "Even a Man Who Is Pure at Heart: Poetry and Danger in the Horror Film." In *Man and the Movies*, New York: W. R. Robinson, ed., Penguin, 1969.

Elley, Derek. *"The Twelve Chairs." Films and Filming*, March 1976, pp. 38–39.

Evanier, Mark, and Jim Brochu. "Sid Caesar: The *Comedy* Interview." *Comedy*, I:i (Summer 1980), pp. 12–20.

Fleishman, Philip. "Interview with Mel Brooks." *Maclean's*, April 17, 1978, pp. 6–10.

Florescu, Radu. *In Search of Frankenstein*. New York: Warner Books, 1975.

Freud, Sigmund. *The Origins of Psycho-Analysis: Letters to Wilhelm Fliess, Drafts and Notes, 1877–1902*, ed. M. Bonaparte, A. Freud and E. Kris. New York: Basic Books, 1954.

Fulford, Robert (as "Marshall Delaney"). *"Blazing Saddles." Saturday Night*, May 1974.

———. "The Juvenile Fixations of Woody and Mel." *Saturday Night*, April 1978, pp. 56–58.

Glut, Donald. *The Frankenstein Legend*. Metuchen, N.J.: Scarecrow Press, 1973.

Gold, Herbert. "Funny Is Money." *The New York Times Magazine*, March 30, 1975, pp. 16–31.

Golden, Daniel. *"Blazing Saddles:* Heading 'em Off at the Cliché." *Jump Cut*, No. 3 (September-October, 1974), pp. 3–4.

Gow, Gordon. *"Blazing Saddles." Films and Filming*, August 1974, p. 43.

———. *"Young Frankenstein." Films and Filming*, April 1975, pp. 35–36.

————. "Fond Salutes and Naked Hate." *Films and Filming,* July 1975, pp. 10–14.

————. "*Silent Movie.*" *Films and Filming.* February 1977, pp. 39–40.

————. "*High Anxiety.*" *Films and Filming,* June 1978, pp. 33–34.

Heller, Franklin. "Mel Brooks," in *Directors in Action,* ed. Bob Thomas. New York: Bobbs-Merrill, 1973.

Hess, Judith. "*Young Frankenstein:* Some Things Just Aren't Funny." *Jump Cut,* No. 6 (March-April 1975), p. 12.

Hirschfield, Gerald. "The Story behind the Filming of *Young Frankenstein.*" *American Cinematographer,* LV (1974), July, pp. 802–5, 840–42, 844.

Holtzman, William. *Seesaw: A Dual Biography of Anne Bancroft and Mel Brooks.* New York: Doubleday, 1979.

Ilf and Petrov. *The Twelve Chairs,* trans. John H. C. Richardson. New York: Random House, 1961.

Kael, Pauline. *Going Steady.* Boston: Little, Brown and Co., 1970; New York: Bantam, 1971.

————. *Deeper into Movies.* Boston: Atlantic-Little, Brown, 1973.

————. *Reeling.* Boston: Atlantic-Little, Brown, 1976; New York: Warner, 1977.

————. *When the Lights Go Down.* New York: Holt, Rinehart and Winston, 1980.

Kleinsinger, George, and Joe Darion. *archie and mehitabel,* in *The Best Short Plays 1957–58,* ed. Margaret Mayorga, 1958.

Lees, Gene. "The Mel Brooks Memoes." *American Film,* October 1977, pp. 10–18.

Logan, Josh. *Movie Stars, Real People, and Me.* New York: Delacorte Press, 1978.

Millar, Gavin. "Uneasy Chairs." *The Listener,* October 9, 1975.

————. "Beyond Lunacy." *The Listener,* January 27, 1977.

Pearlman, Gilbert. *Young Frankenstein,* novelization based on the screenplay by Gene Wilder and Mel Brooks. New York: Ballantine, 1974.

Pilpel, Robert H. *High Anxiety,* novelization based on the screenplay by Mel Brooks, Ron Clark, Rudy DeLuca and Barry Levinson. New York: Ace Books, 1977.

Powell, Dilys. "*The Twelve Chairs.*" *The Sunday Times,* October, 1975.

Richards, Tad. *Blazing Saddles,* novelization based on the screenplay by Mel Brooks, Norman Steinberg, Andrew Bergman, Richard Pryor and Alan Uger. New York: Warner, 1974.

Rivlin, Robert. "Mel Brooks on *High Anxiety*." *Millimeter*, December 1977, pp. 16–20.

Robbins, Fred. "What Makes Mel Brooks Run?" *Show*, September 17, 1970, pp. 12–15.

Rosenblum, Ralph, and Robert Karen. *When the Shooting Stops . . . The Cutting Begins*. New York: Viking, 1979.

Ross, Lillian, and Helen Ross. *The Player: A Profile of an Art*. New York: Simon and Schuster, 1961.

Sarris, Andrew. "Picking the Funny Bone." *The Village Voice*, March 14, 1974, pp. 71, 74.

———. "The Phallic Frankenstein and the Merry Monster." *The Village Voice*, January 6, 1975, pp. 59, 61.

Schickel, Richard. *"Blazing Saddles." Time*, March 4, 1974.

Schjeldahl, Peter. *"Blazing Saddles." The New York Times*, March 17, 1974.

Sennett, Ted. *Your Show of Shows*. New York: Collier Books, 1977.

Shapiro, Jane. "Mel Brooks: 'How Do You Like Me So Far?'" *The Village Voice*, July 19, 1976, pp. 73–74.

Simon, John. *"All-American." Theatre Arts*, May, 1967, p. 58.

———. "Parodies Lost." *Maclean's*, February 6, 1978, p. 60.

Siskel, Gene. "Interview with Mel Brooks." Chicago *Tribune*, November 6, 1971.

Stelzer, Dick. *The Star Treatment*. New York: Bobbs-Merrill, 1977.

Tropp, Martin. *Mary Shelley's Monster*. Boston: Houghton Mifflin, 1976.

Tynan, Kathleen. "Success Is a Great Big Spoof." *Evening Standard*, April 11, 1975.

Tynan, Kenneth. "Frolics and Detours of a Short Hebrew Man." *The New Yorker*, October 30, 1978, pp. 46–130.

Weschler, Lawrence. "Is Mel Brooks Going Crazy?" *The Village Voice*, December 26, 1977, pp. 35–38.

Wilde, Larry. *How the Great Comedy Writers Create Laughter*, paper ed. Chicago: Nelson-Hall, 1977.

Wilson, David. "Sounds Funny." *New Statesman*, January 21, 1977.

Young, Charles. "Seven Revelations about Mel Brooks." *Rolling Stone*, February 9, 1978, pp. 32–36.

Zimmerman, P. D. *"Blazing Saddles." Newsweek*, February 18, 1974, p. 104.

Discography

2,000 Years with Carl Reiner and Mel Brooks. 1961.

2,001 Years with Carl Reiner and Mel Brooks. 1962.

Carl Reiner and Mel Brooks at the Cannes Film Festival. 1963.

The Incomplete Works of Carl Reiner and Mel Brooks. 1973.

2,000 and Thirteen. 1973.

Mel Brooks' Greatest Hits Featuring the Fabulous Film Scores of John Morris. 1978.

Filmography

The Critic, 1962. Created and narrated by Mel Brooks. Produced and directed by Ernest Pintoff.

The Producers, 1967. Director Mel Brooks. Produced by Springtime/MGM/ Crossbow. Producer Sidney Glazier. Associate Producer Jack Grossberg. Production Supervisor Robert Porter. Production Manager Lou Stroller. Assistant Director Michael Hertzberg. Screenplay Mel Brooks. Photography Joseph Coffey. Color by Pathe Color. Editor Ralph Rosenblum. Production Designer Chuck Rosen. Set decorator James Dalton. Music John Morris. Costumes Gene Coffin. Choreography Alan Johnson. Sound Alan Heim. 88 minutes.

CAST: Zero Mostel (Max Bialystock), Gene Wilder (Leo Bloom), Kenneth Mars (Franz Liebkind), Estelle Winwood ("Hold Me, Touch Me"), Renée Taylor (Eva Braun), Christopher Hewett (Roger DeBris), Lee Meredith (Ulla), Andreas Voutsinas (Carmen Giya), Dick Shawn (Lorenzo St. DuBois), Josip Ellic (Violinist), Madlyn Cates (Concierge), John Zoller (Drama Critic), Bill Hickey (Failure).

The Twelve Chairs, 1970. Director Mel Brooks. Produced by UMC Pictures/ Crossbow. Executive Producer Sidney Glazier. Producer Michael Hertzberg. Production Executive William A. Berns. Production Supervisor Fred Gallo. Production Manager Ante Milić. Assistant Directors Bato Cengić, Peter Anderson. Screenplay Mel Brooks. Based on the novel by Ilf and Petrov, as translated by Elizabeth Hill and Doris Mudie under the title *Diamonds to Sit On*. Photography Dorde Nikolić. Color by Movielab. Second Unit Photography Eric Van Haaren Norman. Opticals by Film Opticals. Editor Alan Heim. Art Director Mile Nikolić. Music, Musical Director John Morris. Orchestration John Morris, Jonathan Tunick. Song, "Hope for the Best (Expect the Worst)" by Mel Brooks. Costumes Ruth Myers. Titles Arthur Eckstein. Sound Recording Thomas Halpin, Sanford Rackow, Peter Sutton. Sound Re-recording Richard Vorisek. 93 minutes.

CAST: Ron Moody (Ippolit Vorobyaninov), Frank Langella (Ostap Bender), Dom DeLuise (Father Fyodor), Bridget Brice (Young Woman), Robert Bernal

(Curator), David Lander (Engineer Bruns), Diana Coupland (Madame Bruns), Nicholas Smith (First Actor), Elaine Garreau (Claudia Ivanova), Will Stampe (Watchman), Andreas Voutsinas (Sestrin), Branka Veselinović (Natasha), Paul Wheeler Jr. (Kolya), Vlada Petric (Savitsky), Aca Stojkovic (Captain Scriabin), Mavid Popovic (Makko), Peter Banicevic (Sergeant), Mel Brooks (Tikon), Mladja Veselinović, Rada Djurićin.

Blazing Saddles, 1974. Director Mel Brooks. Produced by Crossbow for Warner Brothers. Producer Michael Hertzberg. Production Manager William P. Owens. Assistant Director John C. Chulay. Screenplay Mel Brooks, Norman Steinberg, Andrew Bergman, Richard Pryor, Alan Uger. Story Andrew Bergman. Photography Joseph Biroc. Panavision. Color by Technicolor. Editors John C. Howard, Danford Greene. Production Designer Peter Wooley. Set Decorator Morey Hoffman. Special Effects Douglas Pettibone. Music, Music Director John Morris. Orchestration Jonathan Tunick, John Morris. Songs: "Blazing Saddles" by John Morris, Mel Brooks, sung by Frankie Laine; "I'm Tired," "The French Mistake," and "The Ballad of Rock Ridge," by Mel Brooks. Costumes Nino Novarese. Choreography Alan Johnson. Titles Anthony Goldschmidt. Sound Recording Gene S. Cantamessa. Sound Re-recording Arthur Piantadosi, Richard Tyler, Les Fresholtz. 93 minutes.

CAST: Cleavon Little (Bart), Gene Wilder (Jim, The Waco Kid), Slim Pickens (Taggart), Harvey Korman (Hedley Lamarr), Madeline Kahn (Lili Von Shtupp), Mel Brooks (Governor William J. LePetomane/ Sioux Indian Chief), Burton Gilliam (Lyle), Alex Karras (Mongo), David Huddleston (Olsen Johnson), Liam Dunn (Rev. Johnson), John Hillerman (Howard Johnson), George Furth (Van Johnson), Claude Ennis Starrett Jr. (Gabby Johnson), Carol Arthur (Harriett Johnson), Richard Collier (Dr. Sam Johnson), Charles McGregor (Charlie), Robyn Hilton (Miss Stein), Don Megowan (Gum-chewer), Dom DeLuise (Buddy Bizarre), Count Basie (himself), Karl Lucas.

Young Frankenstein, 1974. Director Mel Brooks. Produced by Gruskoff/Venture Films/Crossbow Productions. Producer Michael Gruskoff. Production Manager Frank Baur. Assistant Directors Marvin Miller, Barry Stern. Screenplay Gene Wilder, Mel Brooks. Based on the characters from the novel *Frankenstein* by Mary Shelley. Photography Gerald Hirschfield. Editor John Howard. Art Director Dale Hennesy. Set Decorator Robert DeVestel. Special Effects Hal Millar, Henry Miller Jr. Music, Music Director John Morris. Orchestrations Jonathan Tunick, John Morris. Violin Solo Gerald Vinci. Costumes Dorothy Jeakins. Makeup William Tuttle. Titles Anthony Goldschmidt. Sound Editing Don Hall. Sound Recording Gene Cantamessa. Sound Re-recording Richard Portman. Frankenstein laboratory equipment Kenneth Strickfaden. 108 minutes.

CAST: Gene Wilder (Frederick Frankenstein), Peter Boyle (Monster), Marty Feldman (Igor), Madeline Kahn (Elizabeth), Cloris Leachman (Frau Blücher), Teri Garr (Inga), Kenneth Mars (Inspector Kemp), Gene Hackman (Blind Hermit), Richard Haydn (Herr Falkstein), Liam Dunn (Mr. Hilltop), Danny Goldman (Medical Student), Leon Askin (Herr Waldman), Oscar Beregi (Sadistic

Jailer), Lou Cutell (Frightened Villager), Arthur Malet (Village Elder), Richard Roth (Kemp's Aide), Monte Landis and Rusty Blitz (Grave-diggers), Anne Beesley (Little Girl), Terrence Pushman (First Villager), Ian Abercrombie (Second Villager), Randolph Dobbs (Third Villager), John Dennis, Lidia Kristen, Michael Fox, Patrick O'Hara, John Madison, Rick Norman, Rolfe Sedan, Norbert Schiller.

Silent Movie, 1976. Director Mel Brooks. Produced by Crossbow Productions. Producer Michael Hertzberg. Production Manager Frank Baur. Second Unit Director Max Kleven. Assistant Directors Edward Teets, Richard Wells. Screenplay Mel Brooks, Ron Clark, Rudy DeLuca, Barry Levinson. Story Ron Clark. Photography Paul Lohmann. Color by DeLuxe. Editors John C. Howard, Stanford C. Allen. Production Designer Al Brenner. Set Decorator Rick Simpson. Special Effects Ira Anderson Jr. Music John Morris. Orchestrations Bill Byers, John Morris. Costumes Pat Norris. Choreography Rob Iscove. Makeup William Tuttle. Stunt coordinator Max Kleven. 87 minutes.

CAST: Mel Brooks (Mel Funn), Marty Feldman (Marty Eggs), Dom DeLuise (Dom Bell), Bernadette Peters (Vilma Kaplan), Sid Caesar (Studio Chief), Harold Gould (Engulf), Ron Carey (Devour), Carol Arthur (Pregnant Lady), Liam Dunn (Newspaper Vendor), Fritz Feld (Mâitre d'), Chuck McCann (Studio Gate Guard), Valerie Curtis (Intensive Care Nurse), Yvonne Wilder (Studio Chief's Secretary), Arnold Soboloff (Acupuncture Patient), Patrick Campbell (Motel Bellhop), Harry Ritz (Man from Tailor Shop), Charlie Callas (Blind Man), Henny Youngman (Fly-in-soup Man), Eddie Ryder (British Officer), Robert Lussier (Projectionist), Al Hopson, Rudy DeLuca, Barry Levinson, Howard Hesseman, Lee Delano and Jack Riley (Executives), Inga Neisen, Sivi Aberg and Erica Hagen (Beautiful Blondes), Burt Reynolds, James Caan, Liza Minnelli, Anne Bancroft, Marcel Marceau and Paul Newman (themselves).

High Anxiety, 1977. Director Mel Brooks. Produced by Crossbow Productions for 20th Century–Fox. Producer Mel Brooks. Production Manager Ernest Wehmeyer. Assistant Directors Jonathan Sanger, Mark Johnson, David Sosna. Screenplay Mel Brooks, Ron Clark, Rudy DeLuca, Barry Levinson. Photography Paul Lohmann. Color by DeLuxe. Special Visual Effects Albert J. Whitlock. Editor John C. Howard. Production Designer Peter Wooley. Set Decorators Richard Kent, Anne MacCauley. Special Effects Jack Monroe. Music, Musical Director John Morris. Orchestrations John Morris, Jack Hayes, Ralph Burns, Nathan Scott. Song, "High Anxiety," written and performed by Mel Brooks. Costumes Patricia Norris. Makeup Tom Tuttle, Terry Miles. Titles/opticals Pacific Title. Sound Recording Gene Cantamessa. Sound Re-recording Richard Portman. Sound Effects William Hartman, Richard Sperber. Consultant Ron Clark. 94 minutes.

CAST: Mel Brooks (Richard H. Thorndyke), Madeline Kahn (Victoria Brisbane), Cloris Leachman (Nurse Charlotte Diesel), Harvey Korman (Dr. Charles Montague), Ron Carey (Brophy), Howard Morris (Professor Lilloman), Dick Van Patten (Dr. Philip Wentworth), Jack Riley (Desk Clerk), Charlie Callas (Cocker

Spaniel), Ron Clark (Zachary Cartwright), Rudy DeLuca (Killer), Barry Levinson
(Bellboy), Lee Delano (Norton), Richard Stahl (Dr. Baxter), Darrell Zwerling
(Dr. Eckhardt), Murphy Dunne (Piano Player), Al Hopson (Man Who is Shot),
Bob Ridgely (Flasher), Albert J. Whitlock (Arthur Brisbane), Pearl Shear
(Screaming Woman at Gate), Arnold Soboloff (Dr. Colburn), Eddie Ryder
(Doctor at Convention), Sandy Helberg (Airport Attendant), Fredric Franklyn
(Man), Deborah Dawes (Stewardess), Bernie Kuby (Dr. Wilson), Billy Sands
(Customer), Ira Miller (Psychiatrist with Children), Jimmy Martinez (Waiter),
Beatrice Colen (Maid), Robert Manuel and Hunter Von Leer (Airport Police),
John Dennis (First Orderly), Robin Menkin (Cocktail Waitress), Frank Cam-
panella (Bartender), Henry Kaiser (New Groom), Bullets Durgom (Man in Phone
Booth), Joe Bellan (Male Attendant), Mitchell Bock (Bar Patron), Jay Burton
(Patient), Bryan Englund (Second Orderly), Anne Macey (Screaming Woman),
Alan U. Schwartz (Psychiatrist).

Mel Brooks. Directed by Michel Minaud for FR 3, French television, Septem-
ber, 1978. Assistant Director Jean-Noel Despart. In charge of production Nicole
Flipo. Assistant Sophie Chalou. Editor François Ceppi. Sound Gil Plenty.
Photography Tom Harvey. Assistant Photographer Tom Morse. Mixing Domini-
que Hennequin. Sound Effects Serge Canda. Interviewer Catherine Laporte
Coolen. Distributed by Jerry Dexter Program Syndication in United States and
Anthony Morris Ltd. in London.

INDEX